Managing Projects with Microsoft® Visual Studio® Team System

Joel Semeniuk

Martin Danner

PUBLISHED BY
Microsoft Press
A Division of Microsoft Corporation
One Microsoft Way
Redmond, Washington 98052-6399

Library of Congress Control Number: 2007920380

Printed and bound in the United States of America.

1 2 3 4 5 6 7 8 9   QWE   2 1 0 9 8 7

Distributed in Canada by H.B. Fenn and Company Ltd.

A CIP catalogue record for this book is available from the British Library.

Microsoft Press books are available through booksellers and distributors worldwide. For further information about international editions, contact your local Microsoft Corporation office or contact Microsoft Press International directly at fax (425) 936-7329. Visit our Web site at www.microsoft.com/mspress. Send comments to mspinput@microsoft.com.

Microsoft, Microsoft Press, Active Directory, ActiveSync, BizTalk, Excel, InfoPath, Internet Explorer, MSDN, MS-DOS, Outlook, PivotChart, PivotTable, SharePoint, SQL Server, Visio, Visual Studio, Windows, Windows Server, and Windows Vista are either registered trademarks or trademarks of Microsoft Corporation in the United States and/or other countries. Other product and company names mentioned herein may be the trademarks of their respective owners.

CMMI® is registered in the U.S. Patent and Trademark office by Carnegie Mellon University.

The Software Engineering Institute has reviewed MSF for CMMI Process Improvement for completeness and correctness of CMMI V1.1 concepts. However, the Software Engineering Institute and Carnegie Mellon University do not directly or indirectly endorse MSF for CMMI Process Improvement.

The example companies, organizations, products, domain names, e-mail addresses, logos, people, places, and events depicted herein are fictitious. No association with any real company, organization, product, domain name, e-mail address, logo, person, place, or event is intended or should be inferred.

This book expresses the author's views and opinions. The information contained in this book is provided without any express, statutory, or implied warranties. Neither the authors, Microsoft Corporation, nor its resellers, or distributors will be held liable for any damages caused or alleged to be caused either directly or indirectly by this book.

Acquisitions Editor: Ben Ryan
Project Editor: Victoria Thulman
Technical Reviewer: Derek Lakin, Content Master
Copy Editor: Joel Rosenthal, ICC Macmillan

Project Manager: Debbie Abshier, Abshier House
Compositor: Debbie Berman, Abshier House
Indexer: Sharon Hilgenberg, Abshier House
Proofreader: Kelly Hentorne, Abshier House

Body Part No. X12-21110

Dedication

To my wife, who is loving enough to support me in everything and anything I do
To my two sons, who embody everything I want to be when I grow up
I am truly a man who has been blessed.

—Joel

To my wife Peggy and sons Jason, Gregory, and Charlie — whose patience and support
saw me through the temporary insanity popularly known as writing a book.

—Martin

Table of Contents

What do you think of this book? We want to hear from you!

Microsoft is interested in hearing your feedback so we can continually improve our books and learning resources for you. To participate in a brief online survey, please visit:

www.microsoft.com/learning/booksurvey/

What do you think of this book? We want to hear from you!

Microsoft is interested in hearing your feedback so we can continually improve our books and learning resources for you. To participate in a brief online survey, please visit:

www.microsoft.com/learning/booksurvey/

Acknowledgments

We would like to thank the members of the Visual Studio Team System product team who took the time to get us pointed in the right direction: Sam Guckenheimer, Rob Caron, David Anderson, Randy Miller, Jeff Beehler, Ajay Sudan, Michael Leaworthy, and so many others.

Thanks also to the many peers in the Team System MVP community who have contributed ideas and feedback. Special thanks to the staff of Imaginet Resources for keeping the ship afloat while Joel was travelling the world while working with customers who were adopting Team System. A special thanks to Richard Hundhausen and Steven Borg at Accentient for getting Martin on board the Team Systems bandwagon with them. It's been a fun ride!

We would also like to thank Ben Ryan, Valerie Woolley, and Victoria Thulman at Microsoft Press. This book would not have happened without their support and perseverance.

Introduction

Microsoft Visual Studio Team System provides tools for software architects, software developers, software testers, and database professionals; however, perhaps its most important contributions are to project managers. In fact, Visual Studio Team System now provides project managers with tools that interact naturally with the rest of the project team and enable new levels of decision making with little effort when compared to traditional software project management tools.

Whom Is This Book For?

Simply stated, this book is written for your average everyday manager of a software project. This book does not assume that the reader is familiar with any specific project management discipline or methodology. Our focus for the book was to provide an out-of-the-box experience for a typical project manager. We have tried to be as generic as possible with regard to specific processes or methodologies because one of the strengths of Visual Studio Team System is its ability to be adapted to virtually any process or software development methodology. To provide context, however, we followed a generic project life cycle model and, because it represents much of the out-of-the-box experience of Visual Studio Team System from the perspective of a project manager, we made many references to the Microsoft Solutions Framework. That said, if you are involved in the management of a project that uses Visual Studio Team System, and you want to understand how to use the product, this book is for you.

How This Book Is Organized

This book begins by painting a landscape of the dynamic work of software project management, providing some history and theory that helps to put Visual Studio Team System into context. In Chapter 2, we provide you with a" "Lap around Visual Studio Team System," in which we review all of the main features of Visual Studio Team System from the viewpoint of a project manager. Chapters 3 through 5 take you on a journey of Visual Studio Team System following the path of a typical project life cycle. Chapter 3 focuses on how project managers can use Visual Studio Team System during a project's inception, and Chapters 4 and 5 continue this approach through project planning and monitoring. In Chapter 6, we change direction and discuss how to use Visual Studio Team System to improve your organization's software development practices over time. In Chapter 7, we take a slightly more technical look at how to modify Visual Studio Team System to adapt to changing practices. And finally, two detailed appendices discuss two important topics referenced throughout the book, specifically the Microsoft Solutions Framework and the Software Engineering Institute's Capability Maturity Model.

System Requirements

For this book, your computer will need to have only the Team Foundation client software installed and be actively connected to a Team Foundation Server. The requirements for installing Team Foundation Server client software include:

- Microsoft Windows XP Professional with Service Pack 2 or Microsoft Windows Server 2003

- Recommended 1 GB of RAM with 20 GB of free hard disk space on a computer with at least a 2.6-GHz CPU

- Microsoft Office 2003 with Service Pack 1

- Microsoft Internet Explorer 6.0 with Service Pack 1

- Version 2.0 of the Microsoft .NET Framework

- Microsoft Data Access Components (MDAC) 9.0

Support For This Book

Every effort has been made to ensure the accuracy of this book and the companion content. Microsoft Press provides support for books and companion content at the following Web site.

http://www.microsoft.com/learning/support/books/

Questions and Comments

If you have comments or ideas regarding this book or the companion content or have questions that are not answered by visiting the preceding site, please send them to Microsoft Press via e-mail to

mspinput@microsoft.com

Or via postal mail to

Microsoft Press
Attn: Managing Projects with Visual Studio Team System
Editor
One Microsoft Way
Redmond, WA 98052-6399

Please note that Microsoft software product support is not offered through the preceding addresses.

Chapter 1
Managing Software Engineering Projects

- Discuss the challenges associated with building software.
- Describe the opportunities that Microsoft Visual Studio Team System offers to project managers.
- Provide a roadmap to this book.

The Challenges

As a project manager, you have one of the most challenging jobs on the planet. You are responsible for planning the project, keeping it on schedule and within budget, keeping all the stakeholders informed, and ensuring that deliverables are in fact delivered. And if that isn't enough, you must also rise to the unique challenges offered by each software development project.

Almost all software projects start with an incomplete understanding of what exactly will be delivered. Requirements are often vague and frequently change even as the project is in progress. Also, reporting on the status of the project and the health of the software being developed can involve gathering information from a variety of disparate sources and then manually manipulating it into meaningful metrics. This process can be tedious, labor-intensive, and error-prone.

This book introduces a new tool set for managing the software development life cycle. Called Visual Studio Team System, this tool set includes tools for software architects, developers, testers, release managers, and of course, project managers like you. Visual Studio Team System (illustrated in Figure 1-1) consists of four versions of Visual Studio, each for a different team role, and a server application called the Visual Studio 2005 Team Foundation Server. Team Foundation Server acts as the focal point for software project teams, offering services ranging from work item tracking and team Web portals to source code version control, build management, and distributed test execution. Team Foundation Server integrates the information generated by these various services into a single data warehouse and provides a sophisticated reporting system based on the latest data analysis technology.

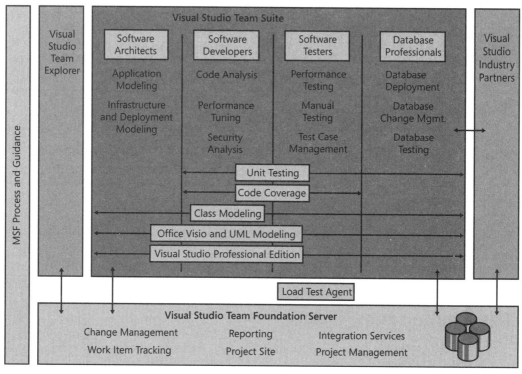

Figure 1-1   Visual Studio Team System

Visual Studio Team System offers compelling benefits to you as the project manager. For instance, it makes gathering information simpler and more accurate. Much of the information gathering is automatic—a by-product of using the tools. Work item tracking is fully integrated into Visual Studio, making it convenient for team members to update work items and link them to the work they are doing, such as checking in code, creating builds, and conducting tests. For the project manager who has to manually gather this sort of information from a variety of sources, this feature alone makes Visual Studio Team System worthwhile.

You can access Visual Studio Team System in a variety of ways using familiar tools. For instance, you can manage work items by using Microsoft Office Project. Or if you prefer, you can manage the very same work items by using Microsoft Office Excel. You can review project reports and access team Web portals by using Windows Internet Explorer. Also, you can use the Team Explorer client application to access all the Team Foundation Server services.

Visual Studio Team System is designed from the ground up to support the latest Agile development methods. It does not impose a specific methodology. Rather, it can be configured to support any number of different methodologies such as Scrum, the Unified Process, and the

Microsoft Solutions Framework. What's more, Visual Studio Team System can evolve as your team's development methodology evolves, allowing the tools to support the process rather than the other way around.

This book is designed to help you get the most out of Visual Studio Team System. You will learn how to use Visual Studio Team System within the context of project management processes: initiating and planning a project, building and stabilizing the software, and closing the project. You will also learn how to tailor Visual Studio Team System to meet the specific needs of the team and the project.

Before we go any further into Visual Studio Team System, let's step back and take a look at some of the other challenges that face software development teams and explore the nature of software engineering projects to see how Visual Studio Team System can help.

The Track Record

Software development projects in general have had a checkered past. As an industry we've had some revolutionary successes, including IBM's O/S 360 operating system, Microsoft Windows and Microsoft Office, and of course, the Internet. Unfortunately, we've also had more than our fair share of spectacular failures over the years. Here are some of the more notorious fiascos:

- A $250 million automated baggage handling system delayed the opening of the Denver International Airport by 16 months. The baggage system software never worked properly, and ultimately the entire system was dismantled and replaced (see *http://www.ddj.com/dept/architect/184415403*).

- The U.S. Federal Bureau of Investigation wrote off more than $100 million for its failed Virtual Case File system, a massive case management system that suffered from poorly specified and slowly evolving design requirements, overly ambitious schedules, and the lack of a plan to guide hardware purchases, network deployments, and software development for the Bureau (see "Who Killed the Virtual Case File?" at IEEE Spectrum Online, September 2005 at *http://www.spectrum.ieee.org/sep05/1455*).

- The U.S. Internal Revenue Service's $8 billion Business Systems Modernization program was its third attempt to modernize its antiquated information systems. The size and complexity of the project coupled with a lack of oversight and user involvement have caused the program to run nearly 3 years late and more than $200 million over budget. The delay and cost overruns have compromised the agency's ability to collect revenue and conduct audits (see "For the IRS There's No EZ Fix" in *CIO Magazine,* April 2004 at *http://www.cio.com/archive/040104/irs.html*).

- The U.S. Federal Aviation Administration canceled its Air Traffic Modernization Program in 1994 after spending $2.6 billion on its Advanced Automation System (see "Observations on FAA's Air Traffic Control Modernization Program," U.S. Government Accounting Office, 1999 at *http://www.gao.gov/archive/1999/r199137t.pdf*).

- Ariane 5 Flight 501, the maiden flight of the Ariane 5 rocket launcher for the European Space Agency, took place on June 4, 1996. Approximately 30 seconds after liftoff, the inertial guidance computer experienced a numeric overflow when converting a 64-bit floating point value to a 16-bit unsigned integer. As a result, the launcher veered wildly out of control and self-destructed, causing a $500 million loss (see "ARIANE 5 Flight 501 Failure, Report by the Inquiry Board," European Space Agency, 1996 at *http://homepages.inf.ed.ac.uk/perdita/Book/ariane5rep.html*).

The loss caused by these failures goes well beyond the money invested in the development project. In some cases in which the software is part of a larger project, the failure caused delays and cost overruns that dwarfed the cost of the defective software. In other cases, the failure hindered the ability of an organization to perform its function, resulting in lost revenue that far exceeded the original software investment. And in a few extreme cases, poor software quality actually resulted in injury and death (see "An Investigation of the Therac-25 Accidents" at *http://courses.cs.vt.edu/~cs3604/lib/Therac_25/Therac_1.html*).

So, how bad is it really? A small research and consulting firm called the Standish Group went about answering that very question. Formed in the mid 1980s, the Standish Group started with a very specific focus: to collect and analyze case information on real-life software engineering projects for the purpose of identifying the specific factors that relate to success and failure. In 1994, the Standish Group published the Chaos Report, which is one of the most often quoted sources regarding the overall track record of software development projects. This report was based on the analysis of more than 8,000 software development projects representing a cross-section of industries. According to the report, a staggering 31 percent of all software development projects were failures, meaning that they were cancelled before the software was completed. Only 16 percent of the projects were completed on time and on budget with all the features initially envisioned.

In 2004, the Standish Group released an update to their Chaos Report. They studied an additional 40,000 projects in the 10 years since the original report was issued. The good news is that project success more than doubled, from 16 percent to 34 percent. Conversely, project failure dropped by more than half, from 31 percent to 15 percent.

Although the trend is encouraging, we still have a long way to go. A 34 percent success rate means that 66 percent of the software projects failed to meet expectations. Very few other industries would tolerate this sort of performance. Would Toyota—or its customers—be satisfied if two thirds of the cars it produced failed to work properly? Of course not. So, why does the software industry get away with it? Perhaps it's because software-based automation has had such a profound effect on improving productivity. Despite the high failure rate, the overall return on investment has been satisfactory because the successes tend to produce huge gains that more than offset the losses due to failures. Just the same, as higher productivity becomes the norm, this sort of project performance will not be tolerated indefinitely. Software development organizations will be expected to improve and will be held to a higher standard. Which is to say that you, the project manager, will be held to a higher standard of performance too.

Visual Studio Team System can help you achieve that higher standard. It becomes another set of tools that you can add to your project management toolbox. Visual Studio Team System gives you unprecedented visibility into the status of work items in addition to the health of the product being developed. Automated reports and diagrams provide at-a-glance information in near real time. Visual Studio Team System not only saves you time by automatically collecting project-related information into a single data warehouse, it also distributes this information to team members in addition to other authorized stakeholders through team Web portals and automated reporting services.

Complexity and Change

Consider where we've come since the IBM PC was introduced in 1981. At that time, the IBM PC shipped with the MS-DOS 1.0 operating system, which consists of approximately 4,000 lines of code (see the Operating System Documentation Project at *http://www.operating-system.org/betriebssystem/_english/bs-msdos.htm*). In 2006, Microsoft introduced Windows Vista, which, according to Wikipedia (*http://en.wikipedia.org/wiki/Source_lines_of_code*), consists of a whopping 50 million lines of code. Although lines of code is a crude measure of complexity, it clearly illustrates the magnitude of the increase in software size since personal computers became popular.

> **Note** Interestingly, the microprocessor of the original IBM PC contained 29,000 transistors, whereas today's modern dual-core microprocessors contain more than 150 million transistors. When you compare lines of code to transistors, you see that the size of the operating system software has increased more than twice the size of the microprocessor that it runs on. One might conclude that the complexity of the software is growing even faster than the complexity of the hardware.

Imagine how many different paths of execution are possible in 50 million lines of code, and you begin to appreciate the fact that modern software rivals biological systems in complexity. Of course, very few of us are building operating systems or software applications this large, but we are all experiencing increasing complexity as we evolve from stand-alone applications to distributed service-based architectures.

Change compounds the challenge of software complexity. Software exists within the context of an ever-changing environment: changing requirements, changing operating systems, changing components and services, changing architectural paradigms, changing hardware platforms, and changing network topologies, to name a few.

This ever-growing complexity and accelerating change place more demands not only on the project team but on the project manager. As the product grows more complex, the project to produce it also tends to grow more complex. There are more tasks for you to coordinate and more deliverables for you to track. Rapid change requires you to be adaptive and keep your projects agile. You need to be able to quickly replan in order to respond to the inevitable changes that will occur.

Visual Studio Team System provides several mechanisms for dealing with complexity and change. Work item tracking allows you to quickly create tasks lists that are instantly available to all team members and easily revise the task lists to reflect changes in the project. Team members can conveniently update their tasks from within Visual Studio, Office Excel, or Office Project or by using a growing number of third-party Team Foundation Server client applications. They can also create their own work items as needed, allowing them to more accurately track their own activities and coordinate work. In some cases, the system can automatically create work items, such as when a build fails. In this way, work item tracking in Visual Studio Team System reduces the effort required by you to manage complex and rapidly changing projects.

You can use work item tracking to manage items other than tasks. For instance, you can manage requirements and track bugs as Visual Studio Team System work items. You can even invent your own work items types as needed or modify existing work item types to better meet the needs of the team and its stakeholders. The flexible nature of Visual Studio Team System work items enabled the team to better handle rapid change and also increases the likelihood that the work items accurately reflect the true state of the project.

Visual Studio Team System offers other team members some great tools for managing complexity. For instance, Visual Studio Team Edition for Software Architects includes the Distributed Systems Designers, which allows solution architects to model sophisticated applications based on distributed, service-oriented architectures. Skeletal implementations can be generated directly from these models, and the models automatically update themselves to reflect changes made directly to the code. In this way, the models provide a visual representation that communicates the intent and design of an application better than does source code alone. Visual Studio Team Edition for Software Developers contains refactoring tools that enable developers to remove unnecessary complexity from applications and unit-test tools to verify that the application is working correctly. Visual Studio Team Edition for Software Testers contains additional test tools that enable software testers to identify defects and monitor stability as the software evolves. Team Foundation Server contains a build system called Team Build, which automates the process of building complex applications. It can also be used to monitor the health of the application by running daily builds and tests to identify any integration issues that may have been caused by recent changes. This early warning system provides the feedback necessary for the team to keep a complex application stable as it evolves. Team Build also records comprehensive build data to the Team Foundation Server data warehouse for analysis and reporting.

The Human Factor

Many organizations have tried to control software development projects by prescribing a detailed methodology. Called by Tom DeMarco and Tim Lister in their 1987 book *Peopleware* (Dorset House Publishing) a *Big M* methodology, it attempts to specify a procedure for every aspect of the software development process in much the same way a cookbook recipe specifies the sequence of steps to produce a cake. At first glance, this approach seems reasonable.

Prescribing the process in this manner should produce consistent, repeatable results. Unfortunately, building software is nothing like baking a cake. The process of baking a cake is well understood and deterministic. If you accurately follow the recipe, you get the same result time after time with little variability.

Unfortunately, building software is far less predictable. Unlike baking the cake, in which the goal is the same result time after time, each software program is a unique creation with its own unique issues. Even the most careful and methodical developers produce software that displays unintended behavior. Occasionally, this unintended behavior is a happy accident that actually enhances the program, but more often than not it's a defect that must be corrected.

Because each software application is new, unique, and somewhat unpredictable, it stands to reason that the activities to produce the software will differ from one application to the next. For this reason, software development does not fit neatly into a prescribed, Big M methodology. It's neither possible nor desirable to create a detailed process that will work for every possible situation. Good things happen when you allow a team to innovate, try new things, learn from their failures, and build on their successes. This sort of team behavior, referred to by Craig Larman in his 2003 book *Agile and Iterative Development: A Manager's Guide, First Edition* (Addison Wesley Professional) as *emergent behavior*, is essential for successful software development, yet it is the antithesis of Big M methodology. The people involved are going to have a far greater effect on the success of a software development project than a prescribed process. If the team members are competent and motivated, they will get the job done regardless of the process imposed upon them. Without a competent and motivated team, however, the results will almost always be unsatisfactory regardless of the process used. Put simply, people trump process every time.

That being said, even a competent and motivated team can benefit from utilizing guidance that describes in general terms its overall approach to software development. This sort of guidance is sometimes referred to as a *little m* or *lightweight* methodology. It tends to focus on describing a process framework without going into too many details. Microsoft's MSF for Agile Development is a good example of a lightweight methodology. It describes a process based on incremental, iterative development. Although MSF includes prescriptive guidance in the form of workstreams and activities, this guidance is cursory, consisting mainly of bullet points designed to serve as a checklist rather than a procedure.

Visual Studio Team System is designed to support a wide range of software development methodologies. Team Foundation Server includes process templates for two different methodologies: MSF for Agile Software Development and MSF for CMMI Process Improvement. Both methodologies describe an iterative, incremental approach to software development. Both methodologies also describe the same team model and the same principles and mindsets. The main difference lies in level of detail that each methodology offers. MSF for Agile Software Development provides a lightweight set of workstreams, activities, work products, and reports. It is designed for self-directed teams operating in an agile environment. CMMI

Process Improvement, on the other hand, is designed for organizations that require a more formal approach. As such, it is more prescriptive, providing a comprehensive set of work-streams, activities, work products, and reports.

Regulatory Requirements

Recent years have seen a significant increase in the number of regulations that impact information systems. As a result, software development organizations that produce these information systems must be diligent in their compliance or run the risk of stiff penalties and in some cases even criminal charges that can result in jail time. Let's take a look at two examples, SOX and HIPAA.

In response to the massive corporate accounting scandals including those of Enron, Tyco, and Worldcom, the United States government enacted the Sarbannes-Oxley Act of 2002. Often referred to as SOX, this federal law requires that the Chief Executive Officer (CEO) and the Chief Financial Officer (CFO) of any publicly traded corporation personally certify the accuracy of the corporation's financial reports. This law has sharp teeth—chief executives face stiff jail sentences and large fines for knowingly and willfully misstating financial statements. What's more, these officers must certify an annual report to the federal government stating that their company has "designed such internal controls to ensure that material information relating to the company and its consolidated subsidiaries is made known to such officers by others within those entities, particularly during the period in which the periodic reports are being prepared."

The law also requires the signing officers to certify that they "have evaluated the effectiveness of the company's internal controls as of a date within 90 days prior to the report." This evaluation requires the implementation of an internal control framework that encompasses all the information systems that generate, manage, or report financial information. In other words, IT organizations must maintain strict controls on all aspects of these systems, including their design, implementation, and maintenance. SOX mandates that any software development project impacting financial reporting in any way is subject to an internal controls audit. As a result, these projects require a great deal of control and record keeping.

But the impact of regulations doesn't stop there. Industry-specific regulations also impact software development projects. For instance, the health care industry in the United States has the Health Insurance Portability and Accountability Act (HIPAA). Enacted in 1996, HIPAA contains a broad-ranging set of reforms designed to protect health insurance coverage for workers and their families when they change or lose their jobs. In addition, HIPAA contains Administrative Simplification (AS) provisions, which address, among other things, the privacy and security of health data. The Privacy Rule regulates the use and disclosure of any health-related information that can be linked to an individual. Organizations that handle private health information must take reasonable steps to ensure confidentiality, make a reasonable effort to disclose the absolute minimum amount of information to third parties for treatment or payment, and keep track of all such disclosures. In addition, HIPAA mandates standards for three types of security safeguards related to private health information: administrative, physical, and technical. Obviously, information systems that contain private health information must comply with the HIPAA privacy and security rules. Failure to do so could result in severe monetary penalties.

Visual Studio Team System addresses the need for control and record keeping through the use of work items. Work items not only help the team manage the flow of work and work products in a project, they also provide historical documentation on the work that was done and the work products affected. Also, the Team System Version Control System can be configured with a policy that requires each set of source code revisions to be associated with a work item, creating an audit trail that extends all the way to individual file changes. In this way, Visual Studio Team System generates compliance data automatically, as a by-product of the normal work flow.

IT Governance

Another challenge that organizations face is how to maximize the value of their investment in IT technology. Perhaps the best way to explore this challenge is to consider the point of view of the Chief Information Officer (CIO). The CIO is responsible for successfully executing business strategy through the effective use of information technology. As such, the CIO has one foot in the business world and one foot in the technology world. Although this executive is responsible for the effective use of technology, the CIO's primary focus is not on technology *per se*. Rather, the CIO is focused on maximizing the flow of value from the IT organization to the rest of the company. To that end, CIOs spend a great deal of time thinking about IT governance because IT governance is the primary vehicle for guiding the performance of the IT organization.

Flow of Value

The term *flow of value* expresses a concept borrowed from the lean manufacturing movement. Actually two concepts are embodied in this term. *Value* refers to the business value a given asset or service offers. *Flow* refers to the ongoing production and delivery of that business value. For instance, a Customer Relationship Management (CRM) system enables a company to do a better job of meeting its customers' needs, which in turn leads to greater revenue for the company. By implementing the CRM system, the IT organization generates business value that benefits the company. In this context, the *flow of value* refers to the delivery of business value from the IT organization to the rest of the company. But *flow of value* can also refer to the process used to create business value within the IT organization. When people start thinking in terms of the *flow of value* within this context, value-added practices start replacing wasteful practices, which in turn leads to increased productivity, increased throughput, reduced costs, improved quality, and increased customer satisfaction.

What is IT governance? Dr. Peter Weill, Director of the Center for Information Systems Research at the MIT Sloan School of Management, describes IT governance as a "decision rights and accountability framework to encourage desirable behavior in the use of IT" (see Weill's 2004 article "IT Governance on One Page," co-authored by Jeanne W. Ross, at *http://mitsloan.mit.edu/cisr/r-papers.php*). He goes on to say that IT governance need not be an elaborate set of policies and procedures. Rather, Dr. Weill claims that an organization can communicate its IT governance in a two-page document that lays out a vision for the IT organization, states who can make what decisions and who is accountable for what outcomes, and describes the desirable behaviors such as sharing, reuse, cost savings, innovation, and growth.

Visual Studio Team System supports IT governance through its process guidance and process metrics. Each Team Project in Visual Studio Team System includes a project Web portal that contains, among other things, process guidance documentation. The process documentation for both versions of MSF describe a team model that specifies roles and responsibilities in terms of advocacy groups. The MSF process documentation also describes desirable behaviors in terms of principles and mindsets and governance checkpoints that serve as process gates. You can customize this process guidance to meet the specific needs of your organization, or you can even replace it completely.

As software development teams use Visual Studio Team System, the Visual Studio Team System data warehouse accumulates a wealth of information about both the development project and the product being developed. Project performance can be measured using work item status and work item history. Product health can be monitored via build status and measured through a variety of quality indicators including bug counts, unit testing statistics, code coverage, and code churn. This information can be incorporated into the IT governance process, providing objective performance metrics that serve as the basis for decision making.

The Opportunities

Visual Studio Team System not only helps you address the aforementioned challenges, it also provides additional benefits to you as a project manager. Visual Studio Team System does not include a Visual Studio Team Edition for Project Managers, primarily because Visual Studio is a software development environment, and the project manager role is not directly involved with developing software. However, the Team Foundation Server client is a Visual Studio shell that contains only Team Explorer and Source Control Explorer. In a way, you can think of the Team Foundation Server client as Visual Studio Team Edition for Project Managers because it provides access to all the Visual Studio Team System resources you need as a project manager, including work item tracking, reporting, and document libraries in the project Web portals. You can also use Team Explorer to load work items into Office Excel or Office Project, in which you can add, modify, delete, and analyze the work items. In addition, the Visual Studio Team System data warehouse gathers a great deal of information that's useful to you as you plan and monitor your projects. You can use the Visual Studio Team System data warehouse to generate ad hoc reports and perform data mining by using your favorite analysis tools, including Office Excel.

Let's take a closer look at a few of the ways that Visual Studio Team System can assist you.

Better Planning and Estimating

One of the strong points of Visual Studio Team System is its ability to gather historical information. As teams use Visual Studio Team System, it collects information about actual project performance. You can measure a team's *velocity*, that is, the historical rate at which it completes work. This information is very useful when estimating how much work the team can take on in a given time period. You can also measure the correlation between estimates and actual time spent, to see whether the estimates tend to be high or low. Most teams tend to estimate low, by the way. This information will help the team calibrate its estimates so that future estimates will be more accurate.

Spend Less Time Tracking Projects

One of your responsibilities as a project manager is to track project status and communicate this information to all interested parties. As I'm sure you well know, this can be a rather time-consuming and tedious process. It usually involves the collection and compilation of status reports from team members. Unless you have a team of perfect angels, you have to constantly remind people to get their reports in on time so that you can update the overall project status. By the time all the information is collected, compiled, and distributed, it's already obsolete because it doesn't really reflect the current status.

Visual Studio Team System reduces your workload in several ways. First, every member of the team can see the current status of all work items at any time. Everyone can see who's doing what, which items are currently in progress, and which items need to be completed. This sort of visibility not only keeps people informed, it encourages people to keep their work items current. In addition, many work items on a software development project result in production of various work products such as source code, unit tests, build scripts, et cetera. These work products have one thing in common: they all need to be checked into the version control system. Visual Studio Team System takes advantage of this fact by allowing you to configure the Visual Studio Team System Source Control to require each set of revisions to be associated with one or more work items. The developer can quickly and easily associate work items with work products during the check-in process and even update work item status at the same time. In this way, work items get updated instantly as a by-product of the doing the work.

There is yet another way in which Visual Studio Team System reduces the time you spend tracking projects. Team Build, the automated build system for Visual Studio Team System, can be configured to automatically create a bug work item whenever a build fails. When this happens, the work associated with fixing the build is automatically added to the tracking system so that it can be assigned and monitored until completion.

Managing Risk

Every software development project has risks associated with it. As a software project manager, you need to identify the risks that can threaten the success of the project, analyze the potential impact of each risk, determine how to avoid the risk if possible, and plan what to do if the risk becomes reality. Visual Studio Team System assists with risk management by providing a tracking mechanism, early warning metrics, and software quality tools.

Visual Studio Team System can be configured to track risks as a work item type. Both versions of MSF include a work item type for documenting and tracking risks. Risk work item fields include Description, Severity, Priority, Assigned To, and State. A Risk work item can also be linked to other work items, such as a Task that mitigates the risk.

Visual Studio Team System also offers a variety of early warning metrics in the form of reports that help identify and monitor risks. For instance, MSF includes a Remaining Work report (see Figure 1-2 for an example) that shows the rate at which work is getting done. By projecting the trend line to the end of an iteration, this report can signal early in the iteration the risk of not completing the work on time.

Remaining Work: Scenarios
Report Generated 11/04/2004 11:25 AM by martin@contoso.com
How much work is left and when will it be done?

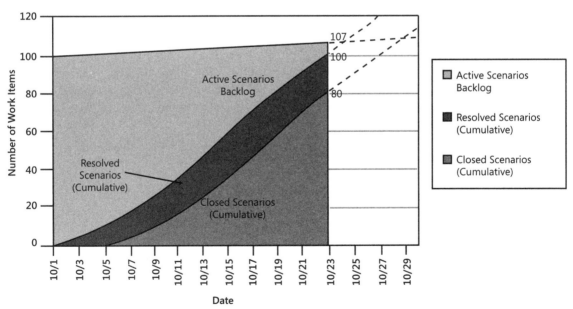

Figure 1-2 MSF Remaining Work report

MSF also includes a Quality Indicators report, an example of which is shown in Figure 1-3, which shows the change in several key quality indicators over time. This report summarizes trends in product health, allowing the team to spot potential problems early and take corrective action.

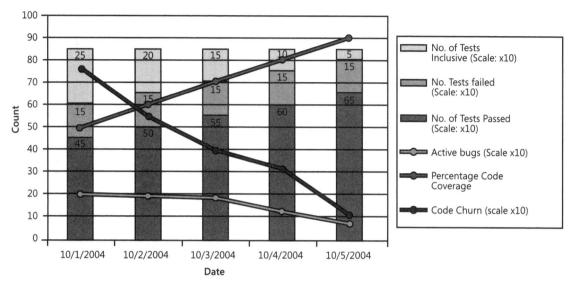

Quality Indicators
Report Generated 11/04/2004 11:25 AM by martin@contoso.com
What is the quality of the software?

Figure 1-3   MSF Quality Indicators report

In addition, Visual Studio Team System includes a variety of automated software quality tools that mitigate the risk of poor software quality. Unit testing tools are included in the Visual Studio Team Editions for Software Developers, Software Testers, and Database Professionals. Visual Studio Team Editions for Software Developers and Software Testers also include a static code analyzer that evaluates source code by using more than 400 rules, in addition to a dynamic code analyzer that measures unit test code coverage. The Studio Team Edition for Software Testers also includes Web test and load test tools and a test case management tool. Team Build, a feature of the Team Foundation Server, can be configured to run builds and smoke tests on a frequent basis. Any issues that break the build become visible in very short order, allowing corrective action to be taken quickly.

Repeating Successes

Visual Studio Team System can help you and your team achieve more consistent results by providing visibility into the process and tools for building quality into the product. The work item tracking system in Visual Studio Team System provides a single authoritative source of project status information that all stakeholders can access using a variety of tools and reports. This sort of real-time, detailed project status information is unprecedented for most organizations. In addition, the abundance of software quality tools in Visual Studio Team System enable the development team to not only build high-quality software but also maintain and verify the quality of the software as it's modified and enhanced throughout its life cycle.

Harvesting Best Practices

Each time a project team completes a development iteration, it's always a good idea to conduct a retrospective, in which the team can discuss what worked well and what needs to be improved. Based on this feedback, you can modify Visual Studio Team System to better meet the needs of the teams that use it.

Updating Process Guidance

The authors of the process guidance contained in MSF for Agile Development and MSF for CMMI Process Improvement knew that they could not create process guidance that would work for all organizations. For this reason, the MSF process guidance is designed so that you can customize it as needed. The MSF process guidance is based on XML files you can edit by using Microsoft Office InfoPath and then compile into HTML Web pages by using a free utility called MSFWinBuild available at *http://www.gotdotnet.com/workspaces/workspace.aspx?id=c0ce8992-2955-4371-904b-1f93a9efffe6*.

You can also completely replace the MSF process guidance with your own custom process guidance if you like. Perhaps your company has its own in-house methodology that includes process guidance, or maybe your shop has decided to create its own process guidance for the first time. As long as the documentation can be accessed using a hyperlink, Visual Studio Team System can incorporate it into any Team Project.

Process Templates

Microsoft wanted Visual Studio Team System to work well for a broad range of development organizations from small informal teams to large highly formal teams spanning multiple continents. To this end, they designed Visual Studio Team System to be highly configurable. The primary configuration mechanism is the process template, which is a collection of XML configuration files that tell Visual Studio Team System how to set up a new team project. The process template tells Visual Studio Team System which process tools to use for a project and how those tools should be configured.

You can install and use any number of process templates on a computer running Team Foundation Server. When Team Foundation Server is installed, it includes two process templates: MSF for Agile Development and MSF for CMMI Process Improvement. In addition, there are a growing number of third-party process templates that you can add to Visual Studio Team System. You can use a process template as-is or modify it to suit the needs of your team.

The most common customization involves work items. Teams often find that the work items they are using either contain unnecessary fields or are missing fields that would be helpful. Maybe the labels on the work item form are confusing, or the status options for a work item are awkward. The Visual Studio Team System process template allows you to specify any number of work item types, specify the fields that each work item type contains, specify the valid states for each work item type, and even control the form layout for each work item type.

The Visual Studio Team System process template can be modified using any XML editor. However, in Chapter 7, "Tailoring Visual Studio Team System," we'll show you a handy utility called the Process Template Editor, which allows you to modify process templates quickly and easily.

Modifying Running Projects

Visual Studio Team System uses the process template only when creating a project. Changes to the process template do not affect existing projects. However, you can modify work item types in existing projects. Let's say a project is underway and the team decides that they need a new field in the Bug work item type allowing them to identify the user who reported the bug. By using the Process Template Editor, you can add and modify work items directly in a Team Project, or you can export a work item to a local XML file, edit the file, and then import it back into a Team Project.

Coming Up Next

The remainder of this book is written in a format that follows the chronological sequence of a software development project. We recommend that you read it in the order presented for the best learning experience. However, you can also use this book as a reference guide on specific topics as needed.

Chapter 2, "Project Management Features of Visual Studio Team System," introduces you to the project management features of Visual Studio Team System. We start with an overview of the features in Visual Studio Team System, emphasizing the features of interest to project managers. Then we discuss how Visual Studio Team System supports the project management role. Specifically, we look at how project managers can use Visual Studio Team System to promote internal standards and facilitate project governance. In addition, we show how Visual Studio Team System supports communications among project stakeholders and helps you manage various aspects of a project such as schedule, budget, quality, scope, and risk.

Chapter 3, "Project Initiation," covers the activities performed during the initiating phase of a project. We'll introduce the Project Management Body of Knowledge (PMBOK) and show how Visual Studio Team System and MSF support the activities in the PMBOK Initiating process group. We'll discuss the structure of a process template and introduce you to several third-party sources. We'll also introduce you to Chase, our fictitious project manager who deals with a variety of real-world project-management scenarios.

Chapter 4, "Planning a Project," deals with project planning. We start by showing you how Visual Studio Team System and MSF support the activities in the PMBOK Planning process group. Then we describe an agile, iterative approach to planning. We show how to use Visual

Studio Team System together with Office Excel and Office Project to plan a project iteratively: starting with requirements, breaking down requirements into an initial release plan, and then performing detailed planning at the start of each iteration. Another important aspect of project planning is risk management, so we describe how to do risk planning using the Risk work item type in MSF. We then revisit our case study to see how Chase puts it all together to plan his project. The chapter finishes up with some final thoughts on project planning, which provide you with useful tips for how to improve your planning process.

Chapter 5, "Monitoring and Controlling Project Execution," shows you how to use Visual Studio Team System to manage execution of the project plan by monitoring and controlling the four dimensions of a project: scope, cost, schedule, and quality. We also discuss how to monitor and control risk during project execution, using Visual Studio Team System to track issues and manage corrective actions. We discuss how to use Visual Studio Team System to manage virtual teams and vendors who are participating in your project. We'll also show you how Chase and his team used Visual Studio Team System to create an information radiator consisting of a graphical display that clearly communicates project status and product health at a glance.

Chapter 6, "Improving Your Process," looks at the various ways you can use Visual Studio Team System to improve your team's processes. We'll show you how Visual Studio Team System can help you harvest lessons learned for process improvement. We'll also introduce a light process improvement framework that complements Visual Studio Team System. To pull it all together, we illustrate these process improvement techniques by using a fictional case study with Chase and his team.

Chapter 7, "Tailoring Visual Studio Team System," shows you how to tailor Visual Studio Team System to meet the specific needs of your teams and your projects. It describes the structure of a Visual Studio Team System process template and explains how the process template controls the configuration of a Team Project when it's created. We also show you how to use the free Process Template Editor utility to customize process templates and to modify work item types in existing Team Projects.

Appendixes A and B provide information about the Capability Maturity Model Integration (CMMI) and the Microsoft Solutions Framework (MSF), respectively.

Chapter 2
Project Management Features of Visual Studio Team System

- Review the common frustrations of a software project manager.

- Understand the basic attributes and functions of all the features of Microsoft Visual Studio Team System

- Understand how Visual Studio Team System supports the software project management role.

Introduction to Visual Studio Team System

In Chapter 1, we looked at some of the results of the Chaos Report (2004) produced by the Standish Group, which shockingly confirmed how poor the industry is as a whole at producing software. Chapter 1 also reflected upon the most common shortcomings of software development teams in addition to some of the key ingredients that can be enforced to help secure the success of a project. Even after these key ingredients have been addressed, which include having an experienced project manager on the team and the reliance on extensive user involvement and executive support, project teams will still be left with a mixture of tools that they must use to support their software development processes. When you think about it, software development teams have always had good tools to help them do their job. What seemed to be lacking is cohesion between those tools—both functionally and with regards to the data they produce. Many software development tool vendors, such as IBM Rational, Mercury, and Borland have attempted to address this gap by providing suites of tools that cover virtually all aspects of the software development life cycle; however, the problem of integrating tools from a changing landscape of tool vendors still poses significant challenges that most organizations do not tackle, leaving project teams with silos of tools that don't work well together and valuable project information that isn't integrated.

Capturing relevant project-related metrics has also traditionally been difficult for many project managers. As a project manager, you would typically rely upon the data given to you by the tools you use, such as Microsoft Office Project or the defect-tracking system used by the developers. Taking the time to consolidate information from all of these disparate systems in a way that provides ongoing meaning and relevance is a difficult and time-consuming endeavor, and for this reason, it is not performed consistently throughout the life of a project or even at all. Even when enough metrics are gathered, such as work completed per week, outstanding bugs, defect rates, and cost/time buffer consumption, making sense of this information as it applies to the successful management of the project is still quite difficult. Project managers must be able to understand whether the metrics that are being gathered result in descriptive (what you have done) or prescriptive (what you should do) perspectives or help to answer daily questions such as, "Will your project be done on time?" and "Will your project go over budget?"

Communication and team cohesion are extremely important elements of successful software engineering projects. One of the roles of a software project manager is to facilitate team cohesion and collaboration by any means. This may mean regular status meetings, detailed task lists that are sent to team members daily, or other activities that force the team to synchronize and focus on the job at hand. Of course, many software development methodologies, especially those based on Agile principles (see *http://www.agilemanifesto.org/*), put a great deal of emphasis on team collaboration; one of the most popular methodologies of this sort is Scrum. Many of these methodologies also stress the usage of some form of tool to help track information that will ultimately be used to drive team effort and focus. For example, Scrum emphasizes the concept of a sprint backlog to track tasks, their assignments, status, and in some cases, effort expended. Sprint backlogs are created during sprint planning meetings in such a way that each task should be able to be completed in about 4 to 16 hours. Within the sprint methodology, the sprint backlog is highly visible and provides a clear picture of the work that the team plans to accomplish during a development cycle called a *sprint*. Project managers will find that effective team tracking and communication tools, such as a sprint backlog, are even more important with geographically dispersed teams or very large projects that require team segmentation.

Continuing the discussion of task tracking, it is also important for project managers to track other aspects of a project such as risks, issues, requirements, and change requests. Many organizations have different tools for tracking each of these, ranging from simple Microsoft Office Excel spreadsheets to expensive off-the-shelf products. In many cases, it is up to the project manager to bring together all aspects of a project from all of their respective sources to build a complete picture of the state and health of a project.

Project managers are also the governors of the process and are selected to guide the software engineering effort. Project managers, with the help and feedback of their team, must be able to choose the correct process for the constraints that they face because you can never expect one process methodology to be used in every situation. After the project manager selects a methodology, the project manager must find a way to explain the process to the team and to help enforce rules and procedures that need to be followed. Far too often, the process that governs the project does not get continually reinforced, resulting in projects getting out of control. A clear sign of a project that has gotten away from the discipline prescribed by an underlying process methodology is the "never-ending status meeting syndrome," in which the team holds a seemingly continual array of status and planning meetings in hopes of getting the project focused and issues resolved. The problem with the never-ending status meeting syndrome project is that it is very hard for people to actually do any work if they are continually in status meetings.

An important aspect of any process is its attention to activities that help drive increased quality in the resulting product. By ensuring that the project team performs tasks related to the quality of the product, you will effectively minimize the size of one of the most dangerous project areas of uncertainty: bugs. In fact, there is no way to predict the number and impact of defects you will have in your software. Because of this, your estimates of your schedule and costs can be only rough approximations at best. Most project managers compensate for uncertainty by adding buffers to time and effort estimates; the bigger the uncertainty, the bigger the buffer. Quality assurance activities, such as developer-level unit testing, regular automated builds, early prototyping, and early-and-often user involvement can all be estimated up front with a fair degree of certainty. As a result, if the team acts upon these quality-related tasks, the impact of the uncertainty of software defects will be minimized, thereby decreasing variation and providing better conditions for success.

With all of this in mind, we have yet to see a tool that can truly help the software project manager deal with the complexity of a project team while at the same time provide flexibility with regard to process and control. This is where Microsoft Visual Studio Team System helps to solve some of the traditional problems faced by project managers by providing a set of tools for helping teams develop software better. In fact, Visual Studio Team System is much more than just a set of tools; it provides a platform and extensible architecture for software development tools that are provided by Microsoft and the entire software tool vendor community, including vendors such as Borland, Compuware, Mercury, and AVIcode, to name a few. Visual Studio Team System was built to enable software teams to focus more on the interaction between team members and the tools they use rather than the tools themselves. Visual Studio Team System also provides project managers with a unique and integrated viewpoint by helping to bring together disseminated tools and data jointly under one environment. Visual Studio Team System also helps to enforce process while at the same time ensuring flexibility across any software development methodology.

Feature Summary

Visual Studio Team System is a set of services and tools that integrate with Visual Studio in a way that can enhance the productivity of developers, testers, architects, and project managers. In this section, we explore the features of Visual Studio Team System at a level designed to give you a perspective of the entire scope of the product.

As you saw in Figure 1-1 in Chapter 1, Visual Studio Team System has two primary components: the client-side components, which extend Visual Studio 2005 Professional Edition, and a brand-new server component called Visual Studio 2005 Team Foundation Server. In fact, Microsoft segments the client-side tools into four SKUs named Visual Studio 2005 Team Edition for Software Architects, Visual Studio 2005 Team Edition for Software Developers, Visual Studio 2005 Team Edition for Software Testers, and Visual Studio 2005 for Database Professionals. Customers can buy each client SKU individually or all of the SKUs together in a package called Visual Studio 2005 Team Suite. Each of the client-side SKUs provide additional functionality to that provided out of the box with Visual Studio 2005 Professional Edition and are intended to be specific to a particular role on a project. Visual Studio Team Edition for Software Architects, for example, provides additional tools for software architects who design Service Oriented Architecture (SOA)–based software applications. Visual Studio Team Edition for Software Developers provides additional tools to help developers write better code and tools to help detect and isolate problems when they occur. Visual Studio Team Edition for Software Testers provides an excellent array of quality assurance tools that software testers can use to help test and validate software.

Team Foundation Server is the component of Visual Studio Team System that project managers will likely spend the most time using. Team Foundation Server provides additional development-focused features such as a new source control engine and an automated build framework; it also provides tools such as work tracking and a consolidated data warehouse and reporting framework. We will explore these features more closely in the following sections.

Work Item Tracking

One of the key features of Team Foundation Server is Work Item Tracking. *Work items* are units of work that are used to identify, manage, and track virtually any piece of work in a project. You can consider a work item to be "something that needs to get done," which you might represent in a tool such as Office Project or Office Excel. Examples of work items include Bugs, Tasks, Risks, Quality of service requirements, and even Change requests. Work items have fields that are used to capture information such as title, description, and work assignments, as shown in Figure 2-1. Work items also specify a workflow that team members must adhere to as they create and modify work items. For example, the Requirement work item type specifies the following states: Proposed, Active, Resolved, and Closed. The Requirement work item also specifies a set of rules that determine what is needed to achieve those states, as depicted in Figure 2-2. The workflow specified within work items is extremely important to process governance because it is in this stage that Visual Studio Team System helps to enforce your process methodology.

When you create a new Team Project, Visual Studio Team System will also prepopulate the project with default work items, which are specified in the process template you used to create the project (we will discuss process templates in more detail later in this chapter). This is very useful when you would like to have similar work performed for all projects of a similar type. For example, you may want every project to have a vision and scope document created. The MSF for CMMI Process Improvement process template comes with a number of default work items for newly created projects, one of which is the Create Vision Statement Task work item.

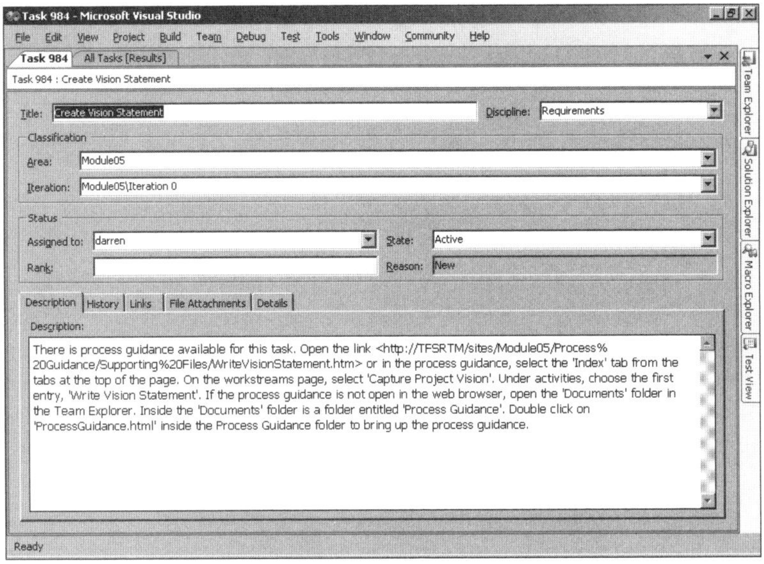

Figure 2-1   The Task work item

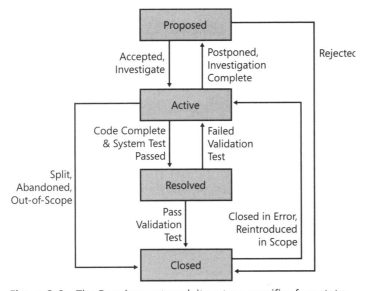

Figure 2-2   The Requirement work item type specifies four states.

Another extremely important aspect of work items is that they can be associated with project documents, source code files, automated build results, test results, or even other work items. The ability to associate work items with virtually any other piece of information within Visual Studio Team System provides an important foundation for traceability and Visual Studio Team System's underlying data warehouse and reporting capabilities.

Work items are specified by something called a process template, which is essentially a stencil that is used to design new projects within Visual Studio Team System. Process templates and the work items that they specify are completely customizable allowing you to add fields, modify workflow, and even change the display form layout. We will be making further reference to process templates later in this chapter because they are an important mechanism for specifying the behavior of Visual Studio Team System.

Source Code Control

Another service in Visual Studio Team System is Team Foundation Version Control (TFVC), which provides an enterprise-scale repository for source code and other file-based documents of the project. The TFVC service is optimized for both in-house and distributed development teams, so network traffic is optimized, and geographically dispersed teams can work together easily. To further support distributed teams, Visual Studio Team System also provides a Team Foundation Proxy Server, which is responsible for caching source code files in remote offices to help optimize the process of fetching files from the central repository. The TFVC service supports advanced source code branching and merging operations. TFVC also supports the new concept of source code management called *shelving*, which a developer can use to temporarily store changes in source code to help facilitate source code reviews or to easily retain current changes while reverting to an earlier state for defect fixes. The TFVC service also supports check-in policies that can be used to enforce quality standards during the code check-in process. For example, policies can be set to require work items and check-in notes to be associated with the check-in operation or to require code coverage and testing to be complete. Other policies can be set to require source code to adhere to coding conventions as specified by the project.

Automated Build

Team Build is another core service in Visual Studio Team System. It is responsible for the automated compilation of source code, execution of automated tests, performance of source code analysis, and production of build statistics that record quality metrics. Team Build can automatically generate new defect work items when tests fail or automatically resolve existing defects when their tests pass. Creating a daily build is now a simple wizard-driven operation that makes it possible to create many different types of automated builds for different needs. For example, your project team may require a daily build in which the source code is compiled and the results deposited into a drop location every night. Your team might also want to specify various other builds that perform specific operations such as performance and load testing, execution of automated tests, or even complex deployment steps.

Metrics and Reporting

Metrics and reporting are likely a project manager's most favored features of Visual Studio Team System. Team Foundation Server ships with extensive reporting services at its core as, illustrated in Figure 2-3. This service transforms operational data, such as work items, automated build results, and test results, into metrics stored within Team Foundation Server's data warehouse. Dozens of reports are included that detail and summarize a Team Project, including reports that provide status, health and defect reports, and other quality metrics. In essence, Visual Studio Team System facilitates the software development processes and provides you with valuable built-in reports that can help you manage and track your projects.

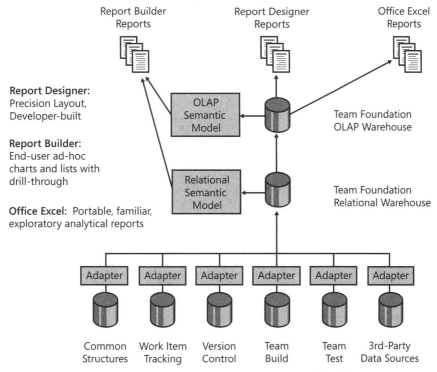

Figure 2-3   Visual Studio Team System reporting is extensible, allowing you to create your own reports or even access the data warehouse directly from Microsoft Excel.

Project Portals

For every Team Project, Visual Studio Team System creates an associated project portal, which is built on Microsoft Windows SharePoint Services. This portal facilitates the maintenance of the documents produced by the project team and acts as a launching pad for project reports and other associated project components. Windows SharePoint Services provides document libraries to store virtually any type of document. When you create a new Team Project, Visual Studio Team System will prepopulate the document libraries contained within the portal with documents that are relevant to the project, which are all specified in the process template used to create the Team Project. Document libraries provide the ability to store metadata information about each document. They also have collaborative functionality such as version history and document check-in and check-out, which prevents other users from viewing partial changes to documents and prevents them from making changes to documents while they are checked out.

The project portal is also a launching pad for project reports, providing easy access to the plethora of reports that are provided by Visual Studio Team System out of the box. In fact, the project portals that are created for each Team Project contain reporting Web parts that embed project reporting directly on the project portal pages, as demonstrated in Figure 2-4. This provides a one-stop shop for business analysts and project sponsors who want to get information about the project quickly.

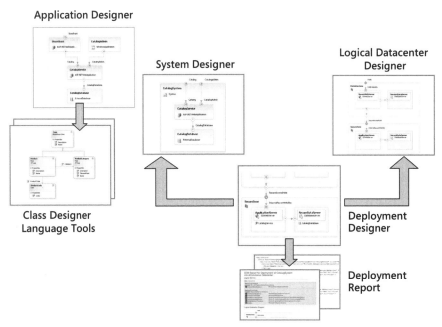

Figure 2-4   The project portal

Office Excel and Office Project Integration

Project managers can use familiar tools such as Office Project or Office Excel to manage their project lists; however, because of the integration with the Visual Studio Team System Work Item service, those lists are now part of the Visual Studio Team System project and are centrally maintained and available for other members to see and update as needed. In fact, the Visual Studio Team System work item repository is fully accessible through Office Project and Office Excel, providing two-way synchronization between work item data and the information stored within the Microsoft Office products. As a project manager, you will be able to use the common features of the product to not only enter and update work item information, but also to analyze and track important project information.

Other roles on your development team will benefit from the integrated toolsets in Visual Studio Team System. These toolsets include Visual Studio Team Edition for Software Architects, Visual Studio Team Edition for Software Developers, and Visual Studio Team Edition for Software Testers.

Tools for Software Architects

Software architects now have access to a new generation of tools that help them create models that accurately represent distributed applications and service-oriented architectures (SOA) by using components such as Web services, Microsoft BizTalk Server Web services, Web applications, Database services, Windows applications, and external Web services. Many of these model components can be used to generate Visual Studio projects. Changes made to applications generated from these models are represented in the model automatically, and correspondingly, changes in the model components are also reflected in the project code and configuration automatically. In this way, the dynamic models accurately represent the application at any point in the life of the project.

Another model type is the Logical Datacenter Diagram, which is used to specify the essential characteristics of a datacenter, especially those settings and constraints that affect the deployment of application components and systems. The Logical Datacenter Diagram can be maintained by the project's architect or the operations managers who understand the communication paths and service endpoints of their datacenter best.

Further, a software architect can create a deployment diagram that maps the components of your software onto a specific logical datacenter and verify that the application's settings and constraints are met by the datacenter's services and endpoints. Architectural changes that may be required in order to have a successful deployment can be identified well before code is even written, and because application diagrams are dynamic, those deployments can be validated at any time during the life cycle of the project, ensuring that changes to the applications in a system will not cause deployment issues later.

The designers available in Team Edition for Software Architects are shown in Figure 2-5.

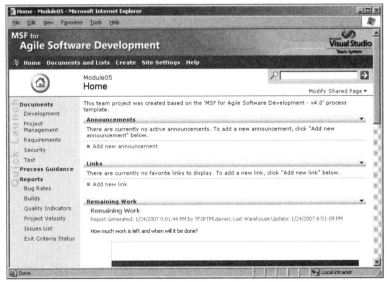

Figure 2-5   Designers in Visual Studio Team Edition for Software Architects

Tools for Software Developers

Developers will enjoy the integration of code quality tools into Visual Studio that will not only help them write higher quality code, but also help detect and track down problems throughout the development process. These include tools for unit testing and code coverage, code analysis, and code profiling. *Unit tests* allow developers to ensure that software components and their interfaces respond correctly and function according to the requirements of the system. *Code coverage* shows the developer the areas of code that have been tested and those that have not. *Code analysis* is a process that assesses code for compliance with various coding and design rules, such as naming conventions, potential security issues, adherence to standards, and common coding mistakes, in addition to custom rules that may be in place. There are also more sophisticated tools for C and C++ projects that can identify common coding errors that cause run-time problems that are difficult to isolate, and other tools that can trap those problems at run time and aid in diagnosis. Figure 2-6 shows some of the code analysis settings available in Team Edition for Software Developers.

Developers commonly find it difficult to debug performance problems while the application is running. Visual Studio Team System includes new features such as code profiling tools, which allow a developer to identify those portions of code that are running, their frequency, and the duration of each call, to assist in diagnosing such problems. The profiling tools can work in two different ways: the sampling mode imposes minimal overhead on the running application and checks into your application at regular intervals, determining with statistical analysis the frequency and duration of code calls during the profiling session. The instrumental profiling mode adds start and end markers to the compiled code to accurately measure all calls and their duration; however, doing so adds the additional expense of performance overhead to the application as it runs.

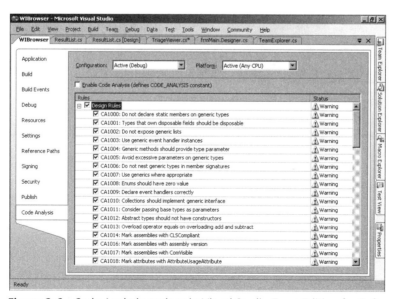

Figure 2-6   Code Analysis settings in Visual Studio Team Edition for Software Developers

Tools for Software Testers

Testers will use the testing framework in Visual Studio Team System to create, maintain, and execute tests of many kinds, including unit tests, Web tests, and load tests, and they will take advantage of the framework to include third-party testing tools or generic executables that perform specific tests. Team Edition for Software Testers even supports manual tests that document the steps in a Microsoft Office Word document for testers to reference manually. All test results can be tracked and maintained in the Visual Studio Team System repository, and they form the basis of a number of quality metrics that are shown on the project portal and common reports. Failed tests can create defect work items (either automatically or manually), and progress of those defects can be tracked throughout their life cycle. Communication of defects and resolutions between tester and developer can happen clearly, easily, and automatically.

As you can see, there are quite a number of new features in Visual Studio Team System designed to maximize the productivity of all team members, helping to impose a repeatable, predictable process for software development projects while minimizing the overhead of the process on the team.

Tools for Database Professionals

Most software development projects have team members who are responsible for developing against some type of database. Visual Studio Team Edition for Database Professionals contains tools that will enable the database developers on your team to be more productive and produce higher quality results. Visual Studio Team System for Database Professionals will allow database developers to fully integrate database projects in the source code management functionality provided by Team Foundation Server. Visual Studio Team System for Database Professionals provides features such as database object refactoring and renaming, database and schema comparison, and data generation. In addition, Visual Studio Team Edition for Database Professionals offers new tools that will enable database-focused members of your team to more easily write and run unit tests that target database objects such as stored procedures and database functions.

How Visual Studio Team System Supports the Project Management Role

First, we should remind ourselves of the range of responsibilities that project managers have on a project. The Project Management Book of Knowledge, or PMBOK, defines project management as follows (from *A Guide to the Project Management Book of Knowledge, Third Edition*):

> *Project management is the application of knowledge, skills, tools, and techniques to project activities to meet project requirements. Project management is accomplished through the application and integration of the project management processes of initiating, planning, executing, monitoring and controlling, and closing. The project manager is the person responsible for accomplishing the project objectives.*

Managing a project includes:

❑ *Identifying requirements*

❑ *Establishing clear and achievable objectives*

❑ *Balancing the competing demands for quality, scope, time, and cost*

❑ *Adapting the specifications, plans, and approach to the different concerns and expectations of the various stakeholders.*

I think it's plain to see that virtually every project should have a project management role. In fact, the role of a project manager is very important even in agile rooted methodologies, and arguably, this definition still holds true, even though the role of the project manager may be distributed across many team members or go by a different name.

Note Is the project manager a role or an individual? In this book, we refer to a project manager as a role instead of an individual on a team to stress that the responsibility of the project manager role can be shared by a number of people on a team depending on the team's size and diversity.

Note In Scrum, the ScrumMaster is equivalent to the project manager. More specifically, the ScrumMaster is responsible for managing the Scrum process instead of simply specifying and managing work. In Extreme Programming, the project management responsibilities are managed by a number of roles: Developers, who own the schedule; the Tracker, who keeps track of the schedule; and the Coach, who guides and mentors the team.

Despite the methodology you choose to implement your software solutions, the project manager will be responsible for managing scope, time, cost, quality, people, communication, and risk. The project manager may also be responsible for tasks such as procurement and setting governance and process models for their teams. Figure 2-7 illustrates the project manager's responsibilities.

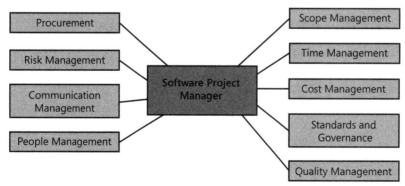

Figure 2-7 The role of a project manager encompasses many areas and is key to project success.

With this in mind, let's take a closer look at how Visual Studio Team System supports each of the just-listed project management responsibilities.

Standards and Governance

Part of a project manager's role is to set up project standards and governance procedures under which the team will operate. Essentially, this is where the project manager declares one or more acceptable patterns that specify the way the team interacts to deliver software. The terms *standards* and *governance* are really quite daunting, especially to a software developer; however, the best way to think about the term *standard* is to correlate it with the term *principles*, which, in most organizations, are reflections of best practices and lessons learned collected by people who have solved similar problems. When a project manager sets up standards for a project, he or she is really choosing the best set of principles for the task at hand. Compare this concept with the job of a software architect. No single software architecture can be appropriate for every application ever conceived—the architect will choose the software architecture based on the constraints and conditions of the problem that needs solving. The same must be true for software engineering process standards. Governance is complementary to this concept. MSF for CMMI Process Improvement defines *governance* as "...utilization of resources through the control of time and money relative to the flow of value." This means that the project manager must take the principles that guide the project and find a way to ensure that they are still effective and be ready and able to make changes when they are not.

One of the unique features of Visual Studio Team System is its ability to support process standards and governance declaratively. This is a fancy way of saying that the product was not built with any particular style of software delivery in mind, relying instead on process templates to help determine exactly how projects are to be delivered. Process templates are simply a bundle of tightly integrated XML files and supporting process documents and reporting definitions. Process template definitions are stored within Team Foundation Server and are used during the creation of a project. Figure 2-8 illustrates what Process Templates specify during this process.

The areas of process templates that support standards and governance include:

- **Work item type definitions** Each work item type specifies its own workflow and field rules that help guide team members through specific parts of the software engineering process. Work item field definitions also specify the metrics that will be stored within the Team Foundation Server data warehouse for project analysis and reporting.

- **Initial project areas and iterations** Project areas and iterations specify ways that you can classify work within a project. Project areas are used to represent functional areas of the software you are building. Iterations are a way of assigning work items to segments of time throughout the project. Project managers can use these classifications to provide a structure for work classifications and reporting dimensions.

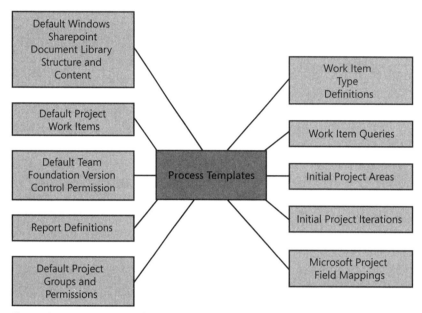

Figure 2-8 Process templates specify virtually every aspect of a Team Project.

■ **Default work items** When you create a new Team Project, the process template can specify a number of default work items that will be created automatically. Default work items help ensure the repeatability of your processes by ensuring that important tasks are never forgotten.

■ **Report definitions** If there is one feature that project managers love about Visual Studio Team System, it's reports, and more importantly, the underlying data warehouse that powers those reports. Visual Studio Team System works to instrument your process and exposes the results through numerous reports that project managers can use to make decisions. The reporting features are extremely important to governance, because some reports reflect the health and status of a project and provide a valuable continual feedback mechanism allowing a project manager to work more proactively.

■ **Default Windows SharePoint Document Library structure and contents** The Windows SharePoint Document Library can be prepopulated with project artifacts. Project managers don't have to worry about having the correct templates because only the appropriate artifact templates will be placed in the store based on the type of methodology used to create the project portal site.

We will get a chance to further explore many of these features in Chapter 3.

Managing Team Communication

One of the most common aspects of a project manager's role is the management of people, which involves forming, organizing, developing, and coordinating project teams. In fact, it has been said that the success of a project is more directly associated with the effectiveness of team communication than to any other factor, a fact that the Agile Alliance embraces in its Agile Manifesto, which is the source of many Agile software development methodologies. In many ways, a psychology degree is more applicable than any other degree when it comes to establishing good team communication; however, providing an effective communication medium is also important. In fact, Visual Studio Team System provides a number of important features that help to support communication management within teams.

First and foremost, project managers need to specify who has appropriate authority to do what on a project and to set the boundaries of how team members will interact with each other and with Visual Studio Team System. More specifically, Visual Studio Team System allows a project manager to configure the groupings, rights, and permissions of their team with respect to Visual Studio Team System activities. For example, the project manager may want to reflect the responsibilities of developers in the rights granted to them on a project, as shown in Figure 2-9. In Figure 2.9, developers are restricted from deleting test results, deleting the project, editing build quality levels, and editing project level information. In Chapter 3, we will explore how to configure project level groups and permissions for your team.

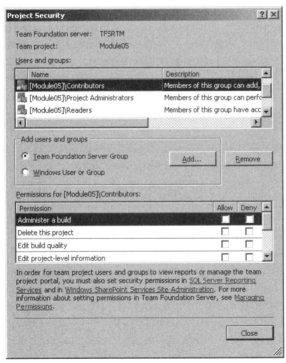

Figure 2-9   Project managers can set specific permissions to restrict the team to performing certain activities with Visual Studio Team System.

As we have previously stated, the work item is the heart of Visual Studio Team System. Project managers will use work items to communicate task assignments and capture issues, requirements, change requests, and risk within work items. Project managers also use features such as work item queries and Office Project and Office Excel integration to facilitate this task. More than likely, project managers will not be using Microsoft Visual Studio as their primary tool for managing projects. In fact, project managers will usually have only the Team Explorer installed and will use the Team Foundation Server work item integration features of Office Project and Office Excel, which all get installed along with the Team Foundation Client to manage specific tasks and assignments. Project managers will then be able to use familiar tools to help break down the project, assign team members to tasks, and get feedback on task level status and tracking. In Chapter 3, we will take a much closer look at how to work with work items, work item queries, and work item integration with Office Project and Office Excel.

A very important role of the project manager is to continually communicate information regarding the chosen software development process to their team. Projects within Visual Studio Team System are created based on a process template, which also provides information about the software methodology the project is based on, represented as process guidance. From a general perspective, process guidance is more like a software development methodology's help system, which is accessed via a Web browser accessing the Visual Studio Team System project portal site for each project. Process guidance provides context, instruction, and details on the methodology associated with a given project and is used as a point of reference for all team members. More specifically, process guidance specifies the core principles and mindsets of the methodology in addition to details of team roles and work item types. This process guidance is accessible via a Web browser and can be accessed by using quick access points scattered across the Visual Studio Team Explorer navigation. Each project's process guidance is located within the project portal that gets created for each Team Project. You will explore the details of Process Guidance in Chapter 3.

Managing Time and Money

Perhaps the most common questions asked of a project manager are, "Are we on time?" and "Are we on budget?" Data that answers these questions is gathered and represented in the form of the all-powerful status report. To create a status report, a project manager typically spends a considerable amount of time gathering status information from project team members based on assignments made within the master project plan. The project manager is then left with the responsibility of correlating this information and making the determination of overall project health, usually expressed in units of time and money. At any rate, consolidating and making sense of status is a time-consuming endeavor, especially when you think of how status reports are consumed. The details within a status report are rarely ever looked at in great detail unless a project is in trouble. In addition, the information within the status report is always a snapshot in time and is usually stale by the time it's consumed.

Getting Accurate Status from Your Team

If you have played the role of a project manager for very long, you have likely realized how difficult it is to solicit accurate status information from your team. The typical responses from many developers to a status request include, "It's almost done, all I have to do is test" or "I'm about 83 percent done." Because of these types of responses, many project managers have changed their form of questioning to be something more like When will you complete your task? The project manager will then be left with the responsibility of determining whether slippage is occurring at the task level and what to do about it. This also suggests that knowing when a task needs to be complete is more important than knowing its progress.

Visual Studio Team System provides a number of features that can help a project manager answer time and money questions. The following list describes these features:

Integration with Office Project and Office Excel   Office Project and Office Excel are considered essential tools for most project managers. Both products play an important role in helping the project managers break down the project and track ongoing activities. As already mentioned, Visual Studio Team System provides access to work items stored in Team Foundation Server from Office Project and Office Excel. Just as important, all of the rules, constraints, and workflow specified with a work item are enforced from within Office Project and Office Excel to help ensure data integrity and validation. Project managers are then free to use the management and analytical features of Office Project and Office Excel to help plan and track time and cost over a project life cycle while at the same providing the ability to work from the same information that rest of the team will use during the project.

Work item fields   The type of work items you will see in a project is determined by the process template you use to create that project. For example, MSF for Agile Software Development includes Scenario, Quality of Service Requirement, Task, Bug, and Risk work items. Task items in MSF for Agile Software Development are the Bug, Change Request, Requirement, and Risk work item definitions. MSF for CMMI Process Improvement specify *Completed Work* and *Remaining Work* fields to help track expected and expended effort. In addition, Visual Studio Team System provides Office Project with mapping of fields such as *Start Date* and *Finish Date* and will automatically record actual completion dates for you based on the rules of the underlying workflow definition of each work item type.

Iterations   Work items are generally assigned to project iterations that typically have a start and end date. You can track slippage by using reports or work item queries to query outstanding work items assigned to a past iteration. Essentially, you have the ability to ask the system questions such as, "What work items that were scheduled for iteration 3 didn't get done?"

Reports   Like work items, reports are specified in a process template used to create new Team Projects. The default process templates that ship with Visual Studio Team System come with a set of very powerful reports that help you understand the health and progress of your projects and are used most often to answer some of the truly difficult questions such as "What is the quality of your software?" "Will you be finished on time?" "Does the project have any constraints that may impede the delivery of the project?" and "How effective is the team?" Some of these reports can help project managers track expended time and effort on a project, helping to get a realistic view of how the project is progressing. One very important report is the Remaining Work report, which helps project managers answer the questions, "How much work is left?" and when will it be finished?" The Remaining Work report, as shown in Figure 2-10, represents a cumulative flow of remaining work measured across a particular dimension such as iteration. We will take a look at more reports and how to interpret them in Chapter 5.

Visual Studio Team System as a Time-Tracking Solution

Many companies rely upon rigorous time tracking along with sophisticated time-tracking software to track time spent on projects either for the purpose of billing customers or for gathering effort-based metrics. Even though certain work item types have fields for the measurement of effort, it should generally not be considered for a time-tracking system.

Remaining Work: Scenarios
Report Generated 11/04/2004 11:25 AM by martin@contoso.com
How much work is left and when will it be done?

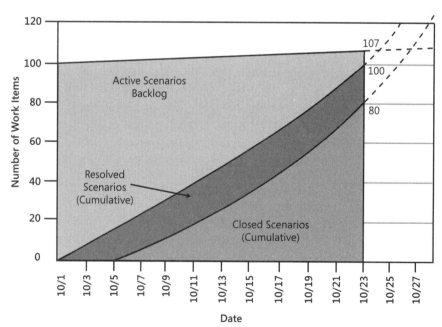

Figure 2-10   The Remaining Work report

Managing Quality

Managing quality in the software industry has never been more important. Today, quality is used as a differentiator because the software industry as a whole has far fewer quality standards than other industries. This is not to say that quality isn't important in virtually every industry—organizations that focus on quality can quickly change their position in the marketplace, providing a substantial edge over their competition regardless of the industry. In the software industry, however, because of the existence of really bad software and the problems it causes, the edge is greater. Quality is a mindset more than a task. You need to have well-defined processes with unanimous commitment from the entire team, including upper management. In addition, those teams that want to focus on quality must do so through the entire life cycle of a project, and it is up to project managers to constantly evaluate quality-control feedback. There are also considerable misconceptions around quality practices in the software industry from those who suggest that to achieve high quality, teams must sacrifice agility and overall velocity of development. However, reports such as "The Economic Impacts of Inadequate Infrastructure for Software Testing" created by the National Institute of Standards and Technology help to solidify the need for practices that enhance the quality of our software and our teams.

Quality of software has always been a difficult aspect to measure properly. Most organizations retrieve metrics from their bug-tracking software. However, one could argue that this is far from adequate because poor testing procedures that miss many defects give the impression that the software is bug free. Other organizations simply look at the quality of the project as it applies to time and money. Are we on budget? Are we going to meet our deadlines? The fact is there are many dimensions to quality that include quality of planning, performance of quality assurance activities, monitoring quality over the life of a project, and even quality of the software development team. Lack of attention to quality assurance practices can also lead to a great amount of uncertainty, which eventually manifests itself into slipped schedules, cut features, and team frustration.

Cost of Defects

A study (*http://www.nist.gov/director/prog-ofc/report02-3.pdf*) commissioned by the U.S. Department of Commerce's National Institute of Standards and Technology (NIST) found that software defects cost the United States economy from $22 to $59 billion annually. The study found that about 80 percent of development funds are consumed by software developers identifying and correcting defects.

From a Project Management perspective, it is much easier to estimate time to conduct quality assurance activities than it is to guess the impact defects will have on a project. In the previous section, we looked at various tools provided by Visual Studio Team Edition for Software Developers and Visual Studio Team Edition for Software Testers that not only help developers write higher-quality code, but also allow developers and testers to more readily continually validate software as it's being constructed. In fact, Visual Studio Team System provides quality-assurance benefits even before we write a single line of code, by providing enhanced designers and deployment validation–modeling tools with Visual Studio Team Edition for Software Architects.

Quality-assurance features can also be found in Team Foundation Server. For example, software testers can publish the results of tests to Team Foundation Server in association with a particular build of software. This information can be used to help measure the quality of each build represented through the many reports that ship with Visual Studio Team System. In fact, Team Build can also be responsible for automatically running tests, such as unit tests, code coverage analysis, and load tests, automatically during its operations. Team Build will also automatically publish the results of all tests, providing a painless approach to continual automated software testing.

Visual Studio Team System's ability to support traceability between work items, test results, and builds also provides us with an important mechanism for helping to implement quality. When making changes to your system, it's often important to understand what other areas are affected. Work item linking, also known as *traceability*, provides the necessary information to produce an impact analysis when change does happen.

Managing Scope

Scope relates to the functionality the team will be responsible for delivering over a certain time period. A project manager must be able to understand what the team is building in addition to the relative priority of each feature to be able to set priority and to construct a work schedule. Visual Studio Team System provides a number of features that will allow better definition, assignment, and tracking of project scope.

Work items shouldn't surprise you as being key to tracking scope with Visual Studio Team System. Depending on the Process Template you chose to use to create your Team Project, you will be able to use work item types such as a Scenario, Quality of Service Requirement, Requirement, and Change Requests to help specify the functionality that your software solution should encompass. Most of these work item types provide you with the ability to set priority or rank on each feature to help you with prioritization. In addition, Team Project areas are an important means of classifying work items within Visual Studio Team System; they are used to help better group scope-related work items together under a hierarchy of feature categories.

There are also numerous reports that can be used by project managers to track scope-related data on a project. These reports can be useful in helping to determine whether scope should be cut in order to meet required deadlines. Reports such as Remaining Work and Unplanned Work are key when it comes to scope management.

Managing Risk

Following the process of risk management falls on the shoulders of every member of a team; however, the project manager takes ultimate responsibility. Even though every project is different, none of them is void of risks. A *risk* is any event or condition that jeopardizes any form of quality, from quality of schedule and cost to quality of product or team. Interestingly, risk is directly associated with uncertainty. This means that the higher the uncertainty of a particular area, the greater the risk of something going wrong or unplanned. It is up to the project manager, with guidance from the project sponsors, to balance risk management with productivity throughout the development process. There are many ways that you can deal with risk; however, the most effective way is to continually anticipate and track risk all the way through a project. As a project manager, you will work to continually identify major risks throughout the life of a project. After a risk has been identified, risks should then be classified and prioritized based on aspects of each risk such as impact or potential reach. Many project managers take this much further and identify mitigation, contingency, and the trigger for each risk. Risk *mitigations* are tasks that the team can perform to prevent the risk from occurring. A *trigger* is an event or a condition that signals that a risk has manifested itself into an issue and is causing work blockage or is impacting some other aspect of quality. *Contingencies* are tasks that the team can, after a risk trigger has been detected, mitigate the impact of the issue to the project and team.

The underlying premise to risk management, and at a higher level, the management of quality as a whole, is managing uncertainty. As stated in the "Managing Quality"" section of this chapter, it is much easier for a project manager to estimate and plan for what they know compared to what they don't know. That is, planning and executing risk-mitigation strategies is much more predictable than reacting to risk triggers and attempting to minimize impact through contingency activities. You can never really predict whether a risk will manifest itself as an issue; however, you can predict the effort required to prevent the risk. The Microsoft Solutions Framework (MSF) 3.0 proposes an evolutionary risk-management model that begins with risk identification and definition and then progresses through analysis, planning, tracking, and controlling, as depicted in Figure 2-11. This risk-management model is certainly not new, and it is supported by Visual Studio Team System out of the box in conjunction with the MSF for Agile Software Development and MSF for CMMI Process Improvement process templates.

By default, Visual Studio Team System supports the risk-management process through process template definitions that specify work item types used to track risks and control the risk-management process and by defining work item queries that help project managers track risks throughout the duration of the software development life cycle. (Only MSF for CMMI Process Improvement includes a Risks work item query. Adding a customized work item query can be accomplished by using Team Explorer.) Specifically, MSF for Agile Software Development and MSF for CMMI Process Improvement process templates both include a Risk work item type. The Risk work item type definition within the process template specifies the fields and rules that will allow you to identify and determine risk and create the Risk management workflow itself, as depicted in Figure 2-12. This means that throughout your projects, you will be able to track risks through Risk work items and use work item queries to help track and monitor those risks as they move through the risk management process.

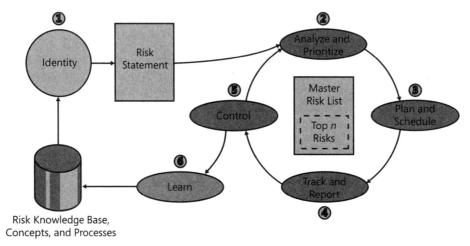

Risk Knowledge Base,
Concepts, and Processes

Figure 2-11 The MSF Risk Management model

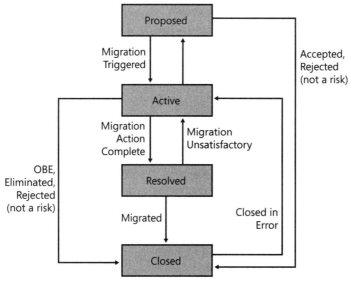

Figure 2-12 The workflow of a Risk work item specified within the MSF for CMMI Process Improvement process template

Summary of the Visual Studio Team System Impact

Even though Visual Studio Team System doesn't have a specific product line dedicated to project managers, its impact on the project management role is significant. Here is a summary of those impacts:

- Increases predictability and reduces variability of your software development projects by providing you with the ability to focus on quality-assurance activities throughout the development life cycle

- Provides visibility into your software development life cycle

- Bridges the gap between IT and Operations, mitigating many risks associated with architecture and deployment

- Effectively manages distributed development team projects

- Responds to changes in business quickly and effectively

- Helps achieve greater levels of CMMI

- Enhances project governance

- Increases team productivity and collaboration during software development

---

Project Management Is Not Just About Managing

There is much more to being an effective project manager than having the ability to manage. In fact, in many ways, a project manager's interpersonal skills will play an even larger role in the success of his or her position. Project managers must be effective communicators, demonstrate the ability to get things done, and they must be talented at developing and reinforcing a shared vision across the team and motivating a diverse team, which is sometimes very difficult with a large group of software developers. Project managers must also be able to negotiate and manage conflict. However, the most important skill for a project manager to have is the ability to solve problems creatively. In some ways, these skills make it difficult for anyone to grow into a project manager role, despite all the procedures and tools in the world.

Summary

In this chapter, we revisited the world of the project manager and took a tour of Visual Studio Visual Studio Team System from end to end. We also mapped the features that are provided by Visual Studio Team System to the common activities of a project manager, setting the foundation for the chapters that follow.

Chapter 3
Project Initiation

- Review the activities performed during the initiating phase of a project.

- Understand how the Microsoft Solutions Framework maps to initiating tasks.

- Understand the role of Microsoft Visual Studio 2005 Team Foundation Server during initiating activities.

- Learn to create and navigate Team Projects.

Initiating a Project

In this chapter, we will discuss what the Project Management Book of Knowledge (PMBOK) refers to as *initiating processes* as they relate to the out-of-the-box experience of Microsoft Visual Studio Team System. In its simplest context, these activities consist of the work required to start a new project or a new phase of a much larger project. Initiating activities focus on finding and recording requirements of the system in addition to attempting to gather and quantify the objectives of a project as set by the project sponsors and ultimately those who are the source of the requirements themselves. Activities performed during initiation also focus on gathering initial assumptions and understanding constraints that will ultimately limit the boundaries of the project and the software that is about to be constructed.

Project initiation might seem very straightforward; however, these activities should not be taken lightly. The work produced during project initiation will form an important foundation for the rest of your project. You will meet with the stakeholders to clarify exactly what you're building, whom you're building it for, the resources you will build it with, and how you will define success. In addition, realizations produced during initiation will also form a baseline from which variations will be tracked.

Traditionally, the primary deliverable from this phase of a project is the *project charter*, which is used by project managers to obtain authorization for a project or phase to begin. To do this, project managers must capture and document the objectives of the project sponsors and the expected results of the project. In the project charter document, the scope of the proposed project is linked into the big picture of the organization detailing information such as the underlying need for the project as it relates to overall organization initiatives or objectives. In large initiatives, where work must be broken into a series of projects or phases, the project charter works to confirm requirements, assumptions, constraints, and expectations for the next phase of the project. To produce a project charter, project managers need to gather base stakeholder and user requirements and constraints regarding budget, environmental, and organizational assets that will be either impacted or required during project execution. A project charter takes as input the overall statement of work and the initial set of constraints that have been identified by the stakeholders.

Another common deliverable produced during project initiation is the preliminary scope of work. This is a more detailed description of the project and includes the constraints captured in the project charter. The preliminary scope statement works to identify deliverables, specific requirements, project boundaries, acceptance methods, and methods by which the team will work to control scope.

The requirements and scope outlines in the project charter need not be extensively specific at this point. Compare building a house to hiring a contractor to build you a new house. The builder will typically ask questions like "How much are you willing to spend?" and "When do you want to take possession?" Given some of these constraints, the builder will also work with you to specify the house plans that can help fit your budget, likely allowing you to fine-tune many of the house's features, such as general type of material that will be used for flooring and cabinetry, before solidifying an overall quote. It is highly unlikely that very specific questions, such as the color of the walls or the style of handles used on the master bathroom door, will need to be asked at this point. Many of these decisions will not significantly impact the cost of the house and can be made much later in the build process. The architecturally significant decisions are the ones that need to be focused on when building a house; the same is true in many ways when building software.

60–80 Percent Rule

Project managers who embrace an iterative requirements-gathering-and-planning approach recognize that you can gather only a certain amount of requirements of the software before it becomes a futile process. You should embrace the fact that it's virtually impossible to specify all aspects of the software you are going to build before actually starting to build that software. A good rule of thumb is if you can specify 60 to 80 percent of what you are going to build, you should likely move on and expect to squeeze the remaining details later in the development process.

Introduction to the Narratives

Perhaps the best method of conveying a message is to wrap it in a story. This book will take you through the life of a typical software project manager named Chase. Chase is an experienced software developer who has played virtually every role on a software development project from software developer and tester to project manager. Chase was recently hired by a startup venture capital–based organization to lead their latest software development effort. For the first time in his career, Chase has been given complete control and has been made responsible for a team of 25 others that consist mostly of developers and testers. Like most software developers, Chase is an extremely smart person and learns quickly—usually as he goes. Chase has a track record of getting things done; however, over the past five years, Chase's interest around project management has been growing to the point where he has taken night courses on project management and has been working to attain project management certification from the Project Management Institute. Agile software development methodologies have always been an interest of Chase's, and he's looking forward to test driving some of his new knowledge on his new job.

Chase's team has been assigned to develop a new commercial, shrink-wrapped software application that targets the insurance industry by using the latest Microsoft .NET technology. The organization for which Chase is now working, Humongous Insurance, has some lofty goals and some very real deadlines and has given Chase the challenge of having the product ready for release within eight months. Needless to say, Chase is excited and up for the challenge. Chase is starting off with a great team; however, he is keenly aware that it will take much more than just smart people to succeed. We will see the launch of Chase's story in this chapter and then follow subsequent phases of the project life cycle through the next three chapters of the book.

Why Chase's Story?

Many different types of organizations use Visual Studio Team System to help build software. Other environments could include software consulting organizations working against fixed-bid tendered contracts, multi-technology platform-based projects, research and development projects, or even multi-geographic and offshoring scenarios. It is the intent of Chase's story to provide enough diversity in approach to help you to adapt the principles and practices prescribed in this book to other more specialized scenarios that you may need to deal with. Because we cannot cover all project types across all possible scenarios, our goal to provide you with a base pattern that you can extend to fit your particular project style and team.

Project Initiation and MSF

Many organizations do not view project initiation activities as part of the project at all. In fact, the end result of project initiation usually marks the beginning of the project or no project at all if the project charter is rejected. With this in mind, it is entirely possible that you may not use Visual Studio Team System at all during project initiation. In fact, your team will probably start using Visual Studio Team System only when the project has been given the green light and the project team is ready to begin collaborating.

As we mentioned in Chapter 2, "Project Management Features of Visual Studio Team System," one of the strengths of Visual Studio Team System is its ability to adapt to virtually any software development life cycle model. Out of the box, Microsoft provides you with the Microsoft Solutions Framework (MSF) as a basis of your software development projects that use Visual Studio Team System. In fact, Visual Studio Team System supports two flavors of MSF: MSF for Agile Software Development and MSF for CMMI Process Improvement, both stemming from the same sets of principles and process mindsets. We will refer to both as the Microsoft Solutions Framework or MSF (unless we need to differentiate one from the other).

Iterations in MSF

MSF specifies a highly iterative method of developing software that promotes a greater ability to adapt to change and refine processes and techniques to best suit the needs of the project. Iterations are fixed-length segments of time in which teams plan, schedule, and perform their work. All aspects of product development, from requirements definition through analysis, design, development, coding, and transition are grouped into these iterations, which typically last anywhere from 2 to 6 weeks. The duration of different iterations within the same project need not be the same length and can be adjusted to best fit the need of the process, team, and scope of the project. The project team simply continues through these mini-development projects until the completion of the project. As you might expect, different iterations can have a different focus as you progress through the development process. For example, the initial iterations of a project might be used simply to specify the requirements and solution architecture of the software you want to build; whereas iterations closer to the end of the project will likely focus more on transitioning the solution to a production environment or to the shelf for your customers to purchase. MSF refers to these themes as *tracks* and specifies five common tracks called Envisioning, Plan, Build, Stabilize, and Deploy. Furthermore, the MSF Agile flavor specifies a Continuous track, and MSF CMMI adds Governance and Operational Management tracks to this list. Tracks can be considered similar to phases in a project except that they can overlap; that is, it is possible for an iteration to be part of the Envisioning and Plan tracks at the same time. This means that activities performed during this block of time will involve both envisioning- and planning-related activities.

Feedback loops are essential to any adaptive system. In MSF Agile, iterations provide the opportunity for feedback to the team and the sponsors or customers who have ultimately requested the features in the software. At the end of an iteration, you should have a working and stable portion of the overall target system. By keeping the time duration of iterations brief (weeks rather than months), you are essentially tightening up the feedback loop thereby providing the opportunity for your team to adjust and adapt to any form of change.

The MSF Envisioning Track

The MSF Envisioning track is similar to PMOK's Initiate process group in that this track's focus is on the capture of the goals of the project and the constraints that help to specify the scope of your project. The primary output of the Envisioning track in MSF is the vision statement. *Vision statements* capture the context for the project and detail the events that have led up to the current business situation or need for the proposed product. The vision statement also specifies the major requirements and time frames that will drive the project and should clearly specify whether the project is driven by feature (software is not released until features are met) or by date (software will be released on a certain date regardless of the features completed by then). Figure 3-1 shows the workstreams in the envisioning track of MSF.

Note   A *workstream* is used in MSF to represent a grouping of activities and roles on a project. For more information about MSF and workstreams, refer to Appendix B, "Microsoft Solutions Framework."

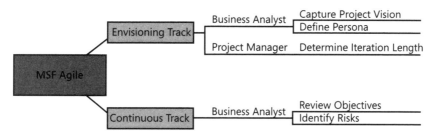

Figure 3-1   MSF Envisioning track workstreams

MSF goes a bit further than what you might find in a traditional project initiation by adding tasks that create personas and set iteration lengths for the project. A *persona* is a more comprehensive way of describing a user of your software. Instead of the more conventional user type labels, such as administrator or corporate user, a persona works to capture the essence of your users by understanding aspects of their personalities such as related knowledge, skills, and general abilities. Personas take this even further by reflecting the essence of your users, detailing life history, personality quirks, interests, and hobbies. Adding deeper aspects of a user's personality makes a persona more realistic. If you are familiar with the Unified Process or the Unified Modeling Language (UML), you might think that a persona is similar to a use case actor; however, personas are much more complete, allowing the traditional actor stick figure to come alive with a personality that your entire team can identify with. In many cases, to help reinforce this concept, teams give names to their personas such as *Frank* or *Nancy* rather than traditional stick figure names such as *IT administrator*.

When creating an initial iteration plan, you will likely use a calendar to determine how much time is available for the project and attempt to divide that time into smaller segments, taking into consideration the time needed to ramp up the team and put together the development and test environments, to construct the project, and to deploy the project. Remember, not all iterations need to be of the same duration. You might even choose to have a 1-week iteration in which the team performs technology assessments that will allow them to make good software design decisions in future iterations. For example, you might want to allocate an iteration for your team to evaluate new *Microsoft* ASP.NET 2.0 Web-based user controls or other recent technical innovations that would be beneficial to your team. Iterations dedicated to writing code usually last anywhere from 2 to 6 weeks depending on the size of your team and the complexity and relative size of the work your team is to undertake.

MSF Agile also specifies a Continuous track, which details a set of workstreams and activities that should happen continually throughout the project. Some of these workstreams can also be included with Envisioning activities in the initiating phase of a project, which involves refining personas, reviewing project objectives, and identifying risks. The Continuous track also specifies activities such as Evaluate Test Metric Thresholds and Triage Bugs; however, these activities truly can't be performed until your team begins constructing the software. One of the more important initiating activities is the Identify Risk activity under the Guide Project workstream of MSF Agile. Sources of risks for a project can originate from usability requirements, reliability requirements, performance requirements, usage scenarios, complex business rules, integration interactions, or even ambiguous requirements. After you have identified risks, you can then do a preliminary impact analysis and prioritization of the risks. You may actually want to combine the vision statement, persona descriptions, initial iteration breakdown, and initial risk assessment into a project charter document to be submitted for project approval and ultimate activation. Risk identification should always have a high priority because these risks will help you to identify some of the finer details of your plan. For example, *risk mitigation*, the process of trying to prevent an identified risk from occurring, manifests itself as additional activities in your plan. *Feature creep* is a common risk identified by many project managers, whereby features are added to software during the software development process without any form of tracking or management. We all know that feature creep can harm our projects, but what can we do to prevent it? Possibilities include a formalized change-tracking process and a functional baselining and sign-off system. Each of these mitigations will result in extra work that will need to be performed by your team and integrated into the overall project plan.

As you can see, tasks associated with the MSF Envisioning track have little to do with Visual Studio Team System. When you do get approval, it will be time to dive into Visual Studio Team System, and when you do, you will start by creating a new Team Project. At this point in the book, however, it makes little sense to fully explain what you and your team will be doing during the MSF Envisioning track without taking a closer look at Visual Studio Team System, and specifically, Team Projects. Once you get a better understanding of the structure of a Team Project, it will be much easier to understand how Envisioning tasks fit into the bigger picture and better prepare you for planning activities. With that said, let's take a break from project initiation activities and pay a little more attention to Visual Studio Team System.

Before You Create a New Team Project

Before you can use Visual Studio Team System for your team, you must first create a Team Project. A *Team Project* will be your repository for everything related to a project such as work items (including scenarios, bugs, tasks, and risks), work item queries, source code, a Microsoft Windows SharePoint Services site used to maintain all of your project documents, and report definitions.

Team Project Creation Checklist

Not all team projects are created equally, and therefore, you will need to address a few issues before creating a new team project. Before creating your project, you should have the following information:

- **The process template** You should select the process template best suited for your project. During the process of template selection, you should also evaluate the need to extend or customize a process template to fit the needs of your project. For example, your project might require additional information, such as a task-tracking code or customer identifier, to be tracked for each work item, requiring the work item definition to be changed within the process template. In addition, you should also evaluate the workflows that are specified for each work item. These workflows specify the mini-processes of your project, such as the change-management process or the defect-management process. You should also evaluate the default reports that are specified within the process template to determine if they fit the needs of your project. If they do not fit your needs, you will need to modify the process template work item type definitions and report definitions to meet your metrics gathering and reporting requirements. More information on this topic can be found in Chapter 7, "Tailoring Visual Studio Team System."

- **The name of your project** This may seem like a trivial decision; however, you really should consider naming guidelines for the Team Projects that you create. In some organizations, the job of considering naming conventions for your projects may not be your responsibility; however, in smaller organizations, the software project manager will likely be responsible for or at least consulted when establishing naming conventions. Considering that you may be using a shared Team Foundation Server architecture and that dozens of different teams might be using the same infrastructure over a long period of time, you will likely want to name your projects to ensure that they are unique over time and easy to find by your project team. Some organizations have chosen to use project codes to identify their team projects; others use a combination of department and project title. Whatever you choose, it should be consistent and make sense to your organization, and it should be resilient enough to last for at least five years. You should also take into consideration how your team members will find your project. The initial release of Team Foundation Server does allow you to delete projects but provides no ability for Team Project archival. For this reason, many organizations simply leave existing projects on computers running Team Foundation Server, even after they have been completed. In addition, a single Team Foundation Server infrastructure can literally support hundreds of projects. If you now consider that when connecting to a Team Project, you must choose from an alphabetically sorted list of Team Projects, you can easily see the importance of naming conventions. Here are some examples:

- ❏ 06-Accounting-TaxAnalysis: *06* denotes the year of the project start, *Accounting* represents the internal department the software is being constructed for, and *TaxAnalysis* represents the name of the project.

- ❏ 07-MySalesForce-CRMv1: *07* indicates the year of the project start, *MySalesForce* is a suite of products, and *CRMv1* indicates the first version of the CRM application within the MySalesForce suite of applications.

- ■ **Source control structure** During the process of creating a new project, a decision must be made on whether to base the new project on existing source code or to start with an empty source code pallet. In this case, if the Team Project represents a new version of an existing application, you will likely choose to branch from an existing Team Project's source code repository. If your project represents a new application, you will probably instruct the Project Creation Wizard to create a new source code repository for your team. Consult with your development team on this and any decision on your source code structure.

Note Most organizations place security restrictions on who can create new Team Projects, and in a lot of cases, this list will exclude project managers. If you do not have enough permissions to create a Visual Studio Team System project on your organization's Team Foundation Server, you should still be familiar with the process and what is required prior to the operation.

Selecting a Process Template

Chapter 2 painted a picture of all of the pieces of Visual Studio Team System, from Team Foundation Server as it applies to the role of the project manager to project tracking and analytical services that come that come out of the box, to the client side components, such as Visual Studio Team Suite, that your team members will likely be using. In Chapter 2, we also talked about how Process Templates act as a blueprint for your project, specifying the type of work items available to your team, the structure and default content of the Windows SharePoint project site, and some default tasks, work item classifications, and report definitions. Obviously, the project template you will choose for your project will be determined by the type of project you will be running. To refresh your memory, Visual Studio Team System ships with two process templates: MSF for Agile Software Development and MSF for CMMI Process Improvement. It is important to note that both built-in process templates are considered to embrace Agile software engineering principles, which are becoming more of the standard than the exception because they encapsulate a great many proven best practices for managing the software construction process.

What Is an Agile Method?

Use of *Agile Software Development* sometimes causes the formation of project teams that have problems predicting cost, quality, or delivery dates. In short, an Agile method is iterative, incremental, self organizing, and ever evolving. Agile methods make it possible for developers to expect and embrace change, not to fear or ignore it. Developers using Agile methods believe that it is better to adapt to changing conditions so they can focus on the value they deliver to their customers rather than attempting to prevent change and sacrifice the additional value the customer would have realized as a result of the change. Proponents of Agile methods believe that it is better to adapt to changing conditions so they can focus on the flow of value delivered as a result of the software than it is to prevent change and sacrifice value.

The following sections describe MSF Agile, MSF for CMMI, and third-party solutions.

MSF for Agile Software Development Process Template

In an MSF Agile–based project, your team will gather requirements in the form of scenarios. A *scenario* is similar to a story that describes a user's interaction with your solution as the user attempts to achieve a particular goal. Successful teams capture scenarios that ultimately lead to the user achieving his or her goal (positive scenarios) and scenarios that prevent the achievement of a user's goals (negative scenarios). Another key concept behind MSF Agile is that it promotes the creation of small teams of highly motivated and skilled individuals. MSF Agile specifies a small number of project roles such as Business Analyst, Project Manager, Architect, Developer, Tester, and Release Manager. MSF Agile doesn't mandate that you have one person for each of these roles; in fact, it assumes that you will likely assign multiple roles to individuals on your team and provides guidance on more likely scenarios for multi-role positions. The MSF Agile team model scales by either adding people to the relatively small number of preset roles or breaking the project into sub-projects and sub-teams, essentially creating a "team of teams" environment.

Scenarios, as we have just defined them, are not enough to describe to the software developer how to construct the software. MSF Agile uses the concept of Quality of Service work item types to capture certain required characteristics of the resulting system such as expected performance, ability to handle load, availability, accessibility, and maintainability. Essentially,

Quality of Service requirements don't describe the functionality of the software but instead help to set constraints on the functionality, the way that functionality is presented and implemented, and the environment under which the functionality should operate.

In short, MSF Agile is an ideal starting point for competitive development environments such as research and development projects, or even off-the-shelf product companies that want to release high-quality software incrementally and are more concerned with being able to adapt to a changing market rather than tracking change. MSF Agile also embraces more of a "walking into the cloud" approach, in which teams plan as they go rather than attempt to plan up front. Projects based on MSF Agile will produce working results quickly but must be highly iterative to continually adjust for newly discovered needs. With this in mind, when you have a project with a relatively short life cycle and a team that can work without a great deal of documentation and that focuses on achieving working software and continual customer validation, choose the MSF Agile process template.

MSF for CMMI Process Improvement Process Template

Capability Maturity Model Integration (CMMI) was developed at the Software Engineering Institute (SEI) to provide organizations with a framework of process improvement. CMMI was formed to provide guidance around improving an organization's processes and their ability to manage the development, acquisition, and maintenance of products and services. MSF for CMMI Process Improvement (MSF CMMI) is an extension to MSF Agile that targets CMMI Level 3–compliance, and for this reason is the world's first CMMI-compliant process based on Agile principles! You shouldn't assume that by simply adopting Visual Studio Team System and using MSF for CMMI that your organization will be compliant with CMMI Level 3. In fact, MSF for CMMI truly provides only process guidance designed to accelerate your achievement of the staged representation of CMMI Level 3 (also known as *Defined Process*) because MSF for CMMI specifies only 17 of Level 3's 21 process areas.

> **Note**   For more general information about CMMI, refer to Appendix A, "Capability Maturity Model Integration (CMMI)."

With MSF CMMI you have more comprehensive work items such as a Requirement, which can be many types, including Functional, Interface, Quality of Service, Safety, Security, and Scenario. In fact, a Requirement work item blends together Scenario and Quality of Service work item types found in MSF for Agile while adding a few more important requirement types. In addition to the enhanced versions of the Bug, Risk, and Task work items, MSF for CMMI provides the Change Request work item, which helps project teams explicitly track and manage the change control process of your project; Issues work items, which are used by project teams to help track any condition that is blocking productivity, quality, customer valued features, or schedule; and the Review work item type, which is responsible for documenting the results of a project or code review. You will also see that MSF for CMMI has also built upon the roles specified in MSF Agile as depicted in Figure 3-2.

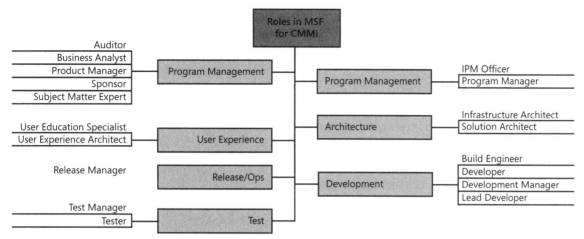

Figure 3-2   Many more team roles are specified in MSF for CMMI.

Understanding that MSF for CMMI focuses more on process and the understanding of variance and the management of process, you should also expect a great deal in terms of reporting. In addition to the reports you get with MSF Agile, CMMI will also give you reports such as Issues and Blocked Work Items, Requirement Details, Requirements Test History and Overview, and Triage. These extra reports provide a heightened ability to track your project by allowing you to better understand issues you must resolve to allow work to continue or quality to increase and helping you to monitor the effectiveness of your quality assurance activities as your project progresses.

Where does MSF for CMMI fit in? Well, to start with, it certainly does not replace a corporate-wide process-improvement infrastructure; in fact, it should work side by side with one. Even though MSF for CMMI has many more steps than MSF Agile, you can still consider using MSF for CMMI even when your organization does not aspire to achieve any CMMI certifications. MSF for CMMI relies more on process and planning than does MSF for Agile. In fact, MSF for CMMI is ideal for any regulated environment and environments which considerable planning needs to be performed up front and in which change, risk, and issues need to be explicitly managed and controlled. For these reasons, the MSF for CMMI process template is also commonly used in software consulting practices, which are typically contract focused and therefore have a greater need for auditing, tracking, and the greater ceremony provided by the template. Many organizations simply use the MSF for CMMI as a more formalized version of MSF Agile.

Other Process Template Options

One of the key benefits of Visual Studio Team System is that the product is not functionally bound by a particular set of process templates. In fact, you have a great deal of opportunity to either modify existing process templates to fit your needs or acquire other custom process templates from Microsoft Partners who have invested in Visual Studio Team System extensibility and customization.

The process templates that you use to create new Visual Studio Team System projects are completely customizable. Each process template specifies the contents and structure of the project portal created for each Visual Studio Team System project in addition to work item definitions, work item queries, default project work items, default project classifications (areas and iterations), and report definitions and security settings. Microsoft encourages customization of the default MSF process templates they ship with the product, and they provide a great deal of documentation and tools to assist you in this process.

> **Note** Many Microsoft partners also provide process templates for Scrum, Feature Driven Development (FDD), and the Unified Process. To see a list of partners and their offerings with regards to customized process templates, visit *http://www.microsoft.com/msf*.

Scrum Process Template

Perhaps one of the more popular process templates available is from a company called Conchango, which provides a Scrum process template for Visual Studio Team System. The Scrum process template provides extensive support for the Agile-based Scrum methodology, because it was produced in conjunction with Ken Schwaber, one of the founding members of Scrum, and the Microsoft Technology Centre in the United Kingdom. Conchango's Scrum process template for Visual Studio Team System is free and can be found at *http://www.scrum-master.com*.

Our Focus Is MSF Agile

As mentioned, MSF for CMMI is based upon all of the goodness of MSF Agile, yet it contains a great deal of specific processes and project artifacts required to help organizations achieve CMMI Level 3 certification and compliance. CMMI compliance with Visual Studio Team System can be a topic for an entire book, so this book will focus on MSF Agile because this flavor of MSF embodies the core principles of MSF for CMMI and can be used as a basis for all future MSF for CMMI learning.

Creating a New Team Project

When you have everything you need to create the Team Project, your next step is to create it in Visual Studio Team System, which you will be able to do only if you have been granted appropriate permissions on the computer running Team Foundation Server. In fact, many organizations restrict the creation of Team Projects to Visual Studio Team System administrators; in this case, you would likely make a request to create your Team Project by supplying your organization's Visual Studio Team System administrators with the Team Project information you have already assembled. If the responsibility of creating new Team Projects lies with you, here are the steps you can take to do so:

> **Note** This book assumes that you have all of the required software installed on your computer. In most cases, project managers will have only Team Explorer installed, which also provides integration between Visual Studio Team System and Microsoft Office Project and Microsoft Office Excel.

1. Launch Microsoft Visual Studio 2005 by choosing Start | All Programs | Microsoft Visual Studio 2005 | Microsoft Visual Studio 2005.

> **Tip** You're a Project Manager, so why are you being asked to launch Visual Studio? Even though you may not have Visual Studio 2005 installed on your computer, when you install the client software for Team Foundation Server, you will get the Visual Studio 2005 IDE shell. It is within this environment that you will access Team Explorer.

2. Connect to the computer running Team Foundation Server by choosing Tools | Connect To Team Foundation Server. If your computer has already connected to a computer running Team Foundation Server, the name of that computer will appear in the drop-down list of computers in the Connect To Team Foundation Server dialog box. If no computers appear in this list, you will need to add the computer by clicking Server and then in the resulting dialog box, clicking Add. At this point, you will be required to type the name of your computer running Team Foundation Server and some technical details regarding the port number and protocol. You should contact your Team Foundation Server administrator for these details. After you have either added a new computer running Team Foundation Server or selected one from the Server drop-down list, click OK.

3. Launch the New Team Project Wizard by choosing File | New | Team Project. The New Team Project Wizard will appear.

4. Type the name of your new Team Project in the first page of the wizard and then click Next.

5. Select a process template from the Process Template list. Only registered process templates will be listed at this point, and by default, you should see two process templates, MSF for Agile Software Development and MSF for CMMI Process Improvement. Click Next to continue. If you have chosen to perform customizations to an existing process template, the modified process template must be properly installed to Team Foundation Server to appear in this list. Please refer to Chapter 7 for more information on process template customization processes.

6. Provide a name for the project portal. By default, the name of the project portal will be the name of the Team Project you specified in step 1. Take note of the Team Project Portal Site Address that appears at the bottom of the Wizard page. This will be the URL by which team members can access the portal through their browser.

7. Specify Source Control Settings for your new Team Project. Here you will have three options: Create an empty source control folder, Create a new source control branch, or Do not create a source control folder at this time. You should consult with your project team when deciding the best action to take. Click Next to continue.

> **Note**   Your decision about whether to create a source code repository for your new Team Project likely depends on whether you are building new software or extending existing software. If you are working on version 2 of a project, you will likely branch from the existing code base, which must reside within the version control system of Visual Studio Team System. Choose not to create a source code repository if your project will not have any new code associated with it.

8. Confirm the settings for your new Team Project, and when you are satisfied, click Finish to create the Team Project. After the project has been successfully created, the Wizard will display a completion message and provide you with the opportunity to view the project's associated process guidance Web page.

Anatomy of a Team Project

Before you dive into your project management duties as part of the initial phases of your project, you should become familiar with Team Explorer, which is the primary interface by which your team will interact with Visual Studio Team System.

Understanding Team Explorer

Team Explorer gets installed when you install the Team Foundation Client software. If you have Visual Studio 2005 installed, Team Explorer will come alive from within Visual Studio providing a new Team Explorer dockable window and new menus such as the Team menu. If you don't have Visual Studio 2005 installed, Team Foundation Client installation routines will set up the Visual Studio 2005 development for you. Figure 3-3 depicts Team Explorer from within Visual Studio 2005.

Team Explorer is the main interface for all of the services provided by Team Foundation Server. It provides you with access to work items and work item queries, documents stored in document libraries on your Windows SharePoint project portal, all project reports, automated Team Build definitions, and access to the source code repository. Team Explorer also acts as a launching ground to Office Excel and Office Project integration and to the project portal and process guidance Web pages.

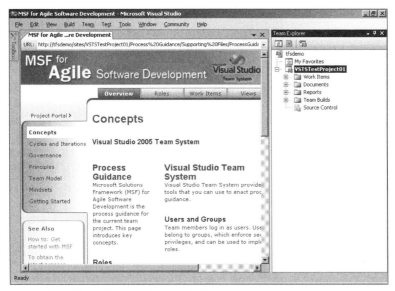

Figure 3-3   Team Explorer in Visual Studio

Accessing Process Guidance

As a project manager, you will likely be interested in how to access the process guidance Web pages. Process guidance provides you and your team with the context of the selected process template and underlying methodology and a wealth of reference information. MSF Agile, for example, provides information such as the core concepts of the methodology, details on how cycles and iterations relate to one another, team model definitions, core team mindsets, and tasks you need to perform to get started with the methodology. MSF Agile process guidance also provides details on each of the roles your team members will play on a project. These role descriptions also provide step-by-step guidance on associated workstreams and activities these roles will participate in. For example, the MSF Agile process guidance specifies that the Business Analyst role is responsible for helping to capture the project vision. It goes further by detailing the activities associated with creating a project vision, such as writing the vision statement and creating and refining personas. You can even see step-by-step how to perform each activity. For example, for the Write Vision Statement activity, the MSF Agile process guidance details how to summarize the project background, explain driving factors, identify users of the system, and determine key value propositions that reinforce the need of the project.

To access the process guidance Web page, perform the following steps:

1. In Team Explorer, right-click your Team Project and choose Show Project Portal from the shortcut menu. Alternatively, you can choose Show Project Portal from the Team menu within Visual Studio 2005. This will launch the Windows SharePoint site that was created for your project by the Project Creation Wizard.

2. From your project portal site, choose the process guidance link from the SharePoint navigation on the left side of the Web page. Your browser should now display the process guidance pages associated with your project.

You can also access process guidance directly from Team Explorer by right-clicking the Work Items folder under your team project and selecting Team Project process guidance from the shortcut menu.

Process guidance pages also go on to describe each work item type you will use in your project, detailing each work item's workflow states and transitions and how to use each field in the work items for your project. Process guidance also provides a few other ways of accessing information—through the Views and Index pages. The Views pages provide an alternate perspective of the content contained within the process guidance pages. Here the information that can also be accessed from other areas of process guidance is organized into different categories. The Index page works as the index of a book, providing you a categorized reference to all aspects of the site.

As a project manager, the process guidance pages are quite relevant because they reinforce the underlying methodology you will be using to deliver software. Many process guidance pages are available for your reference; however, you may want to change the default page that will be displayed to you when you enter the site to make it easier to access the information that is relevant to your role. To configure the process guidance pages to display the Project Manager role page when initially launched, perform these steps:

1. Launch process guidance by right clicking your project and choosing Show Project Portal from the shortcut menu.

2. After the process guidance is displayed in a browser window, navigate to the page that offers a description of the project manager role by clicking the Role tab at the top of the Web page. Then click the Project Manager role from the list of roles on the left side of the process guidance page.

3. In the top right corner of the Project Manager description pages, select the Set As Start Page check box.

After performing this step, whenever you next launch process guidance, the first page you will see will be the Project Manager role page. You can instruct all of the members of your team to configure their Start page as appropriate.

Work Items and Work Item Queries

Team Explorer displays your project in a folder-like structure. If you expand your project, you see that there is a folder for every main set of services provided by Team Foundation Server. The first folder you will see is the Work Items folder, and if you expand it, you will see that here you will be able to access work item information through work item queries. Work items are the heart and soul of Visual Studio Team System, especially for project managers. They specify everything that needs to get done on a project and are the source of virtually all reports and the underlying Visual Studio Team System data warehouse.

To view work items on your projects, you will use work item queries. There are a number of work item queries automatically created by the process template you used during the creation of your project. These queries provide filter criteria to help you determine the list of work items you want displayed. For example, in a project created from the MSF Agile process template, you will see a Project Checklist work item query, which will return a list of work items, regardless of their type, that are set within your current project and are in the "closed" state and that have their Exit Criteria check box selected. Alternatively, if you chose to create your project by using MSF for CMMI, you will see a work item query called Customer Requirements, which will return to you a list of Requirement work items that have a requirement type of either a Scenario or Quality of Service. To view a list of queries and execute a work item query to return a list of work items that meet the criteria specified in the work item query, perform these steps:

1. In Team Explorer, open the Work Items folder under your Team Project. Expand the Team Queries folder to view a list of all queries for your project.

2. Select a query from the list of work item queries that provides the closest search criteria for your needs, such as All Work Items, which will return all work items in your project that are not in the closed state.

3. Double-click the work item query to execute your query against your Team Project. The results of the query will be displayed as a grid within Visual Studio 2005. Click a returned row to view the work item details.

You will also see an area called My Queries. These are work item queries that are not shared with the team or are standard work item queries that you may use often. You can simply drag one of the provided work item queries to the My Queries folder to add an existing query to this list. More importantly, it is very easy to customize existing queries or even create your own to provide you with lists that are unique to your team, project, or organization. To customize a work item query, right-click it, preferably from your My Queries folder, and select View Query from the shortcut menu. This will display a work item query builder window, which you can use to specify filter criteria for your query. Each row in the query builder represents a filter condition. The first column allows you to specify an AND/OR relationship of the filter condition. The remaining columns allow you to specify field matching criteria: the Field column allows you to specify the work item field value you want to evaluate, the Operator column allows you to specify the conditional operator for the field value comparison, and the Value column allows you to specify the target of the field value comparison. Creating your own custom queries is very similar to customization, except that instead of viewing an existing query definition, you would choose Add Query from the Team menu. You will be prompted to save your query when you close the query builder window and will have an opportunity to provide a name and a location for your new query, You can name the query anything you want and store it as a My query that will be visible only to you under the My Queries folder or to a file on your computer." For more information about how to customize work item queries, refer to Chapter 7.

We just looked at how we can view work item information through work item queries. The next step is to understand how to create work items for your team. The good news is there are a lot of ways to do this; however, let's start by looking at how to create work items from within Team Explorer. To create a new work item, select the Work Items folder from Team Explorer and choose Team | Add Work Item. Alternatively, you can right-click the Work Item folder within Team Explorer and choose Add Work Item from the shortcut menu. You should see that you have a choice of a number of different work item types. The type of work item you will be able to add will depend on the process template you used to create your project. At this point, choose a work item type; for example, a Bug, and the work item form will appear inside of the Visual Studio IDE. Every work item type will have a different form for filling out its details.

 Caution   Don't let the name of the work item fool you. The definition of a Bug work item in an MSF Agile project will be different from that of a Bug in an MSF for CMMI project.

Work item forms are broken down into the following sections:

- **Title** Specifies the brief description of the work item
- **Classifications** Help to categorize your work items
- **Status** Provides information on the workflow and assignment of the work item
- **Work item detail** Allows you to specify additional information about the work item and see a work item history of change and its association with other Visual Studio Team System information.

Even though every work item type is different, all work items will share some common traits. For example, all work items have a History tab. Work item history will provide you with a way of understanding all of the changes to the work item during the duration of your project. History will be updated every time you change any detail of a work item and then choose to save those changes. The history section will show you which value changed with every save, as depicted in Figure 3-4. Every time you save a work item, the history tab will display the date and time of the save and detail the changes made to the work item field by field. The history area also provides you with the ability to add open-ended comments to your work items as you make changes allowing you to provide extra information to the work item or to participate in a work item—related discussion.

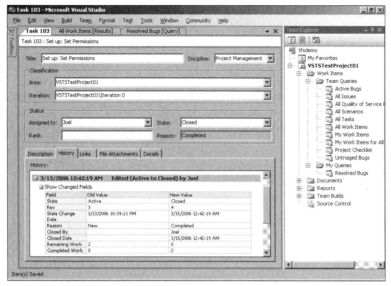

Figure 3-4   Work item history

Work items also have a Links tab. Here is where you will be able to associate a work item with various pieces of information such as other work items, source control change sets, files in the source code repository, and hyperlinks to anything with a URL including Web pages or documents stored within your project portal. In order to jump to the destination of a link, simply select the link and click Open or double-click the link in the list of links for the work item. The File Attachments tab will provide you with the ability to save associated documents along with the work item. A good example of this usage is to attach screen shots of a bug found in your solution to a Bug work item to help give developers assigned to resolve the bug more context and insight into the problem.

In Team Explorer, a *related* work item is simply a work item that has a link to another work item. To quickly create a related work item from an existing work item in your Team Project, right-click the existing work item in a work item query results window in Visual Studio 2005 and choose Add Related Work Item from the shortcut menu. Then choose the type of work item you want to create. The work item form will appear with a link to the original work item already populated in the Links tab (see Figure 3-5). In a similar fashion, you can make a copy of an existing work item by right-clicking the work item in the work item query results window in Visual Studio 2005 and choosing Create Copy Of Work Item in the shortcut menu. In the resulting dialog box, verify the Team Project you would like to make a copy of the item in (by default, it is your current team project) and the work item type of the copied work item (note that the target work item does not need to be of the same type as the original work item type). Again, the new work item will be automatically linked up with the original work item you just made a copy of. This may sound trivial; however, ensuring a healthy degree of traceability between work items means better reporting and a better flow of work. These methods make implementing high-fidelity traceability easier.

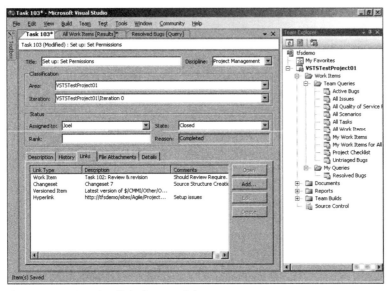

Figure 3-5   Creating links in a work item

Warning   Do not store all your project documentation using files attached to work items. You should use the document libraries in your project portal for all project-level documentation unless specifically relevant to a work item and accessible only by those who can access the details from that work item, such as storing screen shots along with recorded bugs.

As a project manager, you might not feel right managing your work items within Visual Studio, unless, of course, you feel just as at home in Visual Studio as you do in Office Project. For this reason, work items can be managed with both Office Excel and Office Project via a Microsoft Office plug-in that is included in the installation of the Team Foundation Client software. This functionality is very powerful; in fact, many project managers will almost never use Team Explorer to manage work items after the project is underway; they will use Office Excel or Office Project exclusively.

There are two ways that you can integrate Office Excel/Office Project with work items: by either pushing to the Office products or by having the Office products pull work items from Visual Studio Team System. *Pushing* refers to the process of sending the results of a work item query from within Team Explorer. *Pulling* refers to retrieving the results of a work item query initiated from within Office Excel or Office Project. Using either method will result in a two-way link between work item data stored within Visual Studio Team System and the work item information within Office Excel/Office Project. This means that if work item information changes in either Office Excel/Office Project or directly through Team Explorer, the changes will be reflected in both locations after you perform a synchronization.

> **Note**   Conflicts are always a possibility when you are allowed to edit work item information from different locations. For example, one of your team members may by modifying a Risk work item through the Visual Studio interface at the same time you are modifying the Risk item through Office Excel. When you perform a synchronization from Office Excel, a collision will be detected, and you will be given the opportunity to resolve the conflict by choosing which version should be stored in the Team Foundation Database.

To push work item information to Office Excel or Office Project, perform the following steps:

1. Launch Team Explorer from within Visual Studio 2005.

2. Navigate to your project in Team Explorer and expand the Work Items folder.

3. From the Team Queries subfolder, select a query whose results you want to manage within either Office Excel or Office Project.

4. Right-click the work item query definition, and on the shortcut menu, click Open In Microsoft Excel or Open In Microsoft Project.

These steps will then launch Office Excel or Office Project (depending on which command you clicked) and then run the query you specified and return the results to the selected application. Figure 3-6 demonstrates what it might look like in Office Excel. From within Office Excel/Office Project, notice the new Team menu, which was installed with the Team Foundation Client. The Team menu provides you with the options to synchronize changes between Team Foundation Server and Office Excel/Office Project, configure column settings, edit links and attachments, and modify project classifications.

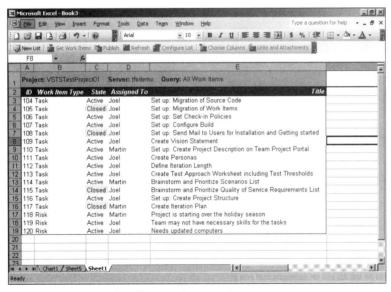

Figure 3-6   Microsoft Office Excel integration

If you wanted to pull work item information to Office Excel or Office Project, perform the following steps.

From Microsoft Office Excel:

1.   Choose New List from the Team menu to display the Connect To Team Foundation Server dialog box.

2.   Select your project from the list of Team Projects and click OK. Note that you also have the opportunity to connect to a new computer running Team Foundation Server at this point.

3.   You will be presented with a dialog box asking if you want to fill your new list with the results of a query or by typing new values you want to publish to Team Foundation Server. For the purpose of this exercise, ensure that Query List is selected and then choose a specific work item query from the Query Office list. Click OK to populate the Excel list with the results of the query.

From Microsoft Office Project:

1.   From the Team menu, select Choose Team Project to display the Connect To Team Foundation Server dialog box.

2.   Select your project from the list of Team Projects and click OK.

3.   From the Team menu, choose Get Work Items to display a dialog box that will allow you to specify the work items you want to bring into Office Project as tasks. Here you will be able to select a work item query in your Team Project, specify work items by their ID, or specify a value that must be contained within the work item title. In this case, select the Title Contains option, and then type **set up:** in the corresponding field with All Work Item types selected in the Type Selection drop-down list. Click Find to retrieve a list of work items that match this criteria.

4.   Select the work items you want to import from the results of the Find command by checking the work items in the results list. You can optionally use Select All or Unselect All to help you with this task if there are a lot of work items. When you have finished selecting the work items, click OK to load the work item information into Office Project.

> **Note**   More information on how to use Office Excel and Office Project will be provided in Chapter 4, "Planning a Project."

There are lots of reasons you might want to manage your work items in Office Excel and Office Project. For example, after you have work items in Office Excel, you can enjoy all of the Office Excel goodness you have come to enjoy such as automatically formatted lists, conditional formatting, filtering, pivot tables and pivot charts, and sorting. In addition, managing your work items through Office Excel or Office Project also means that you can take your work item information with you. By default, Team Explorer cannot be used when you are not connected to Team Foundation Server. When you use Office Excel and Office Project, you can make modifications to work items, add new work items, and delete work items even when you are not connected. When you are able to connect to Team Foundation Server, all you would need to do is to choose Publish Changes from the Team menu to synchronize all your changes and all of the changes to work items that may have been made by others on your team. Another added bonus of using Office Excel and Office Project to manage your work items is that all of the rules specified by the work item type, such as mandatory fields, workflow rules, and reference data, which includes lists of areas and iterations or project team members, are available within the products. Essentially, this means that you will be able to use Office Excel and Office Project for virtually every aspect of work item management.

Classifications

Your project will have a lot of work items of different types. Visual Studio Team System provides a feature called Classifications to better group work items into more manageable buckets. Visual Studio Team System provides two types of work item classifiers, areas and iterations. An *area* is literally a functional area or physical component of your solution. You can have an entire tree of areas which you can assign work items to. The project areas are then used to organize and display work items into logical groupings such as in reports or as a filter criteria in work item queries. *Iterations* are very similar, but they represent segments of time that work items must be completed within. Just as with areas, you can create a hierarchy of iterations that allow you to categorize work temporally. Examples of areas and iterations are show in Figure 3-7.

Area classifications have another really valuable feature relating to security. In order to modify classifications, you must have the appropriate permissions to do so, and by default, any team member who is a part of the Project Administrators group can do this. Areas, however, can take this a step further and even restrict users from editing and viewing work items assigned to specific area nodes. For example, you could prevent certain members of your team to see only work items that are assigned to the Mobile Client area by excluding their View Work Items In This Node permission on all other nodes. Using permissions such as this is just one way that you can logically partition your teams and their work.

You can customize classifications from Visual Studio 2005, Office Excel, or Office Project. From within Office Excel or Office Project, on the Team menu, choose Edit Areas And Iterations. From Visual Studio, select your team project in Team Explorer and then choose Team Project Settings | Areas And Iterations from the Team menu to display the Areas And Iteration dialog box. To add a new area or iteration, simply select the parent of the area or iteration in the corresponding tree list and click Add A Child Node or press Insert. Similarly, you can use the Areas And Iterations dialog box to delete, move, and indent areas and iterations to best fit your project's structure.

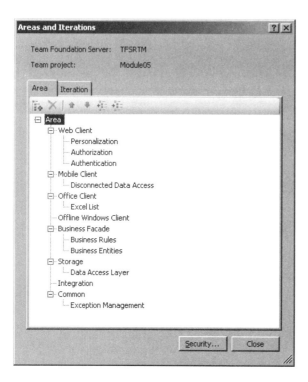

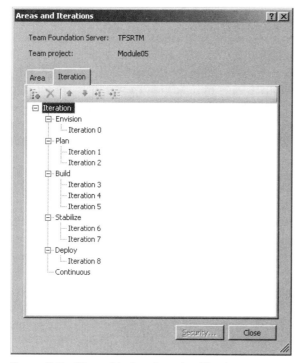

Figure 3-7   Hierarchical project classifications

Project Portal

Your project will undoubtedly create document artifacts, from project charters to meeting minutes and project plans. Visual Studio Team System creates a Windows SharePoint portal for each of your team projects, automatically creating document libraries and populating them with templates ready for use. After the site has been created, it is completely disconnected from the rest of Visual Studio Team System and operates as every other Windows SharePoint site does, with the exception of displaying reports. Once the site is created, you can feel free to create your own SharePoint lists, calendars, or subsites as you would on any other Windows SharePoint site. You can also create your own document libraries and populate them with your own documents.

Note Windows SharePoint Server is a very rich product with lots of options and features. This book will not provide you with details on how to use or configure Windows SharePoint Server other than in areas that directly relate to Microsoft Visual Studio Team System.

Documents and SharePoint

Team Explorer also provides you access to the documents stored on the project portal through the Documents folder under your Team Project. If you navigate to the Documents folder, you will see that you can view and access all of the document libraries and documents contained within directly from Team Explorer instead of being required to access content through your Web browser. The default document libraries and associated content you see when you initially create a Team Project are specified in the process template you used during the creation of your Team Project. You can learn how to modify the default content in Chapter 7.

From the document folder, you will have the option to create new document libraries, create new folders within document libraries, upload new documents into existing document libraries and folders, and open, edit, and delete documents stored within document libraries. To create a new document library by using Team Explorer, right-click the document folder under your Team Project, and choose New Document Library from the shortcut menu. To create new folders within document libraries, which are the root folders listed directly underneath the Documents folder in Team Explorer, right-click a document library folder and then choose New Folder from the shortcut menu. If you want to open a document, you have two choices, Open and Edit, which you can access from the shortcut menu after you right-click a document. If you choose Open, the document is launched in read-only format. If you choose Edit, the document is launched, and you will have the ability to perform check-out/check-in operations from the document library to help maintain document versioning.

Of course, you can still access all of the documents in the project portal from a browser, which will likely be the most common method for those on your team who do not need to interact with Team Foundation Server directly, such as business sponsors. The Documents folder in

Team Explorer provides an interface to documents stored in your document libraries. Note, however, that the documents you see listed in Team Explorer on your system may not always be up to date. To ensure that you're seeing the latest list of document libraries, folders, and documents, right-click the Documents folder under your Team Project and choose Refresh from the shortcut menu. This will instruct Team Explorer to refresh its list of document library contents from your project portal site.

Reports

From a project manager's perspective, Visual Studio Team System's reports are your best friend. As we discussed in Chapter 2, Visual Studio Team System Reports provide you with insight into how well your project is going, providing you with near real-time representations of the work that is being done, the quality of the software being produced, and the overall production trends of your team. These reports will provide you with the ability to monitor the progress of your project in real time without having to continually pester team members for their status. The list of reports for your project are accessed from the Report folder under your Team Project in the Team Explorer. Projects that were created from different process templates will generate different reports. For example, MSF for CMMI has a number of reports that are not provided in MSF Agile, and the Scrum process template from Conchango has an entirely different set of reports that are designed specifically for the Scrum methodology. At project inception, however, reporting will not play any role; because of this, we will provide you with more detailed information on how to interpret and act on the more significant MSF Agile–based reports in Chapter 5, "Monitoring and Controlling Projects Execution."

Builds

In Chapter 2, we discussed the importance of automated builds to the quality of software. The Build folder under your Team Project is where your developers will create and manage automated builds. Creating automated builds is a fairly technical task, and as a project manager, you will likely not be directly responsible for performing this task. You will likely, however, want the ability to see results of an automated build such as what tests passed and failed during the build and details on what features or bugs were included in each of the builds. Before you can do any of this, however, you will need to have created a build, and that means that your team will have already produced code. For more information on how to view and interpret the results of automated builds, refer to Chapter 5.

Envisioning Tasks in MSF Agile

Now that you know your way around Visual Studio Team System, let's take a look at how to perform certain envisioning tasks within Visual Studio Team System. As you might have noticed, Visual Studio Team System provides you with some of the document templates you will need to complete envisioning activities, specifically, a document template that allows you to capture the vision, personas, scenarios, and quality of service requirements.

> **Note**   You don't have to create a new Team Project to get the document templates; you can download them from Microsoft (*www.microsoft.com/msf*) or simply take a copy of the documents that reside in a newly created team project and store them in a safe place to be used during this phase of the project without the need for Visual Studio Team System.

Writing the Vision Statement

Let's start with the writing of the Vision document. If you have already created a Team Project, you can access this document from the Requirements subdirectory of the Documents section in Team Explorer. Alternatively, you can access this document directly from the project portal in the Requirements document store. What is really nice about this document is that instructions on how to fill it out are inside starting with a section called "How To Use This Template." The document is broken down into a few sections. In the "Background" section of the document, you will focus on the needs of the organization sponsoring the project. Here you will try to articulate the current state of the organization and your understanding of its future. This section should include a brief history of the business in relation to the project, the challenges the business faces that relate to the project, and the dependencies this project will have on other projects or vice versa. The template even provides an example of what the Background section could look like with a fictional AdventureWorks project.

The next section of the document is called "Driving Factors." This section expresses all of the major requirements for the project in addition to the constraints such as timelines and budget that will guide scope decisions.

The final section is called "Vision Statement." Your vision statement should be short and to the point and attempt to paint a picture of what life will be like when the project is complete. The default vision document provided for you gives you with plenty of guidance and examples in this area.

Identifying Personas

As we've already mentioned, Personas are representations of the users of your software. MSF provides you with a document you can use to capture persona information called Persona.doc, which is in the Requirements SharePoint document library for your project. You will likely fill out one of these documents for each user type you expect to use your program. The first step, however, is to identify those users. As with capturing the project vision, this job typically falls on the shoulders of the team member playing the role of the business analyst. This job starts by trying to get an understanding of all of the different roles users will play while using the software. A persona document will be created for each of the roles. Each document goes into extensive detail by establishing goals, skills, abilities, knowledge, motives, and concerns for the typical person who plays each role. The persona document also details the usage pattern of the persona with your system that details how often the persona will interact with the system and to what extent. This model is greatly improved over a traditional actor-use case model that you might find on projects that follow the Unified Process methodology.

Determining Iteration Length

As a project manager, you might also attempt to set the durations of iterations on your project. At this point in the project, this will be only a guess used to provide perspective on the entire project. During the planning phase of a project, you will again reaffirm these estimates after your team has more details on the requirements of the software, which will drive more specific estimates and hence a more accurate iteration plan. At this point, you will create an iteration using a common sense approach. You might start by saying "I think we'll need two 1-week iterations for gathering requirements and creating an architecture for the software." You might then take a look at the end of the project and say, "History suggests we're going to need almost two months to stabilize and deploy the software; let's do that over four 2-week iterations." After you set some of the initial iterations and some of the iterations that have to happen at the end, you're left with the available construction time, which you can also break into reasonable time blocks. Your initial iteration estimations might look similar to Figure 3-8.

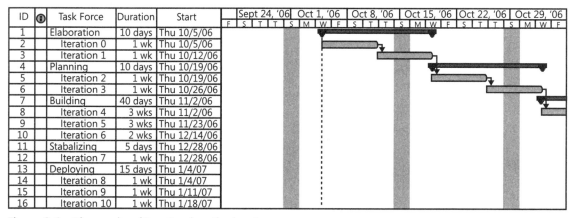

Figure 3-8   The results of iteration length planning

Chase Initiates His Project

Chase has been on the job now for two weeks. His first week was an exciting time. Chase kept busy settling into his office, meeting his team, and working with the human resources department to sort out benefits and insurance details and review the HR manual. Humongous Insurance has been preparing for Chase's arrival for some time and arranged for a week of training for Chase and his team on Microsoft Visual Studio Team System, which was selected by Humongous Insurance's Project Management Office (PMO) and Chief Software Architect as the tool of choice for managing Microsoft .NET 2.0–based projects. Humongous Insurance has always believed in building high-quality software and will not sacrifice this principle in order to go to market earlier than their competitors. That said, Humongous Insurance hopes that the Visual Studio Team System platform will allow them to meet their quality demands while at the same time shorten their development cycles and decrease the burden of software maintenance costs. Intense training consumed his second week of work at Humongous Insurance, and when it was complete, Chase was ready to put some of his new knowledge to work.

Chase is responsible for managing the construction of a new automobile insurance application (code named *Gimli*) that Humongous Insurance plans to take to market within 8 months. After extensive market research, Humongous Insurance identified the need to develop a new software package that helps automotive insurance companies track and optimize their customers' automotive insurance policies. During his initial meetings with the key stakeholders of Humongous Insurance, Chase asked for the business analyst named Dean to be assigned to his project. Dean is extremely familiar with the needs of the target market and will be responsible for helping to deliver the project charter, which will detail the project vision statement, personality profiles, and usage patterns of the primary users of the system. Dean was heavily involved in the initial market research performed by Humongous Insurance and will be responsible for creating a draft of the project charter within two weeks, a time period that Chase refers to as Iteration 0. In fact, Chase has asked Dean to develop the first draft of the project charter in the first seven days, leaving three days for revisions and final approval.

To get Dean started, Chase downloaded the process guidance documentation for MSF for Agile Software Developers from the main MSF Web site (*www.microsoft.com/msf*) and gave Vision.doc and Persona.doc to Dean as a starting point for his work on the project charter document. Everything looked straightforward to Dean with the exception of personas, which was something quite foreign to Dean, who came from a traditional UML background and was more accustomed to UML notation to create actors and their interaction with the system through use cases. Dean thought that creating users in such great detail was a bit strange, but he decided to give it his best effort based on what he knew of potential users of the system.

During Iteration 0, Humongous Insurance hired the same consultant that provided Chase and his development team with Visual Studio Team System training to come into the organization to set up and configure Team Foundation Server to make sure it was done correctly the first time. Chase is excited about his project being the first in the company to utilize Team Foundation Server. He is happy to be working with a new product instead of one that requires significant effort to develop into the next version. Because Chase's was the first project that will use Team Foundation Server, he decided to work closely with the Project Management Office (PMO) to help select the appropriate process template to guide his project. During his Visual Studio Team System training, Chase was exposed to MSF for Agile Software Development and MSF for CMMI Process Improvement. Both methodologies struck a chord with him because they promoted a mindset and an overall iterative delivery pattern that he's always agreed with and tried to achieve ever since he first experienced the Unified Process. Both he and the PMO thought that MSF for CMMI was likely too much for the Gimli project, and they settled on MSF for Agile Software. Because this was their first project using both Visual Studio Team System and MSF, they decided not to make any modifications to the MSF Agile process template and use it out of the box—they expect that they can make the necessary process revisions to their Team Project as the project progresses. Chase was also asked to recommend a naming convention for Team Projects on Team Foundation Server. After considering that the company had a limited set of products, each having a minor release every 6 months and a major version release about every 18 months, Chase suggested a simple naming strategy that was based on the name of the product and its version. The name of Chase's Team Project is *PolicyMonitorV1*, assuming that every major release of the product would result in a separate Team Project, such as version 1.1.

During Chase's initial review of the project charter, he paid particular attention to the constraints he needed to manage, and because Chase tends to be overly cautious, he quickly created a top-10 list of risks that could negatively impact his project. At this point, Chase only identified risks and tried to guess at the overall impact each risk would have on his project if they were to occur. From his review of the project charter and the vision statement produced by Dean, Chase began to realize how strategically important his project was to the future of Humongous Insurance, as the release of Gimli will mark an ushering in of a new technology platform and a new customer base.

As part of the project charter, Dean produced an initial draft of the personas he was asked to identify and detail. After scanning through the personas, he was pleased to see how clear a picture the persona descriptions painted for him of the eventual users of the software. For example, he could literally visualize *Liz*, who is a very intensely focused Auto Insurance Specialist and 35-year old mother of two boys, answering questions from customers on the phone while using the Gimli product to quickly perform what-if scenarios on different arrangements of auto insurance options to help the customers find the options that best suit their individual needs. Dean quickly realized that persona descriptions didn't just detail what the users do with a system but how they do it and why—personas provide a mental image of a real person that the entire team can identify with.

After Team Foundation Server was installed on the Humongous Insurance's internal network, Chase quickly installed the Team Foundation Client software. Because he just completed Visual Studio Team System training, the network administrators have no problem with providing him with the ability to create and manage Team Projects as he sees fit. As Iteration 0 comes closer to completion, Chase decides that it is time to create a Team Project that will facilitate his team throughout the development process and launches the new Team Project Wizard to walk him through this process. During this process, Chase ensures that he selects MSF for Agile Software Development as the process template to base his new Team Project on, and he provides the other necessary information such as the project name (PolicyMonitorV1) and a description of the project portal that will be created simultaneously with his Team Project. After a clarification from the Lead Software Developer at Humongous Insurance, he also indicates that the Team Project will create a new repository for source code and then waits patiently as the Team Project is created. Chase does not have enough skill or permissions to manage security across Team Foundation Server, so he makes a request to the Team

Foundation Administrator to ensure that proper accounts and permissions were set up for his development team, including Dean.

At this point, Team Foundation Server has been installed, a new Team Project has been created, and after a few revisions, the project charter has been reviewed and approved by Humongous Insurance's Lead Product Manager and the company's Chief Financial Officer, a clear sign that work should now begin. Chase takes the final version of the project charter and saves it to the project portal in the Project Management document library. At this time, he also traverses the list of default work items created for him when he created his Team Project, marking the tasks related to project vision and personas as complete while at the same time closing off unnecessary tasks such as those that indicate migration of source code to the new project. Chase also gathers up all of the risks he identified during his review of the project charter and adds them as Risk work items to his Team Project. At this point, he gathers his team together for a kickoff of the planning phase of the project where he goes through every aspect of the project charter including vision statement and personas to ensure that everyone shares the same view of their ultimate destination. During this kickoff, Chase also goes through the list of risks with his team when, to his surprise, some of the risks he identified likely will likely not be risks at all. Chase sets the state of the risk work items to Closed because they are no longer active. During this exercise, however, this team identified a few more risks that he did not predict, which he added as active Risk work items immediately. Chase also takes this time to walk his entire team, from testers to developers, through their new Team Project and clearly reinforces everyone's commitment to the project and to each other.

At the conclusion of the kickoff meeting, his team felt fully prepared for the next phase of the project in which they would work together to establish requirements and more detail to the design, getting them one iteration closer to ship date.

Creating a New Project versus Reusing an Existing Project

Not every new project you undertake will require creating a new Team Project in Visual Studio Team System, and you will need to consider many issues when deciding whether you should. Obviously, if you have a new Visual Studio Team System infrastructure, this decision will likely be much simpler because you may not have an existing project to work with. If you do have existing projects, there are a number of important points you will need to consider when deciding. You might need to make this decision, for example, if you are managing a new version of an existing software product or if you are managing a multi-phase project over a long period of time. If your new project has absolutely nothing to do with any existing Team Project, you should almost certainly create a new Team Project.

Let's assume that you have an option to continue with an existing Team Project. Let's further assume that you would like to have modified work item types for your new project but do not want to affect the information or the display settings of any existing work items in the existing Team Project. Unfortunately, work item types are defined at the Team Project level. If you want to use an updated work item definition, for example, a complex bug work item type definition that captures more information and has a modified workflow, all existing work items of that type in the project will reflect this change. Therefore, if you require conflicting work item type definitions in the same project, your only option is to create a new Team Project and use the updated work item type definitions in the new project, which forces your team to refer to the previous project for work items that were created using the conflicting work item definition.

Somewhat related to work item type definitions is how work item fields specified in the work item types within your project map to fields in Office Project. This mapping, which is specified in the process template used to create a project, is responsible for telling Visual Studio Team System how to map work item information into preset columns within Visual Studio Team System and is essential for any form of synchronization between Office Project and work items within Team Foundation Server. For example, the MSF process template maps the *Assigned To* work item field to the *Resources* field in Office Project and the *State* field to Office Project's *Text13* field. This mapping applies to all integrations between Office Project and work items in a particular project. If you need to make modifications to these field mappings, you will need to create a new Team Project.

The permissions that you can assign to your team members are also done at a project level. Let's assume that you wanted to extend an existing Team Project because it naturally represented the next phase of a much larger project, and that Brian, one of your developers, also happened to be on that project. Brian, however, is a junior developer with limited rights to access certain aspects of the code and is restricted from performing certain tasks such as editing project-level information. If you wanted to give Brian greater permissions on your new project without affecting the permissions set for the existing Team Project, your only choices would be to create a new Team Project or to completely change permissions for the existing Team Project. There is no way to have conflicting sets of permissions for your team within the same Team Project. Similar to Team Project permissions, a Team Project can have only one set of source control policies, which include checkin notes and checkin policies. If your new project will have a completely new set of checkin notes or checkin policies, yet you do not want to affect checkin policies of the existing code base of the project, you must create a new Team Project for your team and apply the new source control settings to the new project.

As mentioned earlier, every time you create a new Team Project, Visual Studio Team System creates a new project portal for your team. There can be only one project portal per Team Project. You may want to have a fresh project portal for a new project; you might not want to reuse an existing project portal site because existing content is not relevant to your new project. In this case, you can either clean up the content of the existing project portal or create a new Team Project and a resulting new project portal for your project.

Of course, one of the most obvious reasons for creating a new team project is if you want to use a completely different process template based on different process guidance. For example, the original Team Project could have been created from the MSF for Agile Software Development process template, but you have decided to base your new project on the Agile Software Development with Scrum process template. There is no way to switch a Team Project from one methodology to another, thus you will need to create a new Team Project for your new project. Of course, when you create a new project, you will see the updated process guidance as part of the project portal created for your team.

Generally speaking, for most corporate environments, it makes sense to create a new Team Project for every new project you undertake, which is slightly different than a company that sells software, which tend to have a more evolutionary process of software development. In fact, deciding to create a new Team Project within a product company could be quite difficult. Do you create a new Team Project for every major release? What if your product has many different subproducts such as with Microsoft Office—would you create a Team Project for each of the subproducts or even components? Do you maintain different delivery schedules for different products? Do you have different teams working on different products? Do you use different technology and methodologies for different products in your product line? The answer to these questions along with some of the technical constraints listed previously will help determine whether you should create new Team Projects. Generally speaking, when creating an entirely new version of a product, you should lean toward the creation of a new Team Project versus creating a "point" release (such as Version 1.1, 1.2, 1.3, et cetera). If your company sells a suite of products that are built by different teams on different schedules, you should also consider using a dedicated Team Project for each of the products in the product suite.

If you do decide to reuse existing Team Projects, there are certain things you should consider to make life a bit easier for you and your team. One of the great benefits of using one Team Project to house many software construction projects is the ability to perform cross-project reporting, because the reports that ship with Microsoft Visual Studio Team System can report only on the project from which they reside. If you decide to use a single Team Project, you must be extra diligent in how you structure your area and iteration because they must be appropriately specified and partitioned to allow both projects to work fairly autonomously if required. For example, a normal project may have a simple area tree and iteration sequence that you can use to categorize your work items, as depicted in Figure 3-9. When you will be managing several projects under the same Visual Studio Team System umbrella, you will likely have area and iteration hierarchies that look more like Figure 3-10, which take into consideration the differing feature areas and release schedules for the different projects. You should also be aware that even though you will have the ability to report on multiple projects at the same time, you will likely be required to set appropriate filter criteria if you wanted to see the progress of any single project within your Team Project.

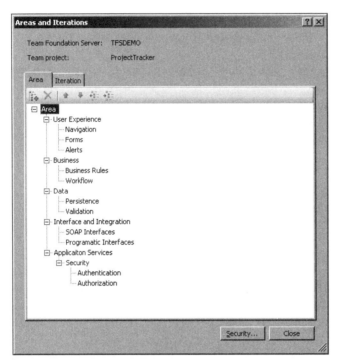

Figure 3-9 A typical area breakdown for a Team Project

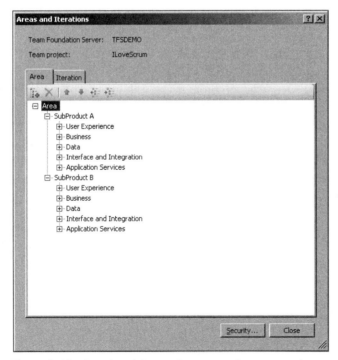

Figure 3-10 Area breakdown when managing two products under one Team Project

Summary

In this chapter we reviewed how project-initiating activities can be performed within a team by using Visual Studio Team System. We learned how to create new Team Projects, and we learned the structure of a Team Project and how to work with work items, work item queries, classifications, documentation, reports, and the project portal.

Chapter 4
Planning a Project

- Review the Project Management Body of Knowledge (PMBOK) definition of project planning.

- Map project planning activities to Microsoft Visual Studio Team System.

- Create a project workbook.

- Enter requirements into Visual Studio Team System.

- Create a release plan with Visual Studio Team System.

- Manage risks with Visual Studio Team System.

Project Planning

In Chapter 3, "Project Initiation," we discussed the work required to start a new project or begin the new phase of a much larger project. In this chapter, we take a closer look at project planning activities and specifically how they relate to Visual Studio Team System. As we did in Chapter 3, let's start by gathering some insight from the Project Management Body of Knowledge, or PMBOK (*http://www.pmi.org/info/default.asp*).

Every project requires some degree of planning. Generally speaking, the more risk and complexity that is involved with a project, the more planning you will perform. PMBOK has broken down project planning into 21 different planning activities, the purpose of each to help to further identify and specify aspects of the project that could not be fully explored during project initiation. Should you plan every project in the exact same way? That's probably a decision you will need to make with your team and your project sponsor, because every project is different with regard to size, scope, complexity, and risk. Planning activities are designed to specify a more concrete view of project scope, cost, schedule, and team activities by working to uncover, explore, and possibly resolve aspects of your project such as activity dependencies, requirements, risks, constraints, and assumptions.

Planning activities should be performed iteratively, because this method ensures an important feedback mechanism that help to guarantee that you are on the right track. It will help you will ensure that you can adapt to realizations that you and your team make as you refine your understanding of what you are delivering and how you should deliver it. You and your team can also gradually adjust your understanding of the customer's needs and help drive decisions regarding the depth and breadth of future planning activities. This approach can be risky because it is possible to plan without actually producing real value. The amount of project planning you engage in should be driven by the value that your team, including your customers, receive as a result of these planning activities.

Important   Do not restrict planning activities to a single planning phase. Planning activities can and should happen throughout a project and can overlap project execution activities in which you will be actually building software.

Note   You can obtain more information about the Project Management Body of Knowledge from *http://www.pmi.org/info/default.asp*.

Let's take a look at the planning activities specified by PMBOK so that we can later map these activities to Visual Studio Team System and the Microsoft Solutions Framework. Start by performing an activity PMBOK refers to as a *Develop Project Management Plan*, which is responsible for outlining the level of planning you will perform for your project and how the resulting plans will be used to drive the remainder of the project. The result of this particular planning activity is a project management plan, in whatever manifestation it takes, such as a document or a list of tasks on a whiteboard, the details of which will vary by project condition and complexity. You will continue to update this plan as needed throughout the life of your project and upon agreed to by you and your project sponsor. These project management plans detail additional information such as descriptions of tools and techniques used to make certain plans, the monitoring and control of changes, and the way that management reviews should be performed to address open issues and pending decisions.

The next cluster of activities specified in PMBOK's planning process group revolves around scope, specifically scope planning and definition. Project scope attempts to specify exactly what you are building and what you are not building. Think of project scope as the view of the finish line in a marathon—you know you must cross it to complete the race. We use the term *initial view* because changes to project scope are almost guaranteed to occur throughout the project, especially after users begin using your software. As with planning in general, the level of scope planning will be different from project to project. For example, an internal research project consisting of a small team working on a fixed-cost and fixed-duration project may have fewer scope considerations than a project delivering financial management software to millions of online subscribers. *Scope planning* typically results in a scope management plan that determines how your team will go about setting scope and developing an initial scope statement, and it establishes the change control process that the team uses to control scope. The *scope definition* activity specifies project scope, which is based on acceptance criteria, constraints, risks, budget, approval requirements, and milestones known at the time. To set the scope, identify a set of requirements (usually in the form of features).

Note   Traditional models of planning suggest that these activities produce a great deal of documentation. Planning is an activity, not a document. Planning must be performed; however, it doesn't have to be a daunting or an extremely boring task. Planning can even be performed in a workshop setting using whiteboards and sticky notes. Every project will have some degree of planning, and it will be up to you and your team to decide how much planning is enough for the conditions of your project. The key outcome of the planning activities discussed in this chapter is to figure out who does what and by when. If you are using Visual Studio Team System, the results of planning will likely be manifested as work items assigned to iterations.

Importance of Good Requirements

This may seem very obvious, but good requirements will be one of the most important factors for a successful project. In his book *Software Requirements* (Microsoft Press, 2003), Karl Wiegers points out a number of benefits to having good requirements, including fewer requirement defects (a *requirement defect* is the building of the wrong solution), less frequent reworking, fewer unnecessary features (keeping the scope as small as possible), lowered enhancement costs, faster development, fewer miscommunications, reduced scope creep, less project chaos, better testing, and higher customer satisfaction. These are clear benefits, and they can be achieved only through good requirements.

What makes a good requirement? Again, Wiegers provides some insight by listing what makes good requirements such as being complete, correct, feasible, necessary, prioritized, unambiguous, and most importantly, verifiable. Verification is extremely important because it ensures that a test can be created for the requirement, and the system can either pass or fail the test. For example, the requirement "The system must respond to every user request within two seconds" is an example of a verifiable requirement, as opposed to "The system must perform adequately," for which no test could ever be written.

The creation of a *work breakdown structure* (WBS) is also another activity specified by PMBOK as a planning activity. Work breakdown structures represent a decomposition of your project's main deliverables and tasks into smaller, more specific pieces. The work breakdown structure represents the entire scope of the project in hierarchical tree format, the leaves of which represent the actual work. Leaf-level detail in a WBS is typically detailed enough to be estimated, scheduled, monitored, and controlled. There are a few different ways that you can organize a work breakdown structure. The first is by phase, in which the primary branches identify the phases of your project, such as assessment, construction, and transition to production. Another way you can organize a work breakdown structure is by functional area of your application, whereby branches represent features of your application, and the highest level of detail represents tasks required to construct each feature or feature area. One of the most common ways to construct a work breakdown structure is by relating it to the underlying process framework by depicting workflows, phases, and deliverables. Here the main branches of the work breakdown structure would depict the type of work, such as management or implementation, further broken down into phases of the project, and then finally by deliverables for each phase, as shown in Figure 4-1.

Task Name	Start	Finish	Duration	Dec 2006				Jan 2007			
				12/3	12/10	12/17	12/24	12/31	1/7	1/14	1/21
Management	11/29/2006	1/23/2006	40d								
Inception Phase	11/29/2006	12/12/2006	10d								
Business Case Development	11/29/2006	12/12/2006	10d								
Elaboration phase release specs	11/29/2006	12/12/2006	10d								
Elaboration phase WBS baseline	11/29/2006	11/29/2006	1d								
Software development plan	11/29/2006	11/30/2006	2d								
Inception Phase Project Control	11/29/2006	12/12/2006	10d								
Elaboration Phase	12/13/2006	12/26/2006	10d								
Construction phase release specs	12/13/2006	12/26/2006	10d								
Construction phase WBS baseline	12/13/2006	12/29/2006	5d								
Elaboration phase project control	12/13/2006	12/19/2006	5d								
Construction Phase	12/27/2006	1/9/2007	10d								
Transition Phase	1/10/2007	1/23/2007	10d								
Environment	11/29/2006	11/29/2006	1d								

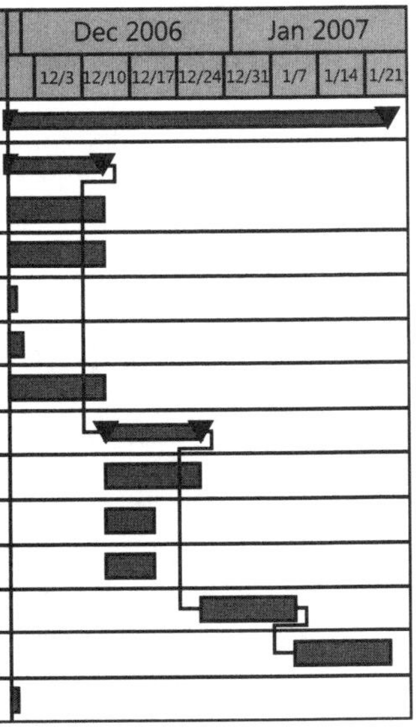

Figure 4-1 A work breakdown structure based on the Unified Process that specifies workflows, phases, and deliverables

Risk planning is yet another type of planning, specified by PMBOK, which is broken down into a number of discrete activities such as *risk management planning, risk identification, qualitative and quantitative risk analysis*, and *risk response planning*. Essentially, the goals of these activities are to try to predict what might go wrong with your project, to decide how to prevent these risks from becoming reality, and to create a strategy for dealing with them if they do become reality. You develop your approach to risk management during the risk management planning activity. Risk identification activities help you predict problems that could affect your project, and qualitative risk analysis prioritizes these risks by estimating the probability of the risk happening and the impact it will have on your project. Quantitative risk analysis is a process that tries to analyze, numerically, how risks will impact the overall objectives of your project. Conduct risk planning continually throughout your project, and integrate risk mitigation tasks continually into your team's activities.

Activity planning is another type of planning specified by PMBOK. Activity planning divides into more specific tasks work in the work breakdown structure; the lowest level of these is called *work packages*. The *activity definition* task decomposes work packages into tasks called *schedule activities*. You can then sequence these activities through the *activity sequencing* activity by performing the *activity resource estimating* and *activity duration estimating* activities. You can compile the activities into an overall project schedule through the PMBOK activity called *schedule development*. It is important to note that activities that represent risk mitigations should also be fed into the schedule even though these activities do not specifically focus on producing work specified by a work package.

PMBOK specifies *quality planning* as another activity that is performed in the planning process group. Quality planning helps to identify the quality attributes your team will try to achieve and the steps you will take to try to achieve them. Quality planning is not a one-time activity and should be addressed throughout the product life cycle. It is important to note that the way you address quality in your life cycle will probably impact the schedule and the cost factors of your project.

The most important aspect of your project is probably your project team because the development of software has more to do with how your team works together than the technology you are using. Because of this, give consideration to *human resource planning*, which logically extends into *contracting*, *purchasing*, and *communication planning*, which are all also specified by PMBOK. Human resource planning specifies the roles and responsibilities on your project, ensuring that all team members understand their commitment to the project and their fellow team members. This activity is related to *communication planning*, which helps to determine the information that is communicated to your team and the project stakeholders. *Contracting* and *purchasing planning* focus on the approaches you will take to obtain resources, in the form of people, knowledge, technology, or tools, that you currently do not have on your project. Obtaining resources must be addressed as an integral part of project delivery.

The activities and the schedule you derive from work packages coupled with risk mitigation activities will form the basis of cost estimating and budgeting activities specified by PMBOK. Unless you are developing software for the open source community, virtually every project will have a cost associated with it. The *cost estimating* activity specifies the process needed to develop an approximation of the costs in terms of people and other resources required to develop your software. *Cost budgeting* creates a baseline of costs from the compiled estimates of activities and work packages. Beyond a doubt, PMBOK acknowledges that cost estimating and budgeting are not static activities and will likely be refined as your team progresses through your process life cycle.

As you can see, PMBOK paints a very comprehensive picture of all the activities normally associated with planning. It cannot be overstressed, however, that PMBOK does not suggest that these planning activities happen in a single phase in your project; many of these planning activities will continue until project completion. In addition, PMBOK functions as a reference manual and does not dictate the level of planning you must perform on each and every project. The specific activities and the depth you must go into in each of these will vary from project to project and from team to team.

> **Note**   A common misconception is that projects based on Agile methodologies do not place as much emphasis on planning as projects based on a more traditional waterfall model project. In fact, with Agile-based projects, you will likely spend a great deal more time planning your project throughout the life of your project because planning and adapting to change is a continual aspect of an Agile project right up until delivery. So no matter what kind of project you will be managing or what methodology mindset you will be using, you will be doing some form of planning.

Planning and Visual Studio Team System

Mapping PMBOK planning activities into Visual Studio Team System without referencing the Microsoft Solutions Framework is very difficult. Virtually all the resulting planning deliverables will be represented as either Visual Studio Team System work items or documents stored on your team's project portal. In fact, all planning activities can be coordinated through work items and tracked within Visual Studio Team System. You can start by creating tasks for you and your team to perform specific planning activities such as determining risk management strategies or planning project resources. In fact, PMBOK specifies the project management plan as a key planning activity. With Visual Studio Team System, this activity would culminate in a set of task work items that specify further planning activities. Virtually every type of planning specified by PMBOK can be performed within the Visual Studio Team System environment. Furthermore, some of these activities have direct correlations to MSF process guidance. In previous chapters, we took a look at the differences between the two different flavors of MSF that ship with Visual Studio Team System: MSF for Agile Software Development and MSF for CMMI Process Improvement, and it's safe to assume that MSF for CMMI puts much more emphasis on planning activities than does MSF Agile. Do not assume, however, that MSF Agile lacks the planning specified by PMBOK. MSF Agile promotes more of a *plan as you go* approach. With Agile methodologies, planning activities are still performed; however, these actions will generally not result in the formality and ceremony you might expect from MSF for CMMI.

Let's take a look at some of the more obvious relationships between PMBOK and Visual Studio Team System with MSF. Activity definition, sequencing, resource estimating, duration estimating, and schedule development will probably all be done using task work items with tools such as Microsoft Office Excel or Microsoft Office Project. Both MSF Agile and MSF for CMMI specify a task work item type that can be used to capture the results of all of the activity-related planning. Risk planning is a first class citizen within MSF–both MSF Agile and CMMI provide guidance on how risk should be managed. Obviously, MSF for CMMI provides a much more comprehensive risk management technique than does MSF Agile. You can identify and analyze risk within Visual Studio Team System by using risk work items–both MSF Agile and MSF CMMI provide risk work item definitions that you can use to create and manage your project's risks. Figure 4-2 shows a diagram of the MSF Agile planning architecture.

Note   The risk work item in MSF for CMMI differs significantly in the amount of detail about a risk you can record in addition to the underlying workflow that determines the process of risk management for your team. In fact, MSF for CMMI allows you to also create Task work items specified as mitigation tasks, which allow you to track tasks that are being driven from risk reduction instead of product requirements.

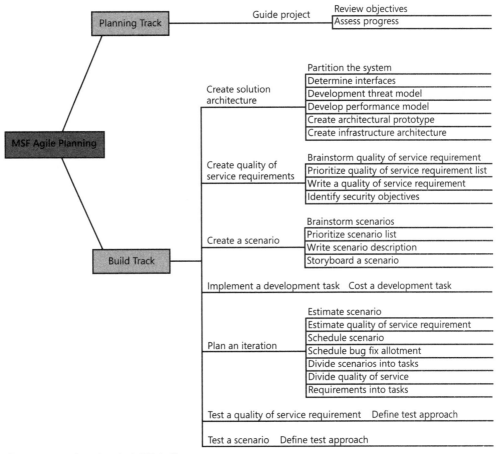

Figure 4-2   Planning in MSF Agile

You can use Visual Studio Team System to effectively plan scope. Both MSF process templates provide you with the ability to store software requirements, and by using the default work flow for each work item, also indicate whether those requirements will be included in the scope of the project. For example, the MSF Agile process template provides a Scenario and a Quality of Service work item type. You and your team can record your requirements in these work items and use the State and Reason fields to help control which of these requirements will be included in the final project and which requirements have been cut because they were beyond the scope. For example, when you enter a new Scenario work item in a project created by using the MSF Agile process template, the state of the work item is Active, which means that it is included in scope. If scope needs to be altered to exclude the scenario from the target application, you can change the state of the work item to Resolved, providing a reason of Deferred or Removed. You could then easily create a new work item query, as discussed in Chapter 3 and in greater detail in Chapter 7, "Tailoring Visual Studio Team System," called In Scope Scenarios, which filters out any scenarios in the Resolved state because of being Deferred or Removed.

Many of the remaining aspects of PMBOK planning activities can be captured as tasks in Visual Studio Team System and formalized in associated documents that you can store in the project portal. When you create a new project, Visual Studio Team System will automatically create a project portal to house the document-based artifacts you will produce during the project. MSF Agile's default list of documents varies greatly compared with the documents provided by MSF for CMMI in this regard. In fact, MSF for CMMI is much more closely aligned with traditional PMBOK deliverables because it puts greater emphasis on up-front planning and formality than does MSF Agile. For example, MSF Agile specifies the following work products that relate to planning: an Office Project–based Iteration Plan and Release Plan, and an Office Excel–based project checklist document. MSF for CMMI however, specifies numerous additional documents that help to capture additional planning information such as audit plan documents, communication plans, corrective action plans, project plans, team charters, and commitment template documents. What is clearly not directly represented by MSF as it relates to a typical PMBOK mindset are cost budgeting, human resources planning, purchase and acquisition planning, contract planning, and quality planning deliverables. With this in mind, however, it would not be difficult to create your own documents to manage these types of planning deliverables and store them within the project portal. If you do not require the formality of the actual planning documents, you can simply use Task work items to ensure that tasks that result from specific planning exercises are captured and tracked.

Note   Of course, Visual Studio Team System can support other process templates such as Scrum; however, this chapter will address planning only as it applies to the out-of-the-box experience, specifically using the MSF for Agile Software Development process template.

Roles Involved in Planning

Before beginning planning activities, you should think about the roles that will be needed for different aspects of planning for your project. Obviously, PMBOK stresses the involvement of business stakeholders during planning activities because they are ultimately responsible for the project. The importance of stakeholder involvement, however, cannot outweigh the involvement of your entire team. Planning is when your team, from business analysts to testers, come together to specify the path they will take with each other to develop great software. By involving your entire team during the planning phase, you are not only sharing the planning workload, you are also working to unify your team's understanding of the project, creating a shared sense of commitment, and ensuring that all perspectives are being addressed. In this way, you will be working to minimize the ambiguity that surrounds every project, which will ultimately help increase the predictability and stability of your project.

It's important to stress that planning is rarely done in isolation and typically requires your entire team, including those playing the Business Analyst role. The MSF process guidance for both MSF Agile and MSF for CMMI provides you with information about planning work streams related to each process type. Each of these work streams identifies the participating roles broken down by the roles responsible for the work stream and those consulted during the work stream to help achieve the desired result. For example, MSF Agile specifies a work stream that is called *Plan an Iteration*. Technically, this workstream is part of the Build track in MSF Agile; however, it clearly incorporates some level of planning that will need to be done by you and your team. The Plan an Iteration workstream focuses on determining the type of work that your team must perform during a particular iteration. This work stream identifies the project manager as ultimately responsible for this work; however, you will need to involve those team members playing the Business Analyst, Architect, Developer, and Tester roles, and these members will be the primary source of most decisions and estimates.

It cannot be overstressed that your team should also include your customer as much as possible throughout planning exercises. Using this method will not only help you produce better planning results, such as better estimates and a more realistic schedule, but it will also create a shared sense of accountability and enhanced communication between your team members and your customer. Developing the "we're all in this together" mentality increases the chances of success. In fact, in *eXtreme .NET: Introducing eXtreme Programming Techniques to .NET Developers* (Addison Wesley), Dr. Neil Roodyn writes that in eXtreme Programming (XP), which is a set of software development practices that extend Agile software development principles, planning activities are performed as part of a planning game. *Planning games* have the entire team including the customer help to derive estimates and timeframes for the delivery of features. In eXtreme Programming, planning takes the form of a cooperative game whereby all participants attempt to work toward the same goal: to produce the maximum value of the software. The planning game works to ensure that all information is out in the open, and more importantly, that everyone is aware of the goals of the project and how to achieve them.

> ### Principles of Agile Planning
>
> Agile planning focuses on customer value and team interaction during the planning exercise. In *Agile Estimating and Planning* (Pearson Education Inc., 2006), Mike Cohn summarized the core approach to planning on an Agile-based project. To start with, an Agile team works as one to develop a shared sense of team and goals, thus planning needs to be done by the entire team. Planning must embrace the fact that Agile teams work in short fixed-duration iterations, each of which deliver value. Iterations aren't just accustomed to box tasks, they are used to focus the team on delivering value one step at a time. Agile teams focus on business priority and customer value and do everything they can to minimize the dependencies between features. Agile teams are introspective and adaptive, and so must be the method of planning.

Getting Started by Creating a Project Workbook

Project managers like lists. Lists keep you focused and consistent, and checking items off your list when your team accomplishes a task feels good. Visual Studio Team System does a great job with lists, as we observed in previous chapters when we learned about work items and work item queries. Using Visual Studio Team System, you can maintain lists of tasks, risks, bugs, issues, and requirements, and because of the customizable nature of work items, you can literally create lists of just about anything you like. The work item queries help you organize our lists to facilitate our quick finding and manipulation of information. Most project managers, however, do not necessarily work with Visual Studio on a regular basis, and for that reason, Microsoft provides support for the use of Office Excel and Office Project to help manage work items on your project.

Creating a Workbook

One of the first things that you should do when you begin working on a new project in Visual Studio Team System is to create a project workbook in Office Excel. This will be the main document you will use to interact with work items. The project workbook will act as a single file that contains full access to work items within your Team Project. The project workbook will be a very simple Office Excel workbook that has one worksheet for every work item query you would normally use to manage your projects.

To create a project workbook, perform the following steps:

1. Launch Office Excel and create a new workbook.

2. From the Team menu, select New List to display the Connect To Team Foundation Server dialog box.

3. Choose the Team Project you want to create a project workbook for and click OK.

4. In the resulting New List dialog box, choose All Tasks from the Query List drop-down list and click OK.

5. From a project management perspective, you will likely want to see some additional columns in your task list. Select Choose Columns from the Team menu in Office Excel to add the following columns to your list: Area Path, Exit Criteria, Issue, Priority, Reason, and Triage. Select these fields in the Available columns list in the Choose Columns dialog box, and then click the > button to add them to the Selected columns list. You can reorder the columns in any way that makes sense to you. Click OK when you are finished adding and rearranging fields. You can also click Add Required to quickly add all required fields to the list of displayed fields.

6. In Office Excel, choose Format | Sheet | Rename, and then rename the worksheet .

7. Save the worksheet to a desired location. Choose the location based on how you will use the worksheet. If you will be using the worksheet in situations when you will not be connected to Visual Studio Team System, save the workbook to your local computer. Otherwise, save it to your project portal.

8. Repeat steps 1–7 for all other queries you would like to have available to you within Office Excel such as All Issues, All Quality of Service Requirements, All Scenarios, My Tasks, Resolved Bugs, and Untriaged Bugs.

> **Note**   You will not be prompted to connect to a Team Project if you are creating lists in the same workbook because the Team Project you specified in step 3 will be used for all subsequent lists you create in the workbook. This means, however, that you cannot have lists from different Team Projects in the same workbook.

Instead of having one list for every work item query, it is also common to have one master list of all work items by referring to the All Work Items query and then adding all required fields as you did in the preceding steps. You will be able to use Office Excel column filters and sorting capabilities to filter and organize the work items on the worksheet. For example, to see all active tasks from a list, select the Task in the Work Item Type column filter (the drop-down box automatically added to each column heading in the list created for you during the steps described above) and Active from the State column filter.

Entering Data into the Project Workbook

After you have created the project workbook, you will be able to use it to enter and view work item data from Visual Studio Team System. When you are entering data, instead of being presented with a work item form, you will type directly in the columns and fields themselves. Fields that provide you with an option of values will display those options in drop-down lists inside the cell. In fact, all of the work item rules, such as mandatory field values or workflow state options, are fully enforced within Office Excel. To enter new rows into a list linked with Office Excel, simply find the last row in the list and start typing data. Optionally, you can insert a new row by selecting a cell you want to insert a row about and choosing Row from the Insert menu.

Work items that you enter into Office Excel do not automatically get saved to Visual Studio Team System. To save any new or modified work items in Visual Studio Team System, you must publish the work items by selecting Publish from the Team menu. By controlling when Office Excel publishes changes to work items in Visual Studio Team System, you have the opportunity to enter a large number of work items without ever needing to communicate with the computer running Team Foundation Server on which the data resides. This makes it possible to use your project workbook in an offline mode, that is, when you are not connected to the network, such as on an airplane or on the bus ride home. When you instruct Office Excel to publish your work items to Visual Studio Team System, all your new and modified work items will be checked for errors. If errors are found, you will be notified with a dialog box and given the opportunity to resolve the problems before publishing the work items once more. Note that you will not be able to publish work items to Team Foundation Server if they contain errors.

When publishing updated work items, you may also experience a conflict while you have Office Excel open if some other member of your team modifies a work item in Team Foundation Server between the time you last refreshed the work item details in Office Excel and the time you are attempting to publish the new information. If such a conflict does occur, you will be prompted to resolve the conflict through the Work Item Publishing Errors dialog box. When you encounter a conflict of this nature, you will be prompted to choose a version of the work item you want to keep—either the version you just modified in Office Excel or the version of the work item that is stored in Team Foundation Server, as shown in Figure 4-3. You will also have the ability to view the version of the work item as it is saved in Team Foundation Server by clicking the View Database Version button.

Usually, one of the first actions you should perform when working with your project workbook is to refresh work item data from the Team Foundation Server. The more often you refresh your copy of the data within Office Excel, the more up to date your work item information will be and the lesser the chance that you can cause a conflict when updating work items. To refresh the work item data stored in a list in Office Excel, choose Refresh from the Team menu. Note that every time you publish your changes to Team Foundation Server, Office Excel will also perform a refresh.

There are a few additional actions you can perform with Office Excel as it integrates with Visual Studio Team System. Both Office Excel and Office Project provide you with the ability to edit areas and iterations on the Team Foundation Server without requiring you to switch to Team Explorer. To do this, you must be connected to a computer running Team Foundation Server (that is, working online). Choose Team | Edit Areas And Iterations in Office Excel or Office Project. Editing areas and iterations from within Office Excel or Office Project is identical to editing this information from within Team Explorer. You can also add links and attachments to work items by clicking the Links and Attachments button on the Team toolbar or by choosing Links and Attachments from the Team menu in Office Excel or Office Project.

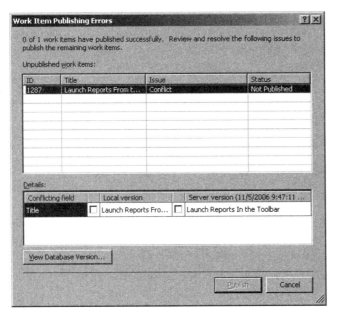

Figure 4-3   A conflict error

Work Item Pivot Tables and Graphs

After you have linked data from your Team Project into Office Excel, you will be free to use other Office Excel features such as pivot tables to help you understand and organize work item information. To create a read-only pivot table of work item data, perform the following steps:

1. From your Office Excel project workbook, click in any cell within a list on a worksheet that contains information on which you want to base a pivot table. A common source of pivot information is the All Work Items list with all required columns added.

2. From the Data menu, choose PivotTable and PivotChart Report to launch the PivotTable and PivotChart Wizard.

3. On the opening page of the wizard, ensure that Microsoft Office Excel List or Database is selected as the data you want to analyze and the kind of report you want to create is a pivot table. Click Next.

4. On the next page of the wizard, you will confirm the range of values you will use in the pivot table. By default, Office Excel will select the list you chose on the previous page. Click Next.

5. Specify the location of the new pivot table report to be a new worksheet and then click Finish to close the wizard.

6. Drag fields from the PivotTable Field List pane to the predefined pivot areas on your new worksheet: Page Fields, Row Fields, Column Fields, and Data Items. For example, if you choose to create a pivot table from the All Work Items list, you might want to drag the

Iteration Path column into the Page Field area; the Work Item Type, Assigned To, State, Area Path, and Title columns to the Row Fields pivot area; Reason to the Column Field; and ID to the Data Item area. By default, the PivotTable report will add a Sum calculation to the field that you dropped in the Data Item area.

7. If you want to change the calculation used for Data Items, right-click the Sum Of ID cell above the Work Item Type pivot table, click the Field Settings button on the PivotTable toolbar, choose the Count function from the functions listed in the Summarize By list, and then click OK.

With a pivot table, you will quickly be provided with the perspective you need to help manage your team, especially if your team is large or you are managing a large number of work items. A common use of a work item pivot table is for task assignments and estimates. This is very handy if you want to look at the amount of estimated work allocated to your team members per iteration. To set up your pivot chart for this, ensure that the Estimate column is one of the columns listed in your Office Excel workbook, and when creating the pivot table, drag the Estimate value to the Data Item area, ensuring that Sum is the operation that will be used for calculations. The result will look very similar to Figure 4-4.

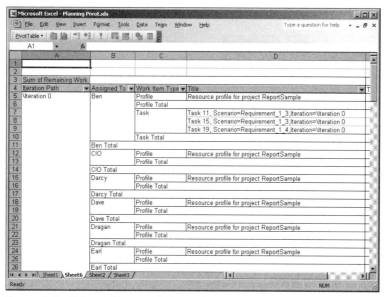

Figure 4-4   Using Office Excel pivot tables to review project estimates

Entering Requirements into Visual Studio Team System

It's virtually impossible to provide estimates on a system without any level of detail of the system unless you are working on a strictly fixed-cost variable-functionality release schedule in which you simply deliver features until you run out of money. Software requirements can take many forms, from screen designs to business and workflow models to usage scenarios and operational needs. Arguably, there is yet to be a single unified method for storing all forms of system requirements. However, Visual Studio Team System allows you to store many of these requirement types as work items. If you are using MSF Agile, you will have two different work items to store your requirements: the Scenario work item and the Quality of Service work item. If you are familiar with more traditional use-cases methods specified by the Unified Process, you should have no problem working with scenarios. A *scenario* is a set of steps that a user (specified by a persona as discussed in Chapter 3) must perform to achieve a goal. Some scenarios will describe a "happy path," wherein the steps in the scenario lead the users to their goal, and others might describe a "less-than-happy path," wherein the steps will not lead the user to a desired outcome. Examples of an undesired outcome are when users enter invalid parameters or certain conditions in the system are not met, causing an error to be reported. These scenarios describe the behavior of the system you are implementing. Quality of service requirements, on the other hand, document what are traditionally called *non-functional requirements* of the software you are going to build, such as load characteristics, availability, accessibility, maintainability, and performance.

Requirements in MSF for CMMI

MSF for CMMI extends the concept of a requirement by providing you with the Requirement work item type. Unlike MSF Agile, you can use the Requirement work item type to store both scenarios and quality of service information by specifying a requirement type attribute on the work item. In fact, by default, MSF for CMMI requirements can be of the following types: functional, interface, operational, quality of service, safety, scenario, and security. Requirement work items in MSF for CMMI also provide you with more areas to capture additional information about the requirement, such as listing related subject matter experts, capturing analysis details, and status of user acceptance testing regarding the particular feature.

Of course, it may not make sense for you to store all of the details of a requirement within a work item. In this case, you should store your document-based requirements, such as user interface flow diagrams or business analysis models created in Microsoft Office Visio, in the project portal. You can then create a Requirement work item in Visual Studio Team System that links to these documents. In fact, this becomes an important practice because this will allow you to track and monitor the state of a requirement stored in document artifacts by using the default work flow specified by the work item type. For example, you can create a user interface flow diagram in Office Visio and store it in your project portal. In Team Explorer, you can create a work item called User Interface Flow of type Scenario. In the links tab of the work item, you can create a hyperlink to the document stored on your Team Project.

Tip   A quick way to get a URL to a document stored on your project portal is by navigating to the document within Team Explorer to view the document properties (right-click the document and choose Properties from the shortcut menu). In the resulting Properties window, select the text in the Url field and copy and paste it into an HTML link to your work item.

This book is focused on the project management perspective of Visual Studio Team System; however, it might be beneficial to talk a bit more about writing scenarios and tracking the quality of service requirements. Scenarios tell a story, and they are meant to come alive in the mind of both the author of the story (business analyst and customer) and the person reading them (developers and testers). Scenarios can be highly descriptive or documented in an abbreviated form, or they can be a combination of both styles. Whatever approach they take, their purpose is to specifically convey the sequencing of events the system must be able to support and to provide context as to how those events fit into the larger picture.

For example, the following represents a highly descriptive story-like example of a scenario:

> *Cindy has two different corporate Wi-Fi networks available to her mobile device. She wants to connect only to the connection supporting WEP, and if that network becomes unavailable, she doesn't want the device to switch automatically to the second one because she does not want to connect to an unsecured network. Cindy opens the Custom Connection Manager on her mobile device and selects the Manual Mode option. She makes sure that her desired network (the WEP enabled connection) is selected. The Custom Connection Manager detects that the device is now in manual mode and will attempt to connect to the manually selected network as specified in Cindy's settings. At the time of attempting to connect, the Custom Connection Manager determines that Microsoft Office Outlook was retrieving e-mail messages from the server. The Custom Connection Manager waits until the application has completed the transfer before continuing with switching to the preferred network.*

> *During Cindy's workday, she enters an area of the building where she has access to a Wi-Fi connection that Terry has configured to be of a higher preference then her currently selected network connection. Since Cindy has set her device to manual mode, her mobile device will not attempt to connect to that more preferred network connection and will instead continue to use her manually selected connection.*

> *Later in the day, Cindy moves to an area in the office where she is unable to access the network connection that she has manually set her device to use. Her device will warn her that she has lost connectivity and will not attempt to connect to any other available network.*

This scenario takes a bit of reading, but it provides excellent context for the developers of the system. In addition, scenarios such as these are very easy to validate by users of the system. Also note the extensive integration of the persona named Cindy in the scenario. Capturing requirements in this way increases the overall understanding of the system and immediately makes the application come alive in the minds of the entire team.

Alternatively, or even in conjunction, we could provide a breakdown of that scenario into something that is a more formal, as shown in Table 4-1.

Table 4-1   More Traditional Scenario Representations

Description	Custom Connection Manager (CCM) Manual Mode Operation
ID	CCM-1
Author	Joel
Date	12/20/2006
Personas	Cindy
Pre-conditions	CCM installed and operational
	Wi-Fi enabled and functioning on the device
Actions	1. Cindy sets CCM to manual mode.
	2. Cindy selects desired Wi-Fi access point.
	3. Device connects to desired Wi-Fi access point. Alternative Flow: If ActiveSync is running, device waits until complete.
	4. Cindy enters area with more preferred Wi-Fi access point.
	5. Device does not switch to Wi-Fi access point.
	6. Currently connected Wi-Fi access point disappears.
	7. Device displays a message to Cindy and does not attempt connections to any other Wi-Fi access points.
Post-conditions	None
Includes	Display alert
Extends	Custom Connection Manager Automatic Mode
Generalizes	None

As you can see, both representations of the requirement are valid—the table-based version provides an easy to read, step-by-step description of the scenario, so it can easily be turned into a test cases for the testers. We suggest that you start writing highly descriptive scenarios with the help of your customer, and then during the requirements realization activities, decompose the requirements into a more organized representation such as the one presented in table format.

The use of area classifications is also extremely important to requirements management in Visual Studio Team System. Areas represent groupings of related functionality in your application that you can use to classify requirements in addition to any other work item in your project. Areas are represented in a hierarchical tree that you can build by using the Areas And Iterations settings of your project. Initially, the Area classification section is empty, and it will be up to your team to decide how you want to group features in your application. For example, some organizations choose to decompose their application into architecturally significant areas such as user experience, business processes, data management, software interfaces, and data migration. Some other organizations choose to decompose their solution into clusters of related scenarios such as breaking a Customer Relationship Management (CRM) solution into areas such as customer management, sales campaign management, reporting, and opportunity management. If you are working on a suite of related products such as Microsoft Office, you might want to break areas into an Area tree that could resemble Figure 4-5.

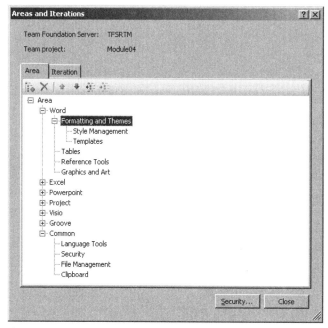

Figure 4-5   A more complex area hierarchy used to classify work items

By properly categorizing your requirements, you will also make your requirements easy to find and provide more filtering capability for your reports. If you manage a large number of requirements, it makes sense to ensure that each of your requirements is in the appropriate area classification. Virtually every report shipped with Visual Studio Team System allows you to provide filter criteria for the report results that include being able to specify one or many area categorizations for your work items. Take the time with your team to structure areas, allowing the structure to change in the early iterations of the project as you gain more understanding of the underlying system requirements. During construction phases of the project, however, try to ensure that the area categorizations do not change. One limitation of areas in Visual Studio Team System is that a work item can belong to only one area, so you must consider this in the structure of area tree. Also note that overly complex area trees may make working with areas cumbersome if you are working in Office Excel or Office Project because the area hierarchy is flattened and appears much like a folder path on your hard drive. These can get very long and quite difficult to work with. Areas also provide another important feature, *requirement hierarchy*. Many other requirement management tools in the industry, such as Borland CaliberRM, provide the ability to create hierarchies of requirements. In Visual Studio Team System, requirements are entered in a table and assigned to a hierarchy, the area tree.

Law of Consumption of Artifacts

Requirements need to be consumable by all members of the team but more importantly, by your users. The methods you choose to represent your requirements should be dependent upon your audience, so you should seriously consider many forms of requirements representation. There are many forms of requirements including UML diagrams, user interface prototypes, whiteboards, and sticky notes. In addition, there are many different types of requirements, including business requirements (usually captured in a vision document), user requirements (usually captured in scenarios), business rules, quality attributes, functional requirements, system requirements, external interfaces, and constraints (Wiegers, 2003). Our experience is to use them all, choosing the best method to capture and communicate the true message of the requirements.

Providing a Rough Order of Magnitude Estimate

After entering requirements into your system, you should record a basic estimate for each of the requirements to capture some general information regarding how difficult or easy a feature might be to implement. If you are using MSF Agile–based projects to record requirements through scenario and quality of service work item types, you will provide only a rough order of magnitude estimate of your requirements. A rough order of magnitude estimate is a value that indicates the complexity of the requirement, represented numerically from 0 to 3, with 0 indicating the lowest level of complexity requiring no effort to achieve and 3 indicating the highest level of complexity. One of the best ways to gather rough order of magnitude values is to open the list of scenarios and quality of service requirements in Office Excel and simply go through each one with your entire team. For each requirement, have a brief discussion with your team, which should include your customer, developers, testers, and business analysts. As Cohn points out, you should act as a moderator during this discussion to ensure that your team doesn't go off track or into too many design and implementation details. It should be clear that working together to establish a rough order of magnitude estimate does not require as much design and implementation details as task-based estimating, which we will describe later in this chapter.

When estimating scenarios at this level, you will be relying on expert opinion, estimate analogies, and requirement breakdown. Your team may have worked on similar projects in the past delivering similar requirements; in this case, their expert judgment is critical to the estimate. The use of estimating analogies refers to comparing scenarios to some known baseline. For example, suppose that the team agrees that the scenario called Enter Production Data has a rough order of magnitude of 2 because this represents a common scenario that the team has worked on many times before. The team would then compare other scenarios with this baseline scenario and ask whether this new scenario is much more difficult or easy than the Enter Production Data scenario. If it is much easier than the baseline scenario, the team would enter 1 as the rough order of magnitude, and if it's much more complex, they would enter 3. Sometimes, the team may indicate that the problem is much too complex to even estimate. This is a clear indication that you will need to decompose the requirement into smaller and more specific requirements that are easier to estimate and understand. This process is called *requirements decomposition*.

Third-Party Requirement Tools for Visual Studio Team System

There are a number of third-party products that help with gathering and representing requirements that plug right into Visual Studio Team System. Here is a list of the more popular tools customers are using today:

CaliberRM from Borland   You can find CaliberRM on the Borland site at *http://www.borland.com.* CaliberRM is a well known requirements management solution that provides a hierarchical representation of requirements and full trace-ability with work items stored within Visual Studio Team System.

Enterprise Architect from Sparx Systems   You can find Enterprise Architect at *http://www.sparxsystems.com.* Enterprise Architect is a superb low-cost modeling tool that integrates with Visual Studio Team System and allows you to graphically represent business requirements in a variety of modeling standards.

stpBA Storyboarding for Microsoft Visual Studio Team System   Found at *http://www.stpsoft.co.uk,* stpBA Storyboarding seamlessly integrates with Visual Studio Team System process templates and generates screen flow diagrams, HTML story-boards, UI specifications, functional specifications, Visual Studio Team System work items, and test scripts.

Prioritizing Requirements

After you have some initial estimates in place, you should prioritize your requirements. Customers are the only people who can prioritize requirements, so you should gather requirement prioritizations in a workshop setting. MSF Agile Scenario and Quality of service work item types allow you to specify the priority of a requirement by using the *Rank* field to capture a numeric value that you can use to help capture requirement prioritization. The Rank field is a free text field that allows you to enter any value you want. For this reason, you must decide upon a prioritization method that will guide how you and your customers rank requirements.

Bucketing Priority

One method of requirement prioritization is to find a requirement that has medium importance and give it a rank value of 500. All requirements that you and your customer decide are more important than the baseline requirement will have a higher rank, starting with multiples of 100 such as 600, 700 and so on. The same will be true for requirements that are deemed less important; you will provide values less than the value you provided for your baseline requirement. Why increments of 100? Prioritization should be done incrementally using a technique called *bucketing*. For example, all requirements you assign 600 to get placed in the 600 bucket. From this point, you can fine-tune your prioritization in the 600 bucket of requirements by using the same general technique just described: find a requirement in the 600 bucket that is average for that group and assign it a value of 650. Compare all other requirements in the 600 group to the 600 group baseline you just selected, resulting in requirements of rank 610, 620, 630, and so on. You can continue this refinement process as long as you want or defer requirement priority refinement until future iterations.

Calculating Priority

Another way of prioritizing requirements is to derive the rank value from a number of other indicators of a requirement. Karl Wiegers in 2003 suggested using a prioritization method based on the value, cost, and risk properties of a requirement. In this method, the rank value for each work item could be a calculated value that would take into account the relative benefit of the requirement compared to other requirements, the relative penalty to the organization of not releasing the requirement, the relative cost of the requirement, and the relative risk of building the requirement compared to other requirements. This method produces some great results and is much less subjective than simply assigning ranks to requirements. The disadvantage, however, is that this method is also much more difficult to implement in Visual Studio Team System. In Chapter 7, you will learn how you can add fields to the work items provided out of the box. However, field level calculations, which would be required to calculate priority based on the four dimensions mentioned, are not supported by work items unless you have Service Pack 1 for Visual Studio 2005 and Visual Studio Team System installed, which allows you to enhance default work items by using custom field controls. This option is beyond the scope of this book. If you do want to use Wiegers' method or some other method to derive rank values, your only option is to use Office Excel. With Office Excel, you can add your own columns to the list of work item fields to capture additional information such as benefit, penalty, cost, and risk in addition to an extra field that would calculate the rank value based on those four requirement properties. You would then need to manually copy and paste the value from the calculated field into the Rank field for each work item.

To set up Office Excel to help calculation of rank, perform the following steps. Note that this example does not implement the entire method set out by Wiegers, but it will give you an idea of how to take advantage of the ability of Office Excel to perform calculations to drive values stored in work items.

1. Start by linking a work item query with an Office Excel workbook. In Team Explorer, right-click the All Scenarios work item query and choose Open in Microsoft Excel from the shortcut menu.

2. When Office Excel is launched and all of the scenarios are listed, for convenience, move the Rank column all of the way to the right. To do this, in Office Excel, select Team | Choose Columns and move the Rank column to the bottom of the Selected columns list.

3. Next, add four new columns to the list to capture values for benefit, penalty, cost, and risk. To perform this step, simply type **Benefit** in the cell to the right of the Rank column heading. If you add a cell directly adjacent to the last column in the work item list, the column will be made part of the work item list, which will affect how the formula will be stored and calculated. Continue this process until you have added a new column for each of the four new values.

4. Add one more field called Calculated Rank next to the four new columns you just created in step 3.

5. Type values in the Benefit, Penalty, Cost, Risk columns adjacent to each of your scenarios.

6. Select the first cell under the new Calculated Rank column heading to add a formula. The formula to enter will be (Benefit + Penalty) / (Cost + Risk), where Benefit, Penalty, Cost, and Risk are the cell references that correspond to the adjacent cells that hold those values. For example, if you followed the above instructions, O3 will be the cell that will hold the calculated rank value, and the formula for this cell will be =(K3+L3)/(M3+N3).

7. Select the cell populated in step 6 and all other Calculated Rank cells in the list. From the Edit menu, selected Fill | Down to copy the formula from the first cell to the remaining cells.

8. Copy each scenario's Calculated Rank value to the Rank cell by typing Ctrl+C; move to the Rank cell and choose Edit | Paste Special | Paste Values.

> **Note** If you try to type a formula directly into a cell that displays Rank or any other work item field, the formulas will be discarded and replaced with literal values when you publish or refresh work item data from Visual Studio Team System.

The method you choose will be entirely up to you and your team. What you are trying to achieve is an accurate representation of feature priority from the perspective of the customer. Weigers' method adds multiple dimensions to this problem to better blend the results, especially if there is a possibility of requiring input from many different, and sometimes competing, customer representatives to your project. Our recommendation is to keep this process as simple as you can without reducing value to your team or your customer.

Requirement Reprioritization

After you and your team have gone through a prioritization exercise of your requirements, you should also consider how you will ensure that you know when these prioritization values change throughout the life of your project. We all know that change will happen, and you should try to set up processes that anticipate and absorb change instead of react to it. One great way of trying to handle changing priorities as you progress through your project is by conducting requirement prioritization reviews as an ongoing part of the project. Iteration planning meetings are a great time to review requirement prioritization with your customer and your team. Don't be afraid to have your customers change priorities on requirements because this is a way of fine-tuning the value you are providing to them, an aspect you can only estimate at the beginning of the project. Of course, changing priorities may have a ripple effect on the entire project providing yet another reason to keep all of these activities simple and easy to change.

Creating an Initial Iteration Plan

An initial iteration plan breaks down your project into fixed time durations and tentatively schedules features for each iteration. The iterations that you can specify in your project are simply labels and have no relation to any particular block of time or duration. For this reason, many organizations change their iteration-naming conventions to include the data ranges the iteration covers. For example, instead of having Iteration 1, organizations would change the name of the iteration to "Iteration1 – Dec18–Dec29". Even when doing this, Visual Studio Team System will still not understand that all requirements assigned to Iteration 1 – Dec18–Dec29 must be performed during that block of time in the calendar. As a project manager, you are likely experienced in using Office Project to aid in project scheduling, and with Visual Studio Team System, you use can use Office Project the way you might have before.

Determining Iteration Length

Before you can begin adding iterations into Office Project, you must determine the duration of each of the iterations. This process is usually best performed with a calendar in front of you and will start with the day you will need to deliver. Most projects have some targeted delivery date in mind, which is captured in the project charter document. The project charter also details the constraints with regard to costs and resources. With these constraints in mind, you should be able to determine the size of your team and how long the project will take from beginning to end. For example, suppose that you had a budget for staff of $100,000 for your project. Let's also assume that the average cost of a team member is $50 per hour. This would indicate that you have about 2000 hours to work with. If you determined that you will need four additional team members, one to act as the business analyst and tester, two developers (who will share the role of Architect), and another full-time employee to act as tester and release manager, this would mean that you have five full-time people employed to deliver the project. Given 5 people (each with a cost of $50 for 8 hours a day) and $100,000 budgeted for effort (which does not include hardware, software, contractors, or any other cost not associated with salary), you will need about 10 weeks of time.

Working backward on a calendar from your required delivery date will give you the date your project should begin. From this point, you can now determine how to specify your iterations. Let's start at both ends of the project. You will make the assumption that it will take at least one week to get the project environment ready for the team, finalize requirements, and refine estimates and assumptions. You might also assume that you will need a week at the end of the project dedicated for bug fixing and release-to-production work. This leaves you 8 weeks of time to spend developing the solution. Based on conversations with your customer, you might also want to dedicate a week to focus on setting requirements regarding the user interface and final architecture. You are told by your developers, however, that this activity can be performed in the same week that the development environment is getting finalized and ready. How you decide to break up the remaining 8 weeks of work will truly depend on the cycles you and your team are accustomed to. Some organizations like to have development iterations set at three weeks, others at one week. In this case, 8 seems like a good number to divide into 4 equal iterations of 2 weeks each. Thus you decide that your project will have six iterations; the first iteration dedicated to requirement finalization and development environment construction, four development iterations, and one stabilization-and-transition-to-production iteration. At this point, you may even want to specify customer release drops. It is normal to have Alpha, Beta, and Release Candidate releases prior to your final release. Each of these will be formalized releases of your software to your customers for the purpose of gathering feedback and discovering defects. Each successive release will obviously be more mature than the previous. An Alpha release typically releases only some of the features of your application, usually the highest-priority features or features that must be developed early in the project because they are architecturally similar to other features in the application. Each subsequent release adds new features while fixing or modifying existing features based on user and testing feedback. The Release Candidate feature typically represents a *feature complete* version of your software, implementing every committed feature. Any subsequent work done to the application after the Release Candidate is bug fixes or changes to deployment, as shown in Figure 4-6.

ID	Task Name	Start	Finish	Duration	Nov 2006				Dec 2006				Jan 2007				Feb 2007		
					11/5	11/12	11/19	11/25	12/3	12/10	12/17	12/24	12/31	1/7	1/14	1/21	1/28	2/4	2/11	2/18
1	Iteration 1	11/6/2006	11/10/2006	5d	■ Alpha Release															
2	Iteration 2	11/13/2006	11/24/2006	10d		■ Beta 1 Release														
3	Iteration 3	11/27/2006	12/8/2006	10d			■ Beta 2 Release													
4	Iteration 4	12/11/2006	12/22/2006	10d					■ Release Candidate											
5	Iteration 5	12/25/2006	1/5/2007	10d						■ Release										

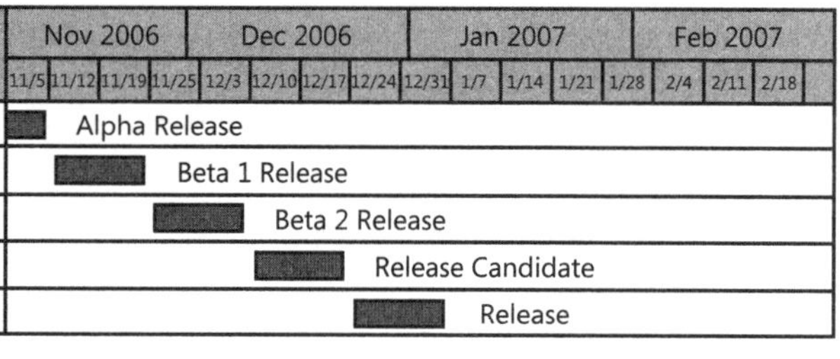

Figure 4-6 Example iteration breakdown

It is extremely important to communicate the release plan to your customers so they can plan to test each release. These major releases are usually provided to as wide a customer base as possible to ensure the most scenarios tested. Because these major releases are quite important in the software development life cycle, they are equally as important as interim releases of the product produced daily and weekly to a smaller group of testers and customers. Interim builds, commonly known as daily or weekly builds, represent an important quality practice your team can practice and will be discussed in great length in Chapter 5, "Monitoring and Controlling Projects Execution."

> ## Buffering Estimates
>
> Up to this point, we have discussed only about how to aggregate estimates from your team, but we have not talked about buffers. A *buffer* is a length of time and money set aside for tasks that take longer or cost more money to complete. If this is the case, then how much buffer is enough? Many organizations look to previous projects to determine an overall percentage of time and money that should be reserved for each project to compensate for unplanned events or underestimated work. Buffers are typically a reflection of certainty. That is, work that your team is less certain of performing will increase the amount of buffer they include in their estimates. Most organizations do not explicitly measure a certainty factor when it comes to estimation; however, you should consider doing so because it will allow you to determine a better estimate for the buffer for your project. Buffers are usually applied against a cycle in a project. For example, some buffers are held at the end of a project to compensate for overall project slippage. Some buffers are worked into each iteration based on the certainty of the work being performed in that iteration. How you decide to integrate buffers into your process will be greatly dependent on how complex buffer management and tracking is because the more elaborate and accurate the method of managing buffers, the more elaborate your tracking system must be.
>
> The details of the various ways that buffers can be calculated and integrated into your estimating practices are beyond the scope of this book. This book's only advice is that you do consider buffers in your planning considerations, even if, for example, you simply call for a 10 percent contingency for your entire project. For some great references on buffers and the theory of constraints as it applies to software engineering, you should read David Anderson's book, *Agile Management for Software Engineering: Applying the Theory of Constraints for Business Results* (Prentice Hall PTR, 2003).

One of the best methods of creating an initial release plan is to use the Office Project integration features of Visual Studio Team System. To use Office Project to create an initial release plan, perform the following steps:

1. Launch Office Project and begin working with a new project plan.

2. In Office Project, select Team | Choose Team Project to display a dialog box that will allow you to specify the Team Project to connect to. Specify your computer running Team Foundation Server and the Team Project and then click OK.

3. Choose Get Work Items from the Team menu in Office Project to display the Get Work Items dialog box. From the Saved query drop-down list, choose All Scenarios, and then

click Find. Here, you are instructing Office Project to import all of the Scenario work items you specified in your project so that you can schedule them into iterations. After the list of work items is retrieved from the server, click OK to add these work items to Office Project.

> **Note**   Even though the work items you just specified were scenarios, they have been added to Office Project as tasks. Notice the updated view in Office Project and how work item data is available, such as Work Item ID, Work Item Type, Area Path, and Iteration Path. In fact, entire new views called Team System Gantt and Visual Studio Team Task Sheet were created in Office Project specifically for Visual Studio Team System integration. You can switch between these views by selecting them in the View menu.

4. Insert a new row at the top of Office Project and provide the name of one of your iterations as the Title. Do not worry about setting the duration or start/end dates for the task at this time. Continue this process for every iteration on your project until you have entered a new task for every iteration.

5. By default, when you add a new task after you have linked to work items on your Team Project, these new tasks will be marked as new work items, and Office Project will attempt to publish them back to Visual Studio Team System. In this case, the new tasks you have just created will be acting as summary tasks in Office Project and do not need to be published to Visual Studio Team System. To ensure that the tasks you just created for your iterations do not get published, move to the Publish And Refresh column (the last in the task list) and change the value from Yes to No. Do this for each of the new tasks you created.

6. Link the Office Project tasks that you just created together by selecting the tasks that specify the iterations and then choose Edit | Link Tasks.

7. Assign scenarios to iterations by moving the tasks that represent the scenarios you imported from Visual Studio Team System as sub-tasks of the iteration task you want the scenario to be developed in. To do this, drag the task row for the scenario to a location under a task that specifies your iteration. On the Formatting toolbar, click the right green arrow to indent the scenario, which makes it a sub-task of the iteration. You must also select the appropriate iteration value from the drop-down Iteration Path list of each scenario. Continue this process until you have moved all of your scenarios under the iteration that they will be released in.

8. Next, select all of the tasks in Office Project, right-click the selected tasks, and on the shortcut menu, choose Task Information. On the Advanced tab, on the Task Type drop-down list, select Fixed Duration, and then click OK.

9. For each of the scenarios listed under each iteration, specify the duration equal to the duration of the iteration. For example, if your iteration length is 3 weeks, set the Duration field for each scenario to **3 w**. You should be left with a project plan that looks similar to Figure 4-7.

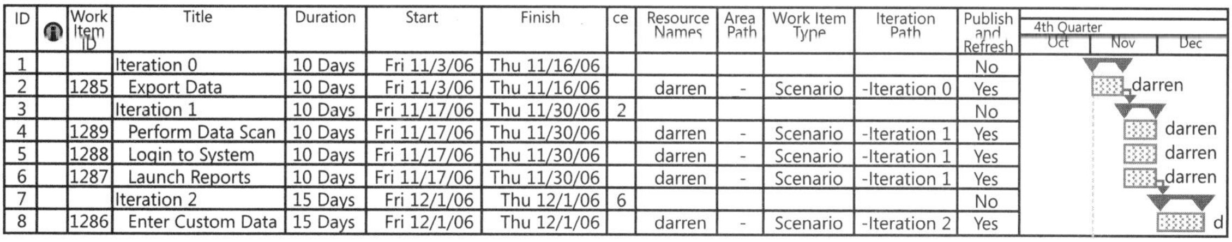

ID	ⓘ	Work Item ID	Title	Duration	Start	Finish	ce	Resource Names	Area Path	Work Item Type	Iteration Path	Publish and Refresh	4th Quarter		
													Oct	Nov	Dec
1			Iteration 0	10 Days	Fri 11/3/06	Thu 11/16/06						No			
2		1285	Export Data	10 Days	Fri 11/3/06	Thu 11/16/06		darren	-	Scenario	-Iteration 0	Yes	▓▓░darren		
3			Iteration 1	10 Days	Fri 11/17/06	Thu 11/30/06	2					No			
4		1289	Perform Data Scan	10 Days	Fri 11/17/06	Thu 11/30/06		darren	-	Scenario	-Iteration 1	Yes		▓▓ darren	
5		1288	Login to System	10 Days	Fri 11/17/06	Thu 11/30/06		darren	-	Scenario	-Iteration 1	Yes		▓▓ darren	
6		1287	Launch Reports	10 Days	Fri 11/17/06	Thu 11/30/06		darren	-	Scenario	-Iteration 1	Yes		▓▓░darren	
7			Iteration 2	15 Days	Fri 12/1/06	Thu 12/1/06	6					No			
8		1286	Enter Custom Data	15 Days	Fri 12/1/06	Thu 12/1/06		darren	-	Scenario	-Iteration 2	Yes			▓▓ d

Figure 4-7   An initial release plan in Office Project

Setting the duration of all of the requirements to the length of the iteration might seem a bit strange at first; however, remember what we are trying to do with this level of iteration planning. We simply want to assign scenarios to be the focus of an iteration. You should not be worried about sequencing these scenarios within an iteration because rarely will developers work on one feature at a time during an iteration. Also remember that the duration of a task is much different than the effort required to complete the task; the tasks were changed to Fixed Duration in step 8 in the earlier procedure because you don't want the duration to change if you make changes to Work and Assignment fields.

Ordering Scenarios

How you choose to sequence scenarios throughout your project will depend on many factors. One of the most important factors is determined by what the customer would like to see first because these scenarios will have most probably scored higher in requirement prioritization. Many organizations start with the highest priority requirements and work their way to the lowest priority requirement when performing scheduling. You should also take into consideration some of the technical details of each of the scenarios. For example, a scenario might have the highest priority but depend upon a number of other scenarios or quality of service requirements to be complete before it even makes sense to begin implementation. In this case, the dependent scenarios will need to be scheduled first. You should ensure that you understand the priority and the dependencies of your requirements to best develop your project plan.

Creating Work from Requirements

Now that you have provided an initial release schedule for your project, you should next derive work from your requirements. In this step, you will determine what the team must do to deliver the feature. Work might include detailing the requirements, performing further analysis, conducting design sessions, writing test cases for the requirement, developing code that implements the test cases, performing user acceptance testing, and so forth.

Your entire team should be involved in decomposing scenarios into tasks. You will first identify tasks that may not be associated with any specific requirement, such as setting up the development and build environments. From there, you will go through all documented requirements and attempt to come up with a list of actions that your team will need to take to implement that requirement. You should also provide an estimate for the amount of work it will take by a team member to complete each task.

It is important to try to maintain traceability between your requirements and all derived tasks. That is, all of the tasks that you create should have a link to the requirement that spawned them. The fastest way to spawn tasks from your requirements is through Visual Studio. Perform the following steps to create tasks that relate to a requirement:

1. In Team Explorer, launch the All Scenarios or All Quality of Service Requirements work item query.

2. Right-click a scenario or quality of service requirement work item from the work item Query Create Results window and choose Add Related Work Item | Task from the shortcut menu.

3. A new task work item will be created for you and given a default name that indicates that it is related to the requirement you originally selected. Notice that in the Links tab of the work item from the original risk are references providing traceability between the requirement and the task. Type the details of your task and save it as a new work item.

On many occasions, one task may be derived from many requirements. For example, you might have a task such as *create user interface prototype*, which would link to every scenario the prototype will demonstrate. To do this, you must add links from each of the tasks to the appropriate scenarios. To perform this task, follow these steps:

1. Create a new task work item from Team Explorer by right-clicking the Work Items folder under your Team Project and selecting Add Work Item | Task from the shortcut menu.

2. Enter the details for your task such as its title, related discipline, and the area to which it belongs to.

3. On the Links tab, click Add.

4. In the Add Link dialog box, specify Work Item as the link type, and then click the Browse button next to the Work item ID field. The Choose Related Work Item dialog box appears.

5. On the Saved query drop-down list, choose All Scenarios and then click Find to return the results of the query.

6. After the work items appear, click the scenario work item you want to associate your new task with and then click OK.

7. Add a comment to the linked work item if you want and then click OK.

8. Repeat steps 3 through 7 for all of the scenarios you want to associate with your task.

Of course, you can always add links to tasks from the scenario, and the method you choose will depend on whether it is easier to link tasks to scenarios or scenarios to tasks on your project. In either case, the results will be the same. In fact, you can also use Office

Project or Office Excel to perform this type of linking. More on this topic will be covered in the next section.

Project Spikes

Sometimes it is very difficult to break a requirement down into the tasks required to develop it because of the uncertainty that may exist around the requirement itself or the approach on its implementation. For this reason you can schedule a *spike*, which is a specific fixed-duration task (usually 3 to 4 hours) with the sole intent of gaining further knowledge or understanding of a problem. For example, your project team may need to use a new technology that no one on the team has used before. Because of this, the team cannot provide a good breakdown of how to use the technology or provide an estimate for any work using the new technology. If this is the case, you can elect one or more people to spike on the technology to gain a better understanding of it so that you can make a more accurate estimate. In its simplest sense, a spike is used to reduce the amount of uncertainty of some aspect of your project. Because higher uncertainty typically drives a greater range of estimates, spiking activities will actually provide you with greater accuracy in your related estimates.

Refining the Project Plan

Now that you have decomposed your requirements into tasks, it's time to add these new tasks to the plan you created when you constructed the initial release plan. In fact, you will use a very similar technique in adding tasks to your project plan as you did when you added requirements to iterations to create an initial release plan. You will add these new tasks to your release plan and make them sub-tasks of the requirements they relate to. If the tasks do not relate to requirements, such as creating a build environment or the construction of a testing lab, these tasks will be set up as sub-tasks of the Office Project tasks that represent iterations. To add tasks to your plan, perform the following steps:

1. Open the release plan you created earlier in this chapter.

2. Add the Remaining Work field to the release plan by right-clicking the column heading of the Duration field in your plan and selecting Insert Column from the shortcut menu. In the Field name list in the resulting dialog box, select the Remaining Work field and click OK.

3. Choose Team | Get Work Items, and then in the Get Work Items dialog box, on the Saved query drop-down list, select All Tasks. Click Find to return a list of task work items.

4. Select the tasks you want to add to your project plan. By default, all of the tasks will be selected indicating that they will be imported into your plan. Click OK to load the tasks into Office Project.

5. All the tasks will be added to bottom of the work area, and you must reorganize the tasks under the appropriate iteration or requirement summary tasks. Before you can do this, select all of the new tasks, right-click, and then select Task Information from the shortcut menu. On the Advanced tab, change the Task type to Fixed Duration.

6. To move the imported tasks to their appropriate location within the Office Project file, drag the individual tasks you just imported as sub-tasks to the iteration in which they will be performed. If you created the majority of these tasks as work items related to your project's scenarios or quality of service requirements, the iteration path of these tasks will automatically be set to the iteration path of the source requirement.

7. If a task has a work item link to a single scenario or quality of service requirement, move the task directly under the scenario in the project plan and indent the task, making the scenario or quality of service requirement a summary task and the new task its child by clicking the green indent arrow on the Formatting toolbar.

8. After rearranging all the tasks, set the Duration field of each task to the duration of the iteration. The resulting plan should look similar to Figure 4-8.

ID	Work Item ID	Title	Remaining Work	Duration	Work Item Type	Iteration Path	Publish and Refresh	4th Quarter Oct	Nov	Dec
1		Iteration 0	126 hrs	10 Days		Alteration	No			
2	1285	Export Data	126 hrs	10 Days	Scenario	Alteration	Yes			
3	972	Define Iteration Length	2 hrs	10 Days	Task	Alteration	Yes	darren [3%]		
4	974	Brainstorm & Prioritize Scenario List	4 hrs	10 Days	Task	Alteration	Yes	darren [5%]		
5	975	Brainstorm & Prioritize Quality of Servic	4 hrs	10 Days	Task	Alteration	Yes	darren [5%]		
6	976	Set up: Create Project Structure	1 hrs	10 Days	Task	Alteration	Yes	darren [1%]		
7	977	Create Iteration Plan	4 hrs	10 Days	Task	Alteration	Yes	darren [5%]		
8	989	Create Vision Statement	4 hrs	10 Days	Task	Alteration	Yes	darren [5%]		
9	971	Create Personas	8 hrs	10 Days	Task	Alteration	Yes	darren [10%]		
10	973	Create Test Approach Worksheet Includ	4 hrs	10 Days	Task	Alteration	Yes	darren [5%]		
11	970	Set up: Create Project Description on Te	4 hrs	10 Days	Task	Alteration	Yes	darren [5%]		
12	963	Set up: Set Permissions	1 hrs	10 Days	Task	Alteration	Yes	darren [1%]		
13	964	Set up: Migration of Source Code	0 hrs	10 Days	Task	Alteration	Yes	darren		
14	965	Set up: Mitigation of Work Items	0 hrs	10 Days	Task	Alteration	Yes	darren		
15	966	Set up: Set check-in Policies	1 hrs	10 Days	Task	Alteration	Yes	darren [1%]		
16	967	Set up: Configure Build	4 hrs	10 Days	Task	Alteration	Yes	darren [5%]		
17	967	Set up: Send Mail to Users for Installatio	1 hrs	10 Days	Task	Alteration	Yes	darren [1%]		
18	1290	Finalize Details on the Data Export Proc	4 hrs	10 Days	Task		Yes	darren [5%]		
19		Iteration 1	243 hrs	10 Days			No			
20	1289	Perform Data Scans	83 hrs	10 Days	Scenario	Alteration	Yes			
21	1128	Set up: Permissions	1 hrs	10 Days	Task	Alteration	Yes		darren [1%]	
22	1177	Set up: Set permissions from 3	1 hrs	10 Days	Task	Alteration	Yes		darren [1%]	
23	1178	Set up: Set permissions	1 hrs	10 Days	Task	Alteration	Yes		darren [1%]	
24	1288	Login to System	80 hrs	10 Days	Scenario	Alteration	Yes		darren	
25	1287	Launch Reports	80 hrs	10 Days	Scenario	Alteration	Yes		darren	
26		Iteration 2	120 hrs	15 Days			No			
27	1286	Enter Customer Data	120 hrs	15 Days	Scenario	Alteration	Yes			darren

Figure 4-8 A project plan showing iterations, requirements, and tasks

9. The Remaining Work fields represent an estimate for the effort for each task. For each task you entered into the project plan, provide the work effort in the remaining field.

10. Using the Resource Name field, select the team member that has been modified to provide you a list of your team members.

11. When you have completed your plan, publish all of your changes to the Team Foundation Server by choosing Publish Changes from the Team menu in Office Project.

> **Tip**   Remember that you can also add new tasks directly into Office Project in virtually the same way you would with Office Excel. You can work with Office Project in an offline mode, publish and refresh work items, and edit areas and iterations all from the Team menu in Office Project.

Notice that the tasks were not sequenced in any further detail than simply being assigned to an iteration or a requirement. You may have also noticed that the duration of each task was set to the length of the iteration itself regardless of how much effort was assigned to the task. The reason for this is to maintain simplicity. In Office Project, the duration of a task does not need to be related to the effort required to complete the task. In addition, your team members will rarely work serially, choosing to perform work in parallel throughout an iteration. This behavior should be encouraged because it allows your team members to remain productive while you are still expecting to have completed work by the end of the iteration. If the iterations are small enough, the order in which work assigned to the iteration must proceed is quite apparent. Our project plan simply states that it must be done by the end of the iteration, saving us the work of going into greater detail by sequencing activity within an iteration. Of course, if the size of an iteration is long and the sequencing is critical, you can go further and specify this in the project plan as you would with any Office Project plan you may have created in the past.

Using Office Excel for Project Planning

As a project manager, your tool of choice might not be Office Project but Office Excel. Office Excel may not provide you with the ability to produce great looking Gantt charts, but it nonetheless provides some very powerful features. These features enable you to plan your project just as effectively as you might with Office Project while forcing you to maintain a simple approach to the planning exercise. Instead of working with task summary tasks and calendar durations, you will simply be left to work with column filtering and ordering features to organize work into iterations.

If you created a project workbook as described earlier in this chapter, you should be ready to start organizing work into iterations. As you did with Office Project, you should start with the All Scenarios tab (assuming that you created a workbook that linked to the All Scenarios work item query). Here, you will simply assign scenarios to iterations by using the drop-down list in the Iteration Path column for each scenario. When you have completed assignment of iterations, you can use the All Tasks tab to perform the same steps to assign task work items to their corresponding iterations. Unfortunately, there is no good way to see how tasks link to requirements from inside Office Excel, or in Office Project for that matter, unless you check for linked work items one work item at a time. If you add the Links & Attachments work item field to your list, you will see only the values Yes or No, which indicate only the existence of a link or an attachment for each work item. If you want to see what those links and attachments are, select the work item that has attachments or links and choose Tools | Links & Attachments in Office Excel.

> **Note** Another limitation of using Office Excel and Office Project to enter work items is the inability to add associated work items as you can in Team Explorer.

Estimating Work and Scheduling with Visual Studio Team System

To this point we've talked about how to create an iteration plan by scheduling scenarios into iterations, splitting the stories into tasks, and then finally estimating the tasks. What happens if you don't have enough time in your iteration to perform these tasks? In fact, there is a big difference between estimating and scheduling. Up to this point we have assumed that since we assigned a scenario to an iteration, all of the tasks that derive from the scenario should get done in that same iteration; however, what if there just isn't enough time? And even more importantly, how much time do you really have to spend working on tasks in an iteration anyway?

Let's start to answer this question by looking at how we work. As asked in *Agile Management for Software Engineering: Applying the Theory of Constraints for Business Results* (Prentice Hall, 2003), during an 8-hour day, is an average person able to complete 8 hours worth of work? Probably not. You should try to take into account team meetings, washroom breaks, e-mail, instant messaging conversations, and hallway conversations, and you are more realistically looking at about 5.5 hours. You should also take into account issues such as vacation, sick time, education and training time, and time for other activities. Therefore, you should likely assume that each team member can productively work 42 to 43 weeks per year and 5.5 hours per day.

Now, assuming this, let's get back to our iteration plan. Let's assume that an iteration is two weeks long. We will need time at the end of the iteration to get our release ready and deploy it to test servers; let's just assume that will take 4 hours. We will need time at the beginning of the iteration to review the iteration plan, our estimates, issues, schedules and so forth. As iterations continue, we will need to allocate time to bug fixing and stabilization. Let's add these up to see what we are left with in Table 4-2.

Table 4-2   Resulting Work Allocation

Activity	Required Time
Iteration planning	.5 days per iteration
Bug fixing	1–3 days per iteration
Stabilization of build	1 day per iteration
Packaging and deploying to test servers	.5 days per iteration
Total	3–6 days per iteration

If an iteration takes 10 days (two weeks), and we are using 3 to 6 days per iteration to work on tasks not related to writing code or testing, that leaves us only about 4 to 7 days to actually write code. If we then take our previous assumption, that the average developer is productive only 5.5 hours per day, we are left with 22 to 38.5 hours of productive work in a two-week period.

When team members provide you with estimates, they are likely not taking into account all of the other factors we just discussed. When asked how long a task will take, the estimate is likely given as if the team member were working on the task uninterrupted, something Cohn refers to as *perfect days*. From these estimates, we can now start assigning tasks to iterations; however, armed with the knowledge that our two-week iteration has only 22 to 38.5 hours of time, we can make a better decision on just how much work to assign to the iteration while ensuring that total work does not exceed 38.5 hours per team member per iteration.

Checking Estimates and Schedules by Using Pivot Tables

Unfortunately, Visual Studio Team System doesn't provide any extra tools to take all these considerations into account when planning iterations. Perhaps the best tool you can use to ensure that you are not over-scheduling work for your team members is an Office Excel pivot table. Earlier in this chapter, you learned how to construct a pivot table from the All Work Item list in Office Excel. Perform the following steps to create a similar pivot table that will help you understand estimated work per iteration for each of your team members:

1. Open the project workbook you created earlier in this chapter and find the All Work Items list.

2. Ensure that the list displays all of the required columns and the Remaining Work field. To do this, click anywhere in the list and select Team | Choose Columns. In the Choose Columns dialog box, click Add Required to add all required fields. From the Available columns list, select the Remaining Work column, click > to move the column to the Selected columns list, and then click OK to continue.

3. Click anywhere in the list and select PivotTable And PivotChart Report from the Data menu in Office Excel to display the PivotTable And PivotChart Wizard.

4. Accept the default settings in step one of the wizard, using an Office Excel list or database as the source of the pivot and a PivotTable as the target. Click Next to proceed to the next step in the wizard.

5. Accept the default range selection provided to you by the wizard. Here the wizard has selected the All Work Items list as its source. Click Next.

6. Accept the default selection of a creation of a new worksheet for the PivotTable report and click Finish.

7. Drag Iteration Path, Assigned To, Work Item Type, and Title fields to the Drop Row Fields Here area of the pivot table. Ensure that you drag the fields onto the Row Area in the same row order as they are specified in this step.

8. Drag the Remaining Work field to the Data area of the pivot table. By default, the formula that will be used to summarize the Remaining Work data on each of the pivots will be the Count function. To change the function to Sum, right-click the Count Of Remaining Work cell and select Field Settings from the shortcut menu to display the PivotTable Field settings dialog box. Select Sum from the Summarized by list and click OK. The value of the Remaining Work field will now be added together for each dimension of your pivot table, as you can see in Figure 4-9.

 Tip If you are using the MSF for CMMI Process Improvement, you should use the Estimate field instead of the Remaining work field.

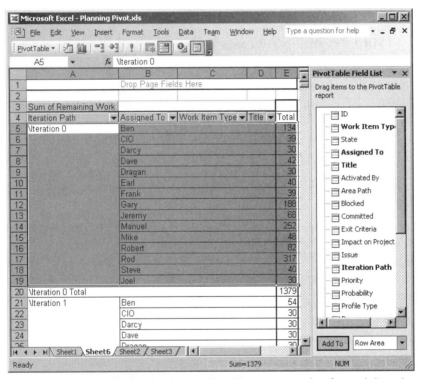

Figure 4-9 Pivot table for viewing workload by team member for each iteration

The pivot table you just created is read only, meaning that you can't make any direct changes to the values that are displayed within it. As you make changes to task assignments and iteration categorization in other parts of the project workbook, you should regularly publish any changes back to Visual Studio Team System, refresh the All Work Items list, and refresh the pivot table you just created by right-clicking anywhere on the surface of the pivot table and selecting Refresh from the shortcut menu. The pivot table will give you a handy representation of the workload as you progress throughout the planning cycles.

> ## More Elaborate Estimating
>
> If there is any aspect of software development that could be considered an art form, it is the estimating process. Very rarely are teams happy with their estimating techniques because most organizations underestimate rather than overestimate work. On the other hand, just as air expands to fill its container, so does work and estimation. That is probably one of the main reasons why overestimating isn't very common. This book is not going to detail the finer arts of estimation because entire books have been dedicated to the subject. If you are interested in fine-tuning your team's estimating abilities, you should read *Agile Estimating and Planning* by Mike Cohn (Prentice Hall PTR, 2006) and *Agile Management for Software Engineering: Applying the Theory of Constraints for Business Results*. Both of these books provide an enormous amount of insight into estimating providing you with a great opportunity to learn about how to improve your approach to this topic.

Managing Risk with Visual Studio Team System

As mentioned earlier, it is tough to talk about project management without discussing how risk is managed. Risk management starts off with risk identification. MSF Agile and MSF for CMMI both allow for this with the Risk work item type. As you might expect, the Risk work item type specified in MSF Agile is quite different than the one in MSF for CMMI; the latter version provides a more comprehensive workflow model and additional fields to manage mitigation plans, contingency plans, risk probability, and estimates. Risk identification starts, however, by simply creating a new risk and providing it with a title and a description.

Creating a Risks Work Item Query

Interestingly, MSF Agile does not include a query that returns all risks. One of the first things you should do in your project is to create a work item query that displays all risks on your project that are not set to closed. Note that if you are working with the MSF for CMMI process template, you will automatically have a risk work item query. To create a work item query that returns all active risks, perform the following steps:

1. In Team Explorer, in the Work Items folder, right-click the Team Queries folder and select Add Query from the shortcut menu. The New Query window will open in Visual Studio.

2. Click the last row of the work item query builder to add a new filter clause.

3. Select Work Item Type from the Field drop-down list and Risk from the Value drop-down list to specify a new clause that will filter out all work items except for risks.

4. Click the last row of the work item query builder to add a new filter clause.

5. Select State from the Field drop-down list, < > from the Operator drop-down list, and Closed from the Value drop-down list to further specify that you want to return only risk work items that are not closed.

6. Add some columns to your query by choosing Team | Column Options. Add the following columns to your query: Assigned To, Severity, Rank, State, Reason, Issue, and Exit Criteria.

7. On the File menu, select Save New Query As and type **Risks** for the name of the new work item query, placing it in the Team Queries location of your project.

One of the best ways to identify risks is with your team during a risk brainstorming meeting. To better facilitate this, you should enter your risks through Office Excel. In fact, if you created a project workbook as discussed earlier in this chapter, you should add a new tab for Risks, linking a work item list in Office Excel to the new Risks work item query you just created. During your risk brainstorming meeting, simply open your project workbook and navigate to the Risk tab. One of the greatest benefits of working with Office Excel in this way that it allows you to add a great number of work items very quickly. It also allows you to enter partial information into the spreadsheet, which must be completed before you publish to Visual Studio Team System. This will allow you to quickly identify risks, recording them as you do, without the worry of having to specify all aspects of a risk at the same time. During risk identification, you may also choose to specify a severity (Critical, High, Low, Medium) and a rank (which is similar to scenario rankings), specify which team member is responsible for the risk in the Assigned To field, and flag the risk as an issue (Issues field) or as exit criteria for the iteration (Exit Criteria field).

Planning from a Technical Perspective

From a technical perspective, your team must also do a considerable amount of planning. This book is not meant to provide the technical details of a project; however, you should be aware of the aspects of technical planning on which your team will likely want to focus on. One of the most important things your developers and testers will want to understand is the technical approach for the solution. Will it be a Web application? Will it run on a mobile device? Will the software be required to support different platforms? What database technology will be used to store data? The list of questions can go on; however, just like customer requirements, these questions are quite significant to your team and answering many of these questions should also be a goal of the planning phase. In the first few iterations, your technical team will likely be focused on the overall solution architecture of the target system and may not be as concerned with the finer details of the solution such as user interface navigation or screen colors.

The establishment of the development and test environment is also critical. Because this activity is usually performed during project initiation, covered in Chapter 3, it will impact other aspects of planning—for example, the source control management plan and the quality plans, of which the automated build and testing environments play a significant role. Your technical team must also ensure that they have time allotted for them to perform any code migrations from previous versions of a product and to appropriately set up and configure the project's source control repository within Visual Studio Team System. You should ensure that the team has sufficient time to make good planning decisions in this area because changes to the development environment after the software development process begins can be detrimental to your project.

When discussing requirements management in Visual Studio Team System previously in this chapter, we discussed how important it is for requirements to be testable. This is a mindset that must permeate its way throughout your team, including your developers. Developers must consider how they will utilize the automated testing features of Visual Studio Team System, specifically unit testing and code coverage analysis, throughout their development processes. Many organizations employ a technique called Test Driven Development to help ensure that every line of code written by developers is covered by at least one test that can be automated. Test Driven Development works to establish a test case first; then it develops a solution that will allow that test case to pass. This will ensure that a number of good practices emerge in your project. First, Test Driven Development demands testable requirements. Second, by writing automated test cases first, it will be easier for developers to regression test their software, which helps to reduce the number of bugs that can get introduced into a system during the normal course of product development.

Finally, ensure that your developers truly understand the user and business requirements for the system they are creating. The greater their understanding, the greater the chance they will produce software acceptable to your customers. Do not simply provide your developers with a mountain of requirement specification documents as the source of their product knowledge because documents alone are rarely enough to transfer the mindset of the user's intent to the creativity of your developers.

Chase's Planning Story

If there is one thing Chase has learned over the years, it's that you can't build great software without great requirements. To emphasize this, Chase calls a meeting with his entire team along with key stakeholders of Humongous Insurance. During this meeting, Chase talks about how requirements form the foundation for everything that follows. Every estimate and every line of code needs to be derived from good requirements. The team is about to embark upon planning activities, and Chase wants to ensure that requirements, not technology, are their focus because without good requirements, the possibility of producing a good plan is remote. Chase tells his team that a good plan involves the entire team and that he expects everyone to contribute to all areas of their plan as they move forward. Chase also emphasizes that planning isn't a phase of a projects, it's an activity throughout the project life cycle. He tells the project team that the initial plan will be the focus of the next few weeks; however, this plan will be reviewed and updated at the end of every iteration right up until the release of their product. Some team members express concern with this approach—they suggest that it will be a waste of time. But Chase convinces them that estimates are only a best guess and that with each subsequent iteration, the guesses will be more accurate.

Chase has a 45-minute train commute every day and has learned to make the best of the commute by focusing on work. To facilitate being able to work on his laptop during his train ride, Chase creates a project workbook in Office Excel that will link to all of the work item queries in Visual Studio Team System he uses every day. This will allow Chase to take work items with him on the train and provide him with the ability to add new work items and modify existing work items while offline. More importantly, when Chase gets back to the office, he will have the ability to synchronize all of his changes with Visual Studio Team System.

To begin the planning process, Chase leads his team through a requirements-gathering workshop in which he brings together his team and a group of people who will ultimately be using the product. Together, they use a whiteboard to brainstorm about the scenarios that the software should provide. At the end of the meeting, Chase works to create Scenario work items in Visual Studio Team System that represent the scenarios that were identified and then assigns these work items to various team members who will be responsible for gathering more information for each scenario.

A week later, after which the team has spent time with their target user representatives to detail each of the scenarios and uncover the many additional quality of service requirements needed by users, such as performance, response time, security, and availability, the team once again comes together to review all of the work in progress and to begin basic estimation and prioritization of the all of the requirements. Chase instructs the team on how to prioritize requirements by using priority buckets and how to perform basic rough order of magnitude estimates on all of the identified scenarios. He also stresses the importance of performing these activities as a group to ensure that everyone's expectations and understanding are the same.

While the rest of the team is busy detailing requirements, Chase is hard at work creating an initial iteration schedule that was based on the general constraints Chase was given to work with. He knew that he had six months to release a new product. Chase also knew his budget would ultimately determine the size of his team. From this information, Chase began to decompose his timelines into iterations. Chase began by allowing time at the end of the project for stabilization and release management activities. Chase also allocated the first few weeks of the project to focus on requirements and initial planning activities. This left his team with about four months to build and test software. Chase further divided this four-month period into three-week iterations and selected iterations that would focus on delivering interim releases of the product. Chase would then use this skeleton iteration plan to schedule the work required to develop the scenarios his team is working to build.

After the initial iteration plan has been constructed and all scenarios have been identified, prioritized, and given a rough estimate, Chase worked with his team to decompose each of the requirements into tasks. Chase made sure that all types of activities related to building each requirement was taken into account, such as design, coding, testing, build integration, reviews, revisions, and bug fixing. Each of the tasks that were derived from each requirement was stored in Visual Studio Team System as a task work item and was linked to the requirement from which they originated. In addition, each Task work item was given an hourly estimate that was agreed to by the entire team. During the course of this process, many risks were identified that would jeopardize aspects of the project. If teams could not provide an accurate estimate on a task, additional work was scheduled that would allow the team to conduct further work to better understand the underlying requirement, technology, or method to help increase the accuracy of the estimates. Each of the risks were recorded in Visual Studio Team System so that they can be tracked and integrated into the overall schedule of the project.

After all of the tasks and risks have been entered into Visual Studio Team System, Chase worked with his team to schedule all of the work into the skeleton iteration plan he created. Chase made sure that his customer representatives participated in this process so that everyone agreed to the ordering and timing of the requirements delivered by the team. During this process, the team discovered that there were too many requirements for the amount of time and money assigned to the project. With the help of the customer representatives, Chase and his team were able to remove lower-priority requirements from the scope of the project, reflecting their decisions in the State fields of corresponding work items. Chase and his team used Office Excel to assign work items to each of the iterations; however, his project sponsors wanted to see the Gantt chart and work breakdown structure in Office Project. After his team completed assignments of work to each of the iterations, Chase then used Office Project to import the task work items and make the appropriate adjustments to the start and end dates of each of the tasks based on the start and end dates of the iteration they are in to produce the appropriate report for management. Chase ensured that the Office Excel workbook and Office Project file he used were safely stored in the project portal for his Team Project so that they can be used in future iterations when they revisit the plan and need to make adjustments.

Final Thoughts on Planning

Here are some final tips on how to improve your planning on your next project:

- Make planning a team event, and make it fun. If planning isn't fun, your team won't want to spend as much time doing it. Making planning fun means that replanning every iteration should also be fun and painless and thus, something your team will want to engage in regularly.

- Keep planning simple. Plans that generate extremely complex results are more complex to communicate and understand. Keep your plans simple and the results of the planning activities easy to consume by all members of your team.

- Don't forget to revisit your plans every iteration. We want to put some degree of emphasis on planning activities before we start developing our software, but always keep in mind that this process should continue throughout the life of your project.

■ Stay flexible and expect change. If there is a single universal constant in software engineering, it is change. Don't run from it. Embrace it when it meets you, and it will be your friend.

We just listed some aspects of planning that should help make it more successful, but what are some planning mistakes you can make to debunk the value of planning on your projects? In D. J. Reifer's *Software Management Seventh Edition* (IEEE Computer Society, 2006), Steve McConnell provided some perspective on this in his article "The Nine Deadly Sins of Project Planning," which we will summarize here:

■ **No planning at all**   This one seems a bit obvious; however, you might be surprised at how common this mistake is. Many organizations rush to implementation without considering the impact on the entire team. Many people have mistakenly thought that Agile software development methodologies reinforce this premise, but it is simply not true.

■ **Not planning enough**   You should take into consideration aspects of your project such as sick time, training, vacations, or staff turnover. Try to start your planning activities with some real-life assumptions that force you to account for some of the minute details that might cause huge problems if not uncovered early.

■ **Failure to plan for risk**   Attention to risks drive further work in either risk preventative activities or risk contingency actives. In any case, risks must be dealt with continually throughout a project.

■ **Using the same plan for every project**   Not every project is created equally. Many organizations assume this and use standard project templates to drive all projects regardless of the project constraints or type.

■ **Allowing your plan to diverge from reality**   On a good project, your team has done enough planning to do a great job developing the product. On a great project, project planning continues right up until deployment, updating project plans along the way.

■ **Planning too much detail too soon**   Don't try to get into too much detail unless that detail provides you or your customer with value. For example, many organizations use a document-based planning approach, that is, planning is complete when the document that contains the plans are complete. The team focuses on filling out the missing sections of the plan instead of on the value they are providing to the project team as a result of planning.

■ **Planning to catch up later**   If your projects get behind schedule, don't assume that you will eventually catch up. It just doesn't happen. When you are behind, you should stop and try to account for why you are behind and rethink your plans.

■ **Not learning from past planning sins**   There are three types of people in the world: ignorant people who do not learn from their mistakes, smart people who learn from their mistakes, and wise people who learn from the mistakes of others. You should try to be smart and learn how to adapt your planning techniques over time.

Cohn extends the list of why planning fails with the following points:

- **Planning is by activity rather than feature.**   Too many plans focus on the completion of tasks rather than the completion of features.

- **Activities do not finish early.**   Air expands to fill its container, and so do tasks in an estimate. Do not plan for some tasks to finish earlier than you have estimated; if you do, it probably demonstrates that you haven't estimated well enough.

- **Activities are not independent.**   Some activities can be done in parallel and some cannot. Make sure that you understand the dependencies between your activities and incorporate these into your planning mindset.

- **Multitasking causes delays.**   Clark and Wheelwrite in *Managing New Product and Process Development: Text and Cases* (The Free Press, 1993) demonstrated that people are most effective when they are multitasking on two tasks and greatly decreasing in productivity as the number of tasks being multitasked increases. Just because someone may be 75 percent utilized on a project does not mean she will be able to carry an additional 25 percent of the workload.

- **Features are not developed by priority.**   Feature prioritization should drive the release schedule because it reflects customer value at the time of the planning activity.

- **Uncertainty is ignored.**   Uncertainty drives the amount of buffer you add to your tasks, iterations, and projects. When estimating, you should incorporate methods of planning that consider uncertainty.

- **Estimates become commitments.**   Estimates are just what they are, a best guess. Commitments cannot be made on best guesses alone

Summary

In this chapter, we described the essentials of project planning according to the Project Management Book of Knowledge. It is important to note that with Visual Studio Team System, you can perform virtually every aspect of project planning by using work items and project documentation. This chapter also described the importance of requirements gathering and steps you can take to turn your requirements into a real, workable project plan broken into timeboxed iterations.

Chapter 5
Monitoring and Controlling Project Execution

- Review the PMBOK process groups for directing and managing project execution and for monitoring and controlling project work.

- Discuss an Agile approach for managing project scope.

- Describe a technique for consistently delivering on time and on budget.

- Describe the difference between quality assurance and quality control and explore how to use Visual Studio Team System to implement both.

- Show how to monitor and control risk.

- Manage a virtual team by using Visual Studio Team System.

- Manage vendors by using Visual Studio Team System.

- Create an Information Radiator by using MSF reports.

Executing the Plan

Chapter 4, "Planning a Project," covered the activities associated with planning a project and showed us how to utilize Visual Studio Team System in the planning process. This chapter focuses on the next step: executing the plan.

The PMI Project Management Body of Knowledge describes two process groups to cover this stage in a project: the Executing Process Group and the Monitoring and Control Process Group. The *Executing Process Group* consists of the processes that implement the project management plan. This process group is where the actual work gets done. In addition to directing and managing project execution, this process group includes acquisition and development of the project team and performance of quality assurance, vendor selection, and distribution of information to all interested stakeholders.

The Monitoring and Controlling Process Group consists of the processes used to observe project execution, measure progress, identify potential problems, and take corrective actions when necessary. In addition to monitoring and controlling project work, this process group includes integrated change control, scope verification, scope control, schedule control, cost control, quality control, team management, performance reporting, stakeholder management, risk monitoring and control, and contract administration.

> **Note** Many people look at the PMBOK and see a monolithic waterfall process full of procedures and documentation—the antithesis of Agile development. It's unfortunate that the PMBOK gives this impression to so many people because that's simply not true. In fact, the PMBOK 3rd Edition states, "The application of the [PMBOK] project management processes to a project is iterative and many processes are repeated and revised during the project. The project manager and the project team are responsible for determining what processes from the [PMBOK] Process Groups will be employed, by whom, and the degree of rigor that will be applied to the execution of those processes to achieve the desired project objective."

The Microsoft Solution Framework (MSF) offers a different yet complementary perspective on project execution. MSF organizes project execution into three tracks: Build, Stabilize, and Deploy. These MSF tracks can overlap and span multiple iterations. Each MSF track includes a governance checkpoint that serves as a go-no-go gate for the project. For instance, the *Build track checkpoint* relates to completing the envisioned scope, the *Stabilize checkpoint* relates to release readiness, and the *Deploy checkpoint* relates to deployment completion. The specific criteria used for each checkpoint is determined during project planning and is updated as needed during iteration planning.

Each MSF track is also associated with activities grouped into workstreams. For more information about MSF tracks, refer to the MSF guidance in Visual Studio Team System. To view the MSF tracks in the MSF process guidance, do the following:

1. Launch Microsoft Visual Studio 2005.

2. In Team Explorer, right-click the name of the Team Project created by using an MSF template and then select Show Project Portal. The project portal appears in a Web browser window, as shown in Figure 5-1.

> **Tip** Add the project portal to the Favorites list in your Web browser so you can easily access the portal in the future.

3. Click the Process Guidance hyperlink from the Quick Launch area of the project portal to show the MSF process guidance home page.

4. On the MSF process guidance home page, click the Views tab to show the About Views page.

5. On the Views menu, click the Tracks link to show the About Tracks page.

6. Click the name of a track to view related information including workstreams and activities, work items, work product examples and templates, and report examples. Figure 5-2 shows the process guidance for the Build track.

Figure 5-1   Home page for a Team Project based on MSF for Agile Software Development

Figure 5-2   MSF process guidance for the Build track

Now let's take a closer look at how Visual Studio Team System and MSF contribute to specific PMBOK processes associated with monitoring and controlling project execution.

Directing and Managing Project Execution

Directing and managing project execution is the process in which the actual work is performed. This process consists of the actions taken by you and the project team specified in the project management plan. In the context of an Agile methodology such as MSF, the *project management plan* is primarily the detailed work plan that the project team produces at the start of each iteration. This iteration plan consists of work items added to the Team Project in Visual Studio Team System. Typically, these work items represent tasks. However, other types of work items can be included, such as risks to be considered and bugs that might be included from the previous iteration. As work progresses, other types of work items are added to the iteration plan: new bugs to be fixed and newly discovered risks to be addressed.

In the Team Foundation Client, you can use the work item queries to produce a list of work items that you can view and update. To produce a list of all the active tasks for a Team Project, do the following:

1. Launch Visual Studio 2005.

2. In Team Explorer, expand your Team Project, expand the Work Items folder, and then expand the Team Queries folder.

3. Double-click the All Tasks query. A query results window (shown in Figure 5-3) appears showing a list of all the active tasks for the Team Project.

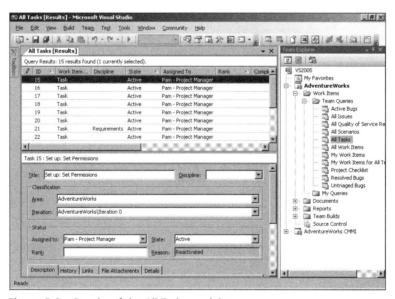

Figure 5-3   Results of the All Tasks work item query

You can click any work item in the query results list to view the details in the work item form below the list. To work with the results in Microsoft Office Excel instead, simply right-click the work item query in Team Explorer and then click Open In Microsoft Excel. Office Excel will launch automatically, and then the results of the query will load directly into the spreadsheet, as shown in Figure 5-4.

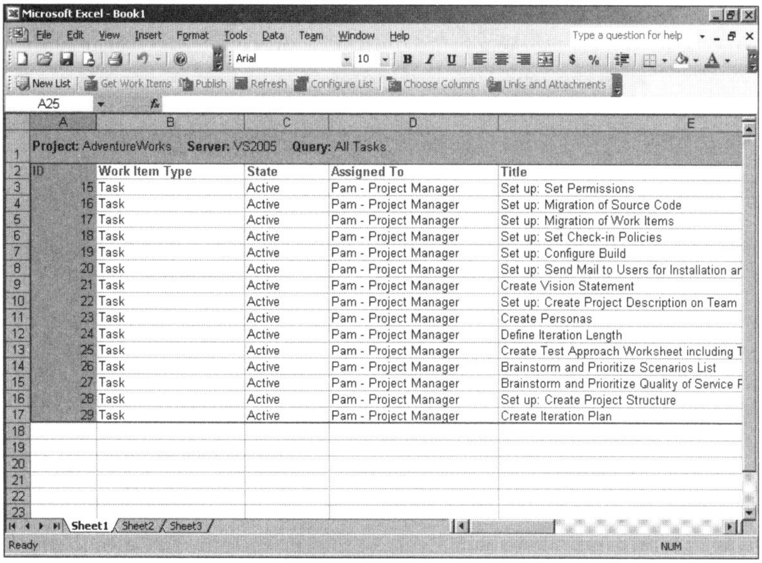

ID	Work Item Type	State	Assigned To	Title
15	Task	Active	Pam - Project Manager	Set up: Set Permissions
16	Task	Active	Pam - Project Manager	Set up: Migration of Source Code
17	Task	Active	Pam - Project Manager	Set up: Migration of Work Items
18	Task	Active	Pam - Project Manager	Set up: Set Check-in Policies
19	Task	Active	Pam - Project Manager	Set up: Configure Build
20	Task	Active	Pam - Project Manager	Set up: Send Mail to Users for Installation ar
21	Task	Active	Pam - Project Manager	Create Vision Statement
22	Task	Active	Pam - Project Manager	Set up: Create Project Description on Team
23	Task	Active	Pam - Project Manager	Create Personas
24	Task	Active	Pam - Project Manager	Define Iteration Length
25	Task	Active	Pam - Project Manager	Create Test Approach Worksheet including T
26	Task	Active	Pam - Project Manager	Brainstorm and Prioritize Scenarios List
27	Task	Active	Pam - Project Manager	Brainstorm and Prioritize Quality of Service F
28	Task	Active	Pam - Project Manager	Set up: Create Project Structure
29	Task	Active	Pam - Project Manager	Create Iteration Plan

Figure 5-4 Results of a work item query in Office Excel

In addition to tasks, the PMBOK refers to three types of actions taken while a project is in progress: defect repairs, preventive actions, and corrective actions. Defect repairs are more commonly referred to as bug fixes. When a defect is found in the software being produced, it is documented as a bug. The act of fixing the bug is the defect repair. Preventive actions are taken as a result of risk planning and monitoring. These actions are intended to avoid a problem by either reducing the probability that the problem will occur, minimizing its impact on the project, or both. A preventive action can occur as a planned task, or it can be triggered by an event. When an unanticipated problem causes the project to deviate from the plan, the team takes corrective action to get the project back on track. Rather than simply reacting to a situation, the project team should apply corrective actions that are deliberate, agreed-upon, and documented in some way.

You can employ Visual Studio Team System to manage preventive actions, corrective actions, and defect repairs in much the same way that you manage tasks—through work items. Both MSF process templates include a Bug work item type for logging and tracking defect repairs. In addition, both MSF process templates include a Risk work item type for documenting and managing preventive actions in addition to corrective actions. MSF calls the preventive actions associated with a risk the *Mitigation Plan* and corrective actions associated with a risk the *Contingency Plan*. In addition, all the work items in MSF for Agile Software Development include a drop-down list to flag the work item as an issue that is impeding progress. The Issue drop-down list is located on the Details tab of the work item data entry form. MSF for CMMI Process Improvement handles issues as a separate work item type that includes additional fields such as *Analysis*, *Corrective Action*, *Target Resolve Date*, and *Actual Resolve Date*.

> **Tip** If you created a Team Project by using the MSF for Agile Software Development process template but wish it had an Issues work item type, you're in luck! You can import new work item types into existing Team Projects by using the Process Template Editor. You will learn how to perform this customization and others in Chapter 7, "Tailoring Visual Studio Team System."

By managing their work items in Visual Studio Team System during project execution, the project team generates work performance information that can be used to produce performance reports. Visual Studio Team System automatically generates additional work performance information through Team Foundation Version Control and Team Build.

Team Foundation Version Control allows the project team to maintain proper version control over the work products it produces. As the project administrator, you can easily configure Team Foundation Version Control to require all source code revisions to be associated with one or more work items when checked in. We highly recommend that you enable this check-in policy because it provides valuable work performance information by linking activities to the resulting work products. To enable this check-in policy for a Team Project, do the following:

1. Launch Visual Studio 2005.

2. In Team Explorer, right-click the name of the Team Project, point to Team Project Settings, and then click Source Control to show the Source Control Settings window.

3. On the Check-in Policy tab, click Add to show the Add Check-in Policy dialog box.

4. Select the Work Items check-in policy, and then click OK to save the setting and close the Add Check-in Policy dialog box. Figure 5-5 shows the Source Control Settings window with the newly added check-in policy.

5. Click OK to save the setting and close the Source Control Settings window.

Team Build is an automated build system integrated directly into every Visual Studio Team System Team Project. By using the New Team Build Type Creation Wizard, the project team can easily configure Team Build to build one or more Visual Studio software projects automatically, run a suite of automated tests against the new build, deploy the resulting executables to a predetermined drop location, and open a Bug type work item if the build fails for any reason. A team member can manually start a build from Team Explorer. With a bit more setup, though, the build can be scheduled to automatically run periodically. The most typical setup is to run the build nightly. Some shops take an even more aggressive approach to automated builds by configuring Team Foundation Server to run a build every time a check-in event occurs.

Each build automatically saves a complete build report to the Team Foundation Server data warehouse. The build report includes a step-by-step log of the build process, a list of source control changesets containing the source code used by the build, a list of work items associated with those changesets, and detailed results of all tests run. When the build is run regularly, these build reports offer a wealth of work performance information related to the health of the product, including current status and historical trends.

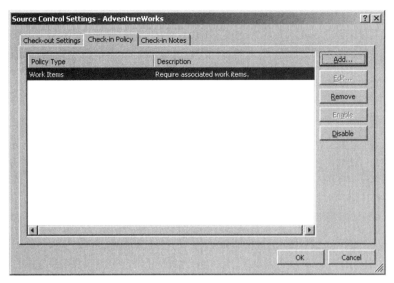

Figure 5-5   Adding a Work Items check-in policy to a Team Project

Monitoring and Controlling Project Work

Whereas directing and managing project execution consists of performing work as specified in the project management plan, *monitoring and controlling project work* involves observing project execution and measuring project performance to identify issues in a timely manner and take corrective action as needed.

> **Note**   Four dimensions of a project need to be monitored and controlled: scope, time, cost, and quality. Historically, the software industry has done a poor job in all four dimensions. The good news is that there is plenty of room for improvement, and we're getting better at applying best practices. The PMBOK provides in-depth guidance for managing each of these dimensions. This guidance is somewhat generalized, designed to apply to a wide range of projects. We'll provide more specific guidance here, based on MSF and other Agile development methods.

When monitoring project work, there are two types of variation to consider: common cause variation and special cause variation. This phenomenon was first described in the 1930s by Dr. Walter Shewart of Bell Labs and was later popularized as a statistical process control method by W. Edwards Deming in the 1980s (*Out of the Crisis*, MIT Press, 1986). *Common cause variation* is predictable based on historical experience. It's the day-to-day variation that occurs on every software project. For instance, the duration of an individual task in an iteration plan almost never matches the estimate—some tasks take longer than expected, whereas other tasks are finished early. This is normal variation that can be anticipated. As long as this variation stays within an acceptable range, it's considered a normal part of executing the project plan, so it requires no corrective action.

Special cause variation, on the other hand, is inherently unpredictable because it is new and unanticipated. Special cause variation signals that something about the project has fundamentally changed and that corrective action is required. One example of special cause variation would be the reassignment of a key project team member to another project halfway through an iteration. Another example would be the discovery of a serious flaw in the software product that requires major rework. Clearly these are unanticipated situations that must be addressed because of their impact on the project plan.

Monitoring and controlling project work is all about detecting special cause variation and taking the appropriate corrective actions. Sam Guckenheimer (*Software Engineering with Microsoft Visual Studio Team System,* Addison-Wesley, 2006) points out the importance of making the distinction between common cause variation and special cause variation. He warns that tampering with a process that's exhibiting common cause variation is counterproductive because it only increases variances, sending the project out of control. On the other hand, ignoring special cause variances can be just as hazardous by allowing the project to remain out of control. For this reason, it is important that you understand the two types of variation and respond to them appropriately.

You can use work item queries to monitor project execution. The MSF process templates include a query called All Work Items, which includes all the work items for a Team Project that are not in a Closed *State*. This work item query is a good choice to see the current status of the project because it lists all the active work items regardless of type. To better analyze the project status, you can sort the query results by clicking the column headings shown in Figure 5-3.

Opening the All Work Items query in Office Excel allows you to further analyze capabilities. You can use the Pivot Table feature of Office Excel to group and summarize work items by any of the fields such as *State, Discipline, Work Item Type,* or *Assigned To*. You can also display the pivot table information as a chart. For more information, see the section titled "Work Item Pivot Tables and Graphs" in Chapter 4.

In addition to work item queries, you can use the Team Foundation Server reports to access work performance information. Team Foundation Server utilizes SQL Server Reporting Services to create sophisticated reports from its data warehouse. The two MSF process templates include a variety of reports that provide many different perspectives on project performance. You can access these reports in several ways. To view a Team Project report directly in the Team Foundation Client, do the following:

1. Launch Visual Studio 2005.

2. In Team Explorer, double-click a Team Project name to expand its folder.

3. Double-click the Reports folder to view a list of available reports, as shown in Figure 5-6.

4. Double-click a report name to view the report.

Figure 5-6   Selecting a report in Team Explorer

To view the reports in a Web browser by using the SQL Server Reporting Services Web site, do the following:

1. Launch Visual Studio 2005.

2. In Team Explorer, double-click a Team Project name to expand its folder.

3. Right-click the Reports folder and then click Show Report Site to open the Microsoft SQL Server Reporting Service Web site for the Team Project in a browser window, as shown in Figure 5-7.

> **Note**   The Work Remaining report has its roots in Lean Production, which is a management philosophy focused on the reduction of waste to improve the flow of value to the customer. This philosophy was first articulated by James P. Womack and Daniel T. Jones (*The Machine that Changed the World: The Story of Lean Production*, Harper Perennial, 1991) in their description of the Toyota Production System (TPS). It turns out that the TPS introduced the Cumulative Flow Diagram as a simple and effective way to visualize the flow of work through a production line. The MSF architects saw the value in the Cumulative Flow Diagram and adapted it to visualize the flow of work in a software development project, renaming it the Work Remaining report.

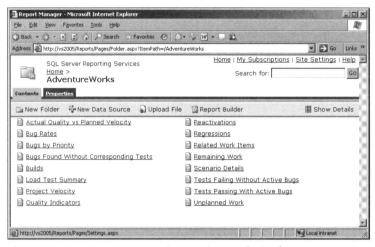

Figure 5-7   SQL Server Reporting Services Web site for a Team Project

By looking at the Remaining Work report, you can quickly assess project performance. First, the slope of the line between Resolved Scenarios and Closed Scenarios indicates the rate at which Scenarios are being closed. By projecting this line to the end of the iteration, you can clearly see whether the rate is sufficient to close all of the Scenarios before the iteration is finished. This provides an early warning that allows the team to take corrective actions if necessary.

Measuring the vertical height of a queue on a given day tells you the size of the queue on that day. Measuring the horizontal width of a queue on a given day tells you the lead time of the queue on that day, that is, how many days it will take for a work item to move to the next queue. If the size or lead time increases for all but the Closed queue, a bottleneck impeding progress. The team should determine the cause of the bottleneck and take corrective action to remove it.

Whereas the Remaining Work report provides at-a-glance information about the status of the *project*, the Quality Indicators report provides at-a-glance information about the status of the *product*. Shown in Figure 1-3 in Chapter 1 (page 13), the Quality Indicators report is actually four diagrams superimposed on one another: test results, percentage code coverage, code churn, and active bug count.

The test results show the number of tests that passed and failed. It also shows inconclusive tests, which are unit test stubs that have been created but not fully implemented. The percentage code coverage shows the number of lines of code that were tested, as a percentage of the total lines of code in the application. Code coverage is a crude measure in that that unit tests might not test all the logic in a block of code even though the block of code was executed at least once. Just the same, code coverage is a good indication of code quality, and most organizations set a minimum threshold for this metric. Both test results and code coverage come from the build history in the Team Foundation Server data warehouse.

Code churn measures the volume of change in the code base. Whenever source code is checked into Team Foundation Version Control, Team Foundation Server automatically measures the lines of code that were added, deleted, and modified, and then it records this information in the Team Foundation Server data warehouse. Code churn is the sum of these changes: lines added + lines deleted + lines modified. Measured over time, code churn is a relative measure of stability in the code base. Code churn is typically high at the beginning of an iteration, when features and being added or changed and unit tests are being added or modified. However, as the code base begins to stabilize, the code churn should taper off, with a corresponding increase in the number of passing tests. If the code churn remains high late into an iteration, that indicates that the software is not stabilizing.

The active bug count comes from the work item tracking system. It shows the number of bugs that have been reported but not fixed. The active bug count should decrease at the end of an iteration. Ideally, it should reach zero, but in practice it rarely does because some bug fixes are either deferred or deemed not worth fixing.

Although the Quality Indicators report is very busy, it's actually easy to interpret, as we see in Table 5.1.

Table 5-1   Interpreting the Quality Indicators Report

Quality Indicator	Healthy Trend
Number of Tests Passed	↗
Percentage Code Coverage	↗
Number of Inconclusive Tests	↘
Number of Failed Tests	↘
Code Churn	↘
Active Bugs	↘

↗ = High and increasing over time,   ↘ = Low and decreasing over time

These two reports give you complete, at-a-glance work performance information for monitoring and controlling project work: the Remaining Work report charts the health of the process, and the Quality Indicators report charts the health of the product. With these reports, you can quickly assess project performance, spot unhealthy trends, and identify the need for corrective actions. The MSF process templates contain additional reports that serve a variety of other purposes including planning and estimating, root cause analysis, process improvement, and capability appraisal. For more information about each of the reports, refer to the MSF Process Guidance. To access report descriptions and examples in the MSF Process Guidance, do the following:

1. Launch Visual Studio 2005.

2. In Team Explorer, double-click a Team Project name to expand its folder.

3. Right-click the Work Items folder and then click Team Project Process Guidance to show the process guidance home page.

4. On the Index tab, click the Reports link in the left pane to show an index of available reports.

5. Click the name of a report in the index to view a description and example of the report.

Managing Project Scope

As mentioned earlier, most software projects begin with a significant degree of ambiguity. Users often don't know exactly what they want, or they cannot articulate their needs in enough detail to clearly specify the requirements. The project team may not fully understand the problem domain, or maybe they are using an unfamiliar new technology. Whatever the reason, there is a good possibility that requirements will change over the course of a software development project.

Iterative and incremental development methodologies address the problem of ambiguity by allowing requirements to be refined and elaborated on as the project progresses, based on knowledge gained in previous iterations. Iterative and incremental development also supports changing business conditions by allowing requirements to be added, removed, modified, and reprioritized on iteration boundaries. This approach is very effective, but it has an insidious downside: scope creep. As users see working software and more fully understand the possibilities, they naturally begin to ask for more features. Developers are sometimes guilty of a form of scope creep called gold plating—embellishing the product with features that were not requested in the hopes that they might prove useful or sometimes just because they are intellectually stimulating to create.

Clearly there is a need to allow changes to the scope of a project while it's in progress, but these changes must occur in a controlled manner. The PMBOK describes a process for managing project scope through an integrated change control process. In a nutshell, the PMBOK scope control process starts with a detailed project scope statement and work breakdown structure and then it manages project scope changes through a formal change control system consisting of a tracking system and documented procedures that include levels of approval for authorizing changes.

MSF for Agile Software Development does not specify a change control process *per se*. Rather, change control is built into the iteration planning process and is managed cooperatively by the Business Analyst and Project Manager. During project planning, the Business Analyst specifies the scope of the project in terms of Scenarios and Quality of Service Requirements, and the Project Manager specifies the project scope in terms of estimated cost and schedule. During an iteration, the Business Analyst updates and reprioritizes the Scenarios and Quality of Service Requirements, adding and changing requirement-related work items and updating their rank values as needed to reflect the current priorities based on customer feedback and changing business conditions. The Project Manager then schedules Scenarios, Quality of Service Requirements, and a bug-fixing allotment for the upcoming iteration, based on the project team's velocity in the previous iteration. After the iteration has started, nobody outside the project team is permitted to make changes until the start of the next iteration. This no-change rule might seem a bit harsh, and some may even perceive its inflexibility as going against the Agile philosophy. This rule is critical, though, because changing the scope of an iteration is very disruptive, causing the team to lose momentum, productivity, and morale.

Even so, there are times when a new opportunity is so compelling that it warrants interrupting an iteration. In his book *Agile Project Management with Scrum, 1st Edition* (Microsoft Press, 2004), Ken Schwaber describes an effective technique for dealing with this situation. If an opportunity comes up that is significantly more important than the work being done on the iteration, management can cancel the iteration completely. This abnormal termination triggers a new iteration planning meeting at which the priorities are re-evaluated and the new opportunity is selected if it becomes the new top priority. Cancelling an iteration is a highly disruptive, highly visible action that management is not likely to take without good reason. What's more, management is not likely to invoke this drastic measure because the opportunity can be addressed at the start of the next iteration, which is no more than a few weeks away.

This approach simplifies the process of controlling and verifying scope. The overall scope of the project is specified by the Product Manager during initial project planning through the vision statement, requirements work items, and other requirements documentation. The scope for each iteration is well defined, based on an elaboration of the high-priority requirements selected during iteration planning. This elaboration involves a collaborative effort between the product manager and the rest of the project team and can be expressed in a variety of ways including additional narrative, flowcharts, models, prototypes, and acceptance tests. At the end of each iteration, the scope is verified, usually through acceptance test results and a formal review with the product manager.

The reason this approach works so well is that the scope is managed in small, incremental chunks that do not change once work is underway. Short iterations of fixed duration not only keep the scope of an iteration small, they also offer the opportunity to frequently re-evaluate priorities and respond to new opportunities. In this way, integrated change control is a highly adaptive process that harmonizes with the overall rhythm of the project.

Another source of scope change is imperfect planning. Even at the iteration level, at which planning is done for a short period in the immediate future, there will be tasks that nobody anticipated. It's not that these tasks are added after the fact; they were there all along but simply didn't make it into the plan. In his book *Agile Management for Software Engineering: Applying the Theory of Constraints for Business Results* (Prentice Hall PTR, 2003), David Anderson calls these unanticipated activities *dark matter*. Project dark matter is an inevitable fact of life that cannot be avoided completely. However, it can be monitored. The Unplanned Work report in Figure 5-8 shows how much work was added to an iteration after it started.

Unplanned Work
Report Generated 11/04/2004 11:25 AM by martin@contoso.com
How much unplanned work do we have?

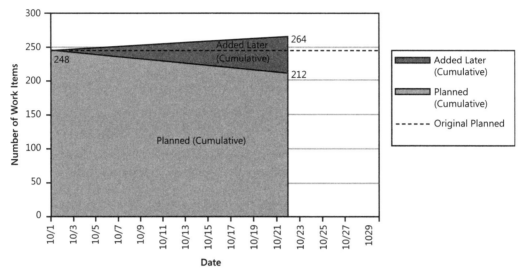

Figure 5-8 Unplanned Work report

Project dark matter can also be seen in the Work Remaining report. Notice how the top line of the Work Remaining report in Figure 1-2 (page 12) rises over time. This increase in the total amount of work is an indication of project dark matter. Both the Unplanned Work report and the Work Remaining report can be used to monitor project dark matter and take corrective actions if necessary. These reports are also very useful during iteration retrospective meetings to review the magnitude of project dark matter and discuss ways to reduce it in future iterations.

Managing Cost and Schedule

The same technique that works so well for managing scope works equally well for controlling cost and schedule, too. One approach that is gaining popularity is to fix the cost and schedule of a project at the outset and then manage the project scope to match the velocity of the project team. Remember, there are four dimensions of a project that you can control: scope, time, cost, and quality. In effect, you hold the time, cost, and quality constant but allow the scope to vary as needed to bring the project in on time and on budget. This approach makes management happy because they know up front when the project will be completed and how much it's going to cost.

But you might be thinking that this approach runs the risk of delivering an incomplete product or a product that does not meet the original specifications. The secret to making this approach work lies in prioritizing the requirements in terms of customer value and then delivering that value incrementally throughout the duration of the project. This is exactly the approach prescribed in Agile methodologies such as MSF and Scrum. The backlog of requirements to be implemented is ranked in descending order based on customer value, and then the requirements to be implemented for an iteration are selected from the top of that list.

To make this work, though, you must make sure that your customer fully understands the advantages and tradeoffs of this approach. The customer should understand that the project will deliver maximum customer value while simultaneously controlling cost and schedule. Further, the project will deliver this value incrementally, which is to say that the customer will realize value from the project early and often. The customer must also understand that building software is an evolutionary process and that the requirements specified at the outset of a project are a vision of the final product that will likely change over the course of the project. Some customers might find this reality difficult to accept. The sweetener that closes this deal is the fact that the customer is in control of that change because the customer controls the priority of the requirements and is allowed to change the priorities for each iteration. This in effect allows the customer to continuously refine and adjust the definition of value throughout the duration of the project. Now who could resist that proposition?

Reprioritizing may cause some requirements to fall out of scope. In other words, there may be features that were originally envisioned but that don't make it into the final product. The good news is that these unimplemented features offer the least value to the customer, as determined by the customer. In some cases, the customer may also have the option of adjusting the project cost or schedule to either increase the number of requirements implemented or decrease them if necessary.

Managing Software Quality

Software quality continues to be an area of particular concern. As stated in Chapter 1, "Managing Software Engineering Projects," our industry's poor track record regarding software quality cannot continue indefinitely—we simply have to get better at building good software. Couple that with the fact that software continues to increase in complexity, and you have a compelling need to build quality into the software and maintain that quality as the software evolves throughout its life cycle. Simply put, complex software of low quality will be hopelessly difficult to maintain, and the cost will be too high. Fortunately, we're seeing a great deal of emphasis put on software quality these days, with unit testing gaining popularity and test-driven development building momentum.

There are two aspects to software quality that need to be managed: *quality assurance* and *quality control*. Quality assurance and quality control are closely related but different in an important way. Quality assurance involves a systematic approach to software quality. It means building the software from the ground up to be easier to test, easier to maintain, and easier to modify as requirements change. To that end, quality assurance involves using proven design patterns and best practices when designing and building software. Quality assurance also involves validating software design and implementation through frequent peer reviews. In an ideal world, quality assurance is a proactive form of defect avoidance. But in the real world, defects happen despite your best efforts. As a result, quality assurance also involves defect repair and taking the appropriate corrective actions when quality become an issue.

Quality control, on the other hand, involves monitoring the quality of the software being produced. Unit tests are a good example of quality control. A good suite of unit tests can quickly verify that an application under development continues to work correctly even as changes are made to it. The Quality Indicators report is another good example of a quality control. It uses a variety of key quality metrics to provide important feedback on the health of the software.

Note   It is interesting to note that test-driven development (TDD) incorporates both quality assurance and quality control. With TDD, the requirements are translated into a list of unit tests that must be satisfied. This test list then becomes the specification for the software implementation. A unit test is implemented first, and then just enough of the application is implemented to satisfy the unit test—but no more. Then the next unit test is implemented, and the application is then modified to satisfy that unit test in addition to the first. This cycle continues until all the unit tests have been implemented and the application is passing all the tests. This approach incorporates quality assurance in several ways. First, requirements expressed in terms of unit tests are clear and unambiguous. Second, building the application to satisfy one unit test at a time avoids defects by ensuring complete code coverage. Third, unnecessary features are avoided by building the application to satisfy the unit tests and no more. Quality control is achieved automatically because TDD produces a unit test suite that can be run at any time to verify that the application is working correctly and meets all of the requirements.

As a project manager, you need to manage quality by making sure the appropriate quality assurance methods are being utilized and the necessary quality control mechanisms are in place. You need to ensure that quality control is monitored and that corrective actions are taken in a timely manner.

Visual Studio Team System provides several important quality control mechanisms. For starters, Visual Studio Team Edition for Software Developers provides a variety of test tools for developers, including an extensive unit test framework complete with code coverage analysis, a rule-based static code analyzer that warns of potential problems, and a performance profiler that identifies the source of performance issues. Visual Studio Team Edition for Software Testers also includes unit testing and code coverage. But in addition to a Web test framework, a distributed load test framework, and test case management, Visual Studio Team Edition also offers an innovative unit testing framework that automatically creates a test database at the start of each test run, populates the database with test data, and then runs any number of unit tests against the database.

Team Build takes the test suite one step further, making it possible to automatically build and test the application frequently, save the results for reporting and analysis, and send alerts if the build or test fails. Finally, the Quality Indicators report gives the project team unprecedented ability to monitor key aspects of software quality.

Other Things To Consider

In addition to managing the four dimensions of a project, there are other aspects of a software development project that you need to monitor and control. In this section we'll consider three of these: monitoring and controlling risk, managing a virtual team, and managing vendors.

Monitoring and Controlling Risk

A risk identifies only a potential problem that could impact schedule, cost, or the quality of your team, software, or project. When a risk becomes reality, it is said to be *triggered* and at this point becomes an issue. MSF Agile uses an issue flag on work items to track issues on a project. Risks are one of the work item types that have a field called *Issue* that you can use to flag that a risk has been triggered and some contingency action should take place. When you mark a risk or any work item type as an issue, the work item will appear when you execute the All Issues work item query from Team Explorer. Every work item in MSF Agile can be marked as an issue by any member of your team who encounters problems with any aspect of the work item. You should run the All Issues query every morning before your team meeting to ensure that the issues get discussed as a team and to plan action to resolve the issues. This is when your project workbook comes in very handy because before your team meetings every morning, all you would need to do is open your project workbook and refresh all of your work item lists to get a fresh perspective on all work, risks, issues, and requirement status on your project.

MSF for CMMI tracks issues very differently by providing an Issues work item type for your team to record any concerns that must get resolved. Like MSF Agile, MSF for CMMI provides a handy query, called Issues, that will display all issues on your project, allowing you to keep track of problems that require special attention before they get out of control or are missed.

Deriving Work from a Risk   Similar to scenarios and quality of service requirements, risks generate work, in fact, two types of work: work that mitigates the risk and attempts to prevent it from becoming an issue and work that must occur if a risk becomes reality. Just as with work derived from requirements, it is important to trace work derived from risks back to its source. Creating tasks from risks is identical to the job of creating tasks from requirements. In Team Explorer, simply right-click the task you want to decompose into mitigation or contingency tasks, point to Add Related Work Item, and then click Task.

You should try to ensure that your team adheres to establishing traceability in this manner all the time—it doesn't take much effort, just discipline to remain consistent. If you establish good traceability between your risks and work that is derived from them, the Related Work Items report becomes a valuable project management instrument, as shown in Figure 5-9.

Related Work Items

Report generated: 11/04/2004 11:25 am by martin@contoso.com

How are the work items linked?

Title	State	Type	Linked Work Items		
⊟ Inventory Tracker	Active	Feature	5 Scenarios		

Title	State	Assigned To	Priority	Type
Browse products by category	Active	Brian Cox	1	Scenario
Order for in-store pickup	Active	Brian Cox	2	Scenario
Search local inventory	Active	Brian Cox	1	Scenario
Set preferences for pickup	Active	Brian Cox	1	Scenario
Search inventory for multi	Active	Brian Cox	2	Scenario

Title	State	Type	Linked Work Items	
⊟ Inventory Updater	Active	Feature	2 Scenarios	

Title	State	Assigned To		Type
Edit distributor directory	Active	Judy Lew	2	Scenario
Shipment status notification	Active	Judy Lew	2	Scenario

Title	State	Type	Linked Work Items
⊞ Distribution Status Tool	Active	Feature	6 Scenarios
⊞ Vendor Notification	Active	Feature	7 Scenarios
⊞ Vendor Tracker	Active	Feature	7 Scenarios

Figure 5-9   Related Work Items report

Managing a Virtual Team

An ever-increasing number of software development projects involve geographically distributed project teams, also known as *virtual* teams. Although this approach offers a great deal of staffing flexibility, it also introduces significant communication challenges. Team members are not only separated physically, they may also be in different time zones, making it difficult to schedule conference calls and live meetings.

Visual Studio Team System helps you get a handle on managing a virtual team. It doesn't replace conference calls and live meetings, but it does significantly increase the bandwidth of communication between team members in different locations. In effect, the Visual Studio Team System Team Project becomes the communication hub for the team. Work items coordinate team activities; the team portal keeps everyone informed; document libraries provide a repository for various work products; and the reports give all involved visibility into many aspects of the project.

Visual Studio Team System was created with virtual teams in mind. The product team realized that Team Foundation Server had to work well through enterprise firewalls and virtual private networks. To that end, they implemented Team Foundation Server as a set of Web services designed to work efficiently over the Internet. In this way, team members across the globe can access their Visual Studio Team System Team Projects with minimal setup and good performance.

> **Note**   Team members do not need to log onto Team Foundation Server because it utilizes Integrated Windows Authentication. This means that the credentials a team member uses to log on to the Microsoft Windows workstation are transmitted automatically and securely to the Team Foundation Server Web services. In other words, the user accesses Team Foundation Server through the same Windows account that was used to log on to the workstation. This feature makes accessing Team Foundation Server convenient because the user need not supply a user name and password. However, it does require that the user log on to the Windows workstation with a Windows account that is either in the same Active Directory domain as the Team Foundation Server or in an Active Directory domain that is trusted by the domain containing the Team Foundation Server. In most cases this is not a problem. However, a virtual team might include a member from an outside organization who logs on to a Windows workstation in a non-trusted domain. Unfortunately, this team member cannot access the Visual Studio Team System Team Project from this workstation. One option for resolving this problem is to have IT set up a trust between the domain containing the Team Foundation Server and the domain that the team member logs on to. However, setting up such a trust may not be a good idea from a security standpoint. A simpler option would be to have the team member use the Remote Desktop Client through a Virtual Private Network to log on to a Windows workstation using a Windows account on the same domain as the Team Foundation Server. This allows the remote team member to access a Visual Studio Team System Team Project as if working locally, and it has the added benefit of keeping all the work products on the local domain where they can be properly secured.

Managing Vendors

If your project utilizes external vendors, you can use Visual Studio Team System to facilitate vendor management. First, you can utilize work items to manage all the vendor-related activities, from vendor selection to work assignments to vendor ratings. Next, you can utilize the document libraries in the project portal to organize vendor-related documents including the request for proposal, vendor responses, vendor selection criteria and worksheets, and contracts. After work has begun, you can use the security features in Visual Studio Team System to provide vendors controlled access to Team Projects and source control. Better yet, you can set up a separate Team Project for each vendor and then use the branch and merge capability of Team Foundation Version Control to move work in and out of the vendor Team Project. This approach provides maximum isolation while allowing the vendor unhindered use of the features in Team Foundation Server. You can also use the reporting features of Visual Studio Team System to monitor vendor performance.

Case Study: Creating an Information Radiator

Back in Chapter 3, "Project Initiation," you met a project manager named Chase who was planning a development project for a new automobile insurance application code-named "Gimli." The project is now underway, and the first iteration has just wrapped up. Chase asked another project manager, Sue, to facilitate a retrospective meeting for the iteration. Having participated in many retrospective meetings and even led a few, she eagerly accepted the invitation because she knows that these meetings are not only worthwhile but they can be fun, too. Sue schedules a two-hour meeting and invites the entire team. She starts the meeting by explaining that the purpose of the retrospective is to constructively evaluate the team's process and look for ways to improve it. She sets some ground rules to keep the discussion constructive and to make sure everyone gets a chance to participate. Next, Sue goes to the whiteboard and draws two columns, one for things that went well and one for things that didn't go so well. She then asks the team, "If you could do this iteration all over again, what changes would you make?" A lively discussion ensues, and soon both columns are filled. The group takes a few moments to consider this information, and then Sue moves into the next phase of the meeting: brainstorming improvement ideas. She goes around the room and asks for one idea from each person, writing all the ideas on the whiteboard. She continues to solicit ideas until everyone passes. Next she gives everyone five votes that they can use to vote for the ideas they like the best. Before voting begins, though, Sue invites the group to ask questions about any of the ideas listed. Chase is intrigued by an idea listed as Information Radiator, but he's not sure what it is so he asks for clarification.

Mark, the software developer, contributed the idea. He explained that he read about the concept in a book by Alister Cockburn (*Agile Software Development: The Cooperative Game*, 2nd Edition, Addison Wesley Professional, 2006). The term comes from the idea that the flow of information is analogous to the swirl and flow of convection currents in gas or heat. An Information Radiator is a source of information positioned so that the information flows freely to those who need it. Just as a heat radiator in a building is designed to keep people warm, an Information Radiator is designed to keep people informed. In the case of software projects, an Information Radiator is typically a bulletin board or display set up in a high-traffic area such as a hallway where people notice it as they pass by. The Information Radiator should be set up in such a way that a passerby can see at a glance what is going on—the information flows as a convection current.

The project team finds the idea of an Information Radiator appealing. Sue calls for a vote, and the Information Radiator tops the list. Mark is put in charge of setting it up. The first thing Mark does is consult with Chase on what information should be included in the Information Radiator. They look over the reports available in their Team Project, which was created using the MSF for Agile Development process template. They then decide to start with two reports: the Work Remaining chart and the Quality Indicators report. Mark decides to start with a low-tech approach for the next iteration, printing the two reports and posting them on the bulletin board in the hallway daily. The Information Radiator is an instant hit. Every time a project team member passes by, he or she looks at the reports to see how things are progressing. But what's even better is that people outside the project team notice the Information Radiator and stop to have a look. Some folks are just curious, but others are managers and marketing professionals who have a vested interest in the project. You can spot the latter type because they stop and study the report a bit longer than the average passerby, and they come back regularly.

At the end of the iteration, the team discusses the Information Radiator. The comments are all favorable. The feedback and visibility provided by the Information Radiator has had a positive effect on team performance and morale. The only negative comment came from Mark, who was getting tired of having to print out and post updates to the Information Radiator every day. The team discusses alternatives and decides to allocate some time in the next iteration to go high tech by replacing the bulletin board with a large video display that shows the reports. Mark will program the display to update periodically so that it automatically shows up-to-date information.

Summary

We reviewed the two process groups in the PMBOK for monitoring and controlling project execution. The first process group, Directing and Managing Project Execution, consists of performing work as specified in the project management plan. The second process group, Monitoring and Controlling Project Work, involves observing project execution and measuring project performance to identify issues in a timely manner and take corrective action as needed.

We explored the two types of variance that can occur on a project: common cause variance and special cause variance. Common cause variance is normal part of every project and requires no corrective action. Special cause variance, on the other hand, indicates something out of the ordinary that must be monitored and corrected.

We described the four dimensions of a project that must be monitored and controlled: scope, cost, schedule, and quality. These dimensions are interrelated, so changing one affects the others. We discussed an Agile approach for managing project scope that involves incremental and iterative development and a change control process that allows changes to scope only between iterations. We described a technique for consistently delivering on time and on budget by holding to a fixed cost and schedule and adjusting project scope as needed.

We described the difference between quality assurance and quality control, and we explored how to implement both by using Visual Studio Team System. Quality assurance is the use of tools and methods to avoid defects, whereas quality control involves detecting defects that require corrective action.

We discussed methods for monitoring and controlling risk by using MSF and Visual Studio Team System. Risk mitigation involves taking actions to prevent a risk from occurring, whereas risk contingencies specify the actions to be taken after a risk occurs.

We discussed techniques for using Visual Studio Team System to manage a virtual team. And on a related note, we explored ways to use Visual Studio Team System to manage vendors who are working on the project.

Finally, we explored a case study in which MSF reports were used to create an Information Radiator, which displays at a glance project-related information in a public area so people both inside and outside the team can see how the project is going at any time.

Chapter 6
Improving Your Process

- Establish the key principles of a lightweight process improvement framework.
- Create a lightweight process improvement framework.

Improving your Processes and Teams

Up until this point, this book has focused on how to manage projects with Microsoft Visual Studio Team System. Managing projects, however, also involves fine-tuning the way you develop software so that it can adapt to changing teams, technologies, tools, and processes. This chapter discusses that process of fine-tuning, which involves understanding and reflecting upon lessons learned—those best practices your team will naturally uncover as they develop software. The goal, then, is not only having great processes but also learning how to adjust those processes and practices over time so that your organization can move from proficiency in delivery to proficiency in adaptation. In this chapter, we will discuss how to turn the learning and adapting process into something much more deliberate and controlled, which will help identify the most valuable aspects of change for your organization and teams.

Harvesting Lessons Learned

At the end of your projects, you conduct a project review in which your team discusses their accomplishments as well as in what areas they could have done a better job. You work with them to complete the sentence, "If I had to do it all over again, I'd change...." This exercise has the potential to be extremely beneficial to everyone on the team; however, in most cases, these meetings gather only subjective feedback and do not address essential lessons or how these lessons can be integrated into the next project. How can you be sure that the information gathered during this meeting will increase the success of your next project? You will have a better chance if you keep the same team together, and this team works with the same technology and business problem. But what if you want to ensure that these best practices are adopted by all teams within an organization? If you are not interested in larger-scale process improvement initiatives, harvesting best practices from your projects is a good place to start initiating change. You can use a few techniques to make this process more concrete—techniques that allow you to extract more value from the review process and more easily integrate your lessons learned into project delivery. Review your projects throughout their lives rather than only at their completion. If you wait until your projects are finished before you review them, you can affect only future projects. Try to perform project reviews in the transition between project iterations or phases if you can so that you can integrate any changes to your software development practices before the start of the next iteration.

When you are conducting a review session with your team, treat the lessons you learn as project requirements so that they can be expressed, recorded, tracked, and implemented as any other project-level requirement would be. Using this method ensures that you can assign responsibility for these new best practices and gives you the opportunity to integrate resulting task assignments into your project schedule.

Of course, you and your team must evaluate the impact of each of the lessons learned you want to gradually work into your project, because they could cause your project more harm than good. Just like any change to requirements during a project, integrating lessons learned may create a ripple of changes throughout your project. Some of these changes may increase your team's efficiency, but some of them may have the exact opposite effect. For example, let's say that your team is making a large number of manual code changes because of significant code revision. Halfway through the project, you realize that using a code generation engine to generate your business object code would have been a better choice. Switching to a code generation engine halfway through a project, however, is probably not a best practice because it will introduce a great deal of rework and significant restructuring of your project's source code, and you would doubtfully see any benefit from this change in the current project. With this said, you must evaluate every change you introduce to your project, including those changes that represent best practices. Don't forget that if you change how your team works, you will need to revisit all your estimates to ensure they all still make sense.

Improving Your Software Development Process Over Time

Instead of improving your development processes one project at a time, you may want to create a process improvement initiative that exists independently of any specific project. Of course, this is not a new concept; it has been happily happening within Project Management Offices (PMOs) for decades. Again, CMMI provides an excellent roadmap for you to follow if you are a large organization looking to gradually improve your processes. However, many organizations do not want to use CMMI because it has a very steep learning curve and can be overly complex and structured.

 Note   For more information about CMMI, refer to Appendix A, "Capability Maturity Model Integration (CMMI)."

Many organizations want to improve their software development processes without the complexity and ceremony of CMMI-based Improvement processes. These organizations want to start with a structured yet common-sense approach to their development processes but might be left with a "there are lots of things I can improve upon, but I don't know where to start" feeling. This book introduces a process improvement framework that is less complex than CMMI and relies on a more *chaordic* (chaotic, yet organized) approach to process improvement. We are not discouraging the use of CMMI in any way; rather, we are proposing an alternative method to process improvement that is easier to adopt yet inspired by many aspects of CMMI.

A Lightweight Process Improvement Framework

A key to developing a great organization is to build a framework and cultivate a mindset on which all decisions are based. The same is true for a process improvement framework. The following sections present some of the critical mindsets important to the success of any process improvement process.

Focus on the Goal   Improving your software development processes is much more like a never-ending journey than it is a destination. But never-ending journeys do not seem very exciting if there aren't some specific stops, and for this reason, process improvement should identify specific goals your team can achieve along its way. This means that process improvement is less about doing work than it is about accomplishing goals. When working with your team to plan out process improvements, it is important to first identify team goals such as being able to measure the quality of software as it compares to the velocity of your team. How you choose to accomplish these goals is secondary to the goals themselves. In fact, from the perspective of the team, goals should be absolute reference points, and you should provide whatever flexibility is needed to achieve them; ultimately, these goals are crucial to process improvement, not the tasks you complete to achieve them.

Get Support from the Business   Absolutely no process improvement initiative can be successful without the full support of the entire organization. Process improvement activities may initially take team members away from their primary responsibilities, because members will need to plan and execute process improvement–related activities. Team members' work will be slowed as a result, which could have a negative effect on other areas of the business. Process improvement cannot happen overnight, nor is it accidental, and for these reasons, the entire organization must realize that effort, time, and resources will be required to produce long-lasting results. It also should not happen in a vacuum or focus on the needs of a particular group within the organization such as software developers and testers. All process improvement activities must support the needs of the business from a holistic perspective. The plans and activities generated as a result of process improvement must also reflect the constraints of the organization, which will likely include allocations of time, budget, resources, existing commitments, and schedules. The success of the process improvement exercise should not be measured by the increased efficiency of your software engineering teams but by the value those efficiencies bring to the entire organization.

Embrace Change   Such as it is with any Agile process, the lightweight improvement scenario should expect and adapt to change. When planning your process improvement roadmap, ensure that the team understands that you will need to revisit the plan after every phase of the process to allow for necessary adjustments because of changing technology, teams, or business conditions.

Strive to Achieve Success   When planning for process improvement goals, it is very easy to try to accomplish more than is possible. Always make each goal easily achievable every step of the way, especially in the beginning of the process improvement process when it might be tough to build momentum and acceptance from your team. Otherwise, you risk discouraging team members or the organization. Never risk success. If you or your team feels that a particular goal is unrealistic, rethink your objectives and your plan because failure in any respect will have a greater impact on your team than success. With every team achievement, celebrate with your entire team and ensure that each success resonates throughout the organization.

Work as a Team of Peers   Process improvement will affect your entire team and probably the entire organization in one way or another. The team you select to help guide and implement process improvement activities must realize that everyone is working for a common set of goals. They must work together as equals to bring about change. A business analyst's process improvement should not take precedence over the needs of developers and testers. In a similar way, developers have no dominion over the sales and account management teams. Everyone's opinion must be heard and count equally and objectively.

Treat Process Improvement as a Project   Process improvement activities should be managed similarly to other types of projects in your organization. Each process improvement project should have a specified set of roles and be managed by a project manager. Projects should have budgets, schedules, resources, deliverables, plans, and people assigned to them. Your organization must consider process improvement projects when considering resource management and work allocations across all employees and projects. If you ensure that a process improvement project is treated in the same way as every other project in your organization, you minimize the risk that process improvement activities will be treated as higher priorities than other projects and thus lead to ongoing organizational change.

Learn from the Experience of Others   You are not alone. Many organizations have either gone through or are going through process improvement and will be more than willing to share their experiences. There are many proven practices that are available to you regarding ways to improve your software development practices. Empower your entire team to search for reference material or advice from others. Consider hiring an outside organization that specializes in process improvement to jump start and guide your team's activities, help get everyone into the right mindset, and act as a coach as the process improvement practice grows and continues.

Agile Maturity Model

In *Agile Management for Software Engineering: Applying the Theory of Constraints for Business Results* (Prentice Hall PTR, 2003), David Anderson suggests that the Software Engineering Institute's Software Capability Maturity Model (CMM) is inadequate for Agile approaches to project management and conformance to quality as well as human factors. From this perspective, Anderson introduced a maturity model that is more aligned with all types of software development business, which he calls *The Learning Organization Maturity Model*. This new maturity model is summarized in Table 6-1.

Table 6-1   The Learning Organization Maturity Model

Stage	Capability
Stage 0	Analysis Ability
	Decompose system input into basic units of measurement.
Stage 1	End-to-End Traceability
	Implement system for capturing and monitoring measurements.
Stage 2	Stabilize System Metrics
	Demonstrate basic statistical process control, and show that system is stable against a target and within a tolerance.
Stage 3	System Thinking and a Learning Organization
	Focus on continuous improvement.
Stage 4	Anticipated ROI and the Failure Tolerant Organization
	Encourage risk taking. Focus on throughput of process, not production quantity.

As you can see, like CMMI, this model also has five levels and is compatible with any Agile method or rigorous software methodology.

Overview of the LPI Framework

The Lightweight Process Improvement (LPI) framework suggested by this book provides simple-to-use guidelines you can use to begin the ongoing discipline of perpetual process improvement. LPI's goal is to allow you to begin process improvement with minimal effort and is designed to produce value to your entire team early and often. LPI takes an iterative approach whereby iterations are further grouped into one of four phases: Initiate, Plan, Execute, and Review. These phases are very similar to the PMBOK-inspired practices already discussed throughout this book. The LPI framework promotes a continual life cycle model, meaning that after the review phase of the life cycle, the LPI project continues by entering the planning phase once again, as shown in Figure 6-1.

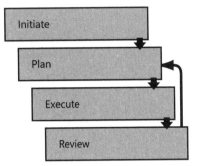

Figure 6-1 The LPI Framework life cycle

Similar to the Initiate process group specified by PMBOK, the primary goal of LPI's Initiate phase is to align the team members and business sponsors so they can produce a project charter document and hold a team kickoff event. The project manager is responsible for most of the work and deliverables produced during the Initiate phase and works with the project sponsors to establish a clear business case for process improvement, which typically evolves from the need to increase productivity, reduce waste, provide better estimates, be better positioned for innovation, and ultimately increase profit and profit-earning potential.

The Plan phase of LPI begins with an assessment that scrutinizes the strengths, weaknesses, threats, and improvement opportunities of the existing software development processes. It is in this phase that you must continually reinforce the needs of the business to help align your team. To provide input to the assessment, you must involve all the key members from all major disciplines including product managers, project managers, software architects, software developers, software testers, and business analysts. The assessment phase should quantify your current state and identify a desired state to help provide direction and focus for planning activities. After the assessment is complete, your team uses assessment results to construct a goal-focused action plan that will guide it throughout the process improvement life cycle. The resulting plan should take into account different perspectives of the improvement process such as process management, project management, engineering, and support.

During the Execution phase, the team will work together to achieve the goals outlined in the Plan phase. This phase is similar to the traditional execution and monitoring in which the team works together, and it requires the same level of project management and governance as a non-process improvement project. The Execution phase should be broken down into a series of iterations to ensure that the team has time to regularly synchronize and adjust to changing circumstances or priorities. Iterations will also help to focus the team's delivery cycle and allow for execution milestones to be created. Each process improvement goal achieved during the Execution phase needs to be clearly identified and celebrated.

The Review phase begins when the final iteration of the Execution phase ends. During this phase, you and your team will take time to reflect on the results of the Execution phase. Did your team meet all its goals? Did you encounter any major issues that could have been prevented with better planning? What were your accomplishments? What are some of the outstanding goals you would like to focus on next? Were there any lessons learned during the execution phase that will make subsequent phases more successful? The results of the Review phase will be used as inputs to the Plan phase discussed earlier.

Continual improvement represents moving from the Review phase back to the Plan phase of the LPI framework and is usually required, because rarely is a single pass through the LPI life cycle enough to cause your software development practices to mature. You must embrace process improvement as an ongoing repetitive process. Process improvement should be like the heartbeat of a software development organization, continually pumping new life and vitality into it as it grows and matures.

Roles Involved with the LPI Framework

Process improvement needs the dedication of people to be successful. Rarely can a single individual effectively guide process improvement across all aspects of the software development skills spectrum. Recognize that for the most part, most of your team members already have a great deal of understanding of and insight into how certain processes can be improved. For this reason, successful processes for process improvement involve a wide breadth of individuals from differing disciplines. Table 6-2 summarizes the roles and responsibilities on a LPI-based project.

Table 6-2   LPI Roles and Responsibilities

Role	Responsibilities
Business Sponsor	Clearly articulate business objectives of the process improvement initiative.
	Establish project constraints such as budget, time, resources, and people.
Project Management	Facilitate all aspects of an LPI-based project.
	Gather business objectives and project constraints.
	Produce the project charter.
	Manage timelines, budget, resource allocation, and commitment to work.
Team Leads	Act as representatives of their teams or divisions during all phases of the project.
	Gather information that will be used during the assessment of current processes from their team.
	Contribute to the process improvement plan.
	Lead activities specified in the process improvement plan to help the team reach their goals.

Table 6-2 LPI Roles and Responsibilities (Continued)

Role	Responsibilities
Remainder of the team: Software and IT Architects Developers Development Managers Build Engineers Testers Test Managers Quality of Service Specialists Release Managers Product Managers Business Analysts	Provide insight into the current software engineering practices and tools. Carry out assigned tasks specified by the process improvement plan. Provide continual feedback and open opinion on the LPI project.
Process Improvement Coach (Optional)	This role is typically played by an external consultant who has extensive experience with helping software development teams and organizations improve their processes. Plays the role of a facilitator and coach throughout the duration of the process improvement project.

First Who...Then What

Finding outstanding people should be the primary focus of any company. The "First Who...Then What" concept is promoted by Jim Collins in *Good To Great: Why Some Companies Make the Leap...and Others Don't* (HarperCollins Publishing Inc., 2001)

Collins argues that companies that progress from good to great recognize that their biggest constraint is their ability to attract and keep enough of the right people, beyond constraints that might be imposed by markets, technology, competition, or products. Collins goes on to say that organizations should put their best people on the biggest opportunities, not the biggest problems. It's also been well accepted that some software developers are higher producers than others—best-of-breed developers have been documented to outperform average developers by 10 to 20 times (see Sackman, Erikson, and Grant: "Exploratory Experimental Studies Comparing Online and Offline Programming Performance," *Communications of the ACM,* January 1968). So you should be extremely diligent about how you compose every team, including your process improvement team.

Initiating Process Improvement

The Initiate phase of the LPI framework is very similar to Initiating activities specified by PMBOK. In this phase, the focus is on establishing the scope and objectives of the process improvement project by trying to establish the business value that can be achieved as a result of the project. The Initiate phase also establishes the constraints of the project that must be taken into account during ongoing project planning such as budget, time, and level of team commitment. For example, the organizational sponsor for the project may specify that the first phase of process improvement should take place during the months of the year the business is least busy. It could also specify that employees involved in the process improvement project can spend no more than 25 percent of their time over a given month on process improvement activities. The project manager creates a project charter to capture the business objectives and constraints on which the project will focus, helping to establish a clear set of success criteria the project will target.

During this phase, the project team is also selected from different functional areas across the organization such as project managers, software and IT architects, developers, development managers, build engineers, testers, test managers, quality of service specialists, release managers, and business analysts. The participants of this team will be responsible for providing guidance and feedback and for participating in process improvement workshops and reviews. Some team members may also be responsible for collecting information such as current process definitions or existing process metrics that will be used during the planning phase. This phase will culminate with a kickoff to align the entire project team with the project charter produced during this phase. During this meeting, the project manager is responsible for educating the team about the structure of the project and expected commitment and responsibilities. This phase is further summarized in Table 6-3.

Table 6-3   Summary of LPI's Initiate Phase

When can you begin?	Commitment obtained from the organization to move forward with the initiative.
	Budget allocated.
	Time set aside for team members on existing projects.
How do you know when you have finished?	Project charter complete and accepted.
	Team assigned and time allocated.
	Kickoff meeting held.
Typical activities	Assign a project manager.
	Meet with project stakeholders to gather business objectives and constraints.
	Create project charter document.
	Form team.
	Schedule kickoff meeting.
Deliverables	Project charter.

Note   You may want to consider using Visual Studio Team System to help manage and track the process improvement project just as you would any other software development project.

Planning Process Improvement

Before you can begin any planning activities, you need to first assess where you are today. A simple way that you can gather this information is through a standard Strengths, Weaknesses, Opportunities, Threats (SWOT) Analysis. One of the most effective ways you can perform a

SWOT analysis with your team is through a series of facilitated workshops. In these workshops, your entire process improvement team comes together to analyze how they develop software by identifying what they do well (strengths), practices that the team does not perform well (weaknesses), areas that they can improve upon (opportunities), and aspects of their environment that may prevent them from achieving their goals of process improvement (threats). Prior to the SWOT workshop, your team should spend some time creating an inventory of the processes and tools currently used to create software. This information could include a list of tools developers and testers use to perform their job, bug-tracking tools and processes, and any existing process-related documentation or document templates.

The SWOT workshops should be very focused and assess each aspect of the development process individually. For example, you might choose to categorize how your team develops software into the following: Program Management, Architecture, Development, Testing, Release and Operations, and User Experience. To stay focused, you should conduct a SWOT analysis on each of these categories individually. Each time you identify a strength, weakness, opportunity, or threat, your team should also assign an associated level of impact and priority. Using this technique will allow you to help better quantify your results and help drive decisions and direction. For example, Table 6-4 demonstrates a number of weaknesses and their relative impact and priority.

Table 6-4   Sample Weakness List

Impact	Area	Description
High	Project Management	Customers are not involved throughout the project life cycle.
Medium	Project Management	Not all development work performed by the team can be traced back to requirements.
Medium	Project Management	Risk, not activity, managed throughout the project.
Medium	User Experience	No formal training in the design of modern user interface designs.
High	Testing	No automated build process.
High	Testing	Not enough test cases created to cover all known requirements.
High	Testing	Lack of automated testing tools.

Tip   You can use a numeric scale (for example from 1–9) to represent impact if you prefer because this will give a greater ability to fine-tune SWOT prioritization.

SWOT workshops such as these have the possibility of getting out of control. To compensate for this, ensure that your team members understand that they are there to gain perspective on the current software development model, not to engage in heated debate or establish blame. Meetings should last no longer than two hours to ensure focus and productivity, and a facilitator needs to be on hand to help maintain that focus. Also, prior to each SWOT workshop, consider allowing time for your team members to harvest their own thoughts regarding the SWOT analysis so that their time in the workshop is as fruitful as possible.

When you have identified and ranked all strengths, weaknesses, opportunities, and threats, the next step is to decide on actions for each issue. For example, if one of the weaknesses you identified during your SWOT workshop was that your team lacked automated testing tools, actions that can be taken to resolve this weakness could include conducting research on available testing tools on the market, setting a budget for the purchase of testing tools, purchasing the tools, and providing training for using the tools. Produce an action plan that will address each weakness, opportunity, and threat you identified during your SWOT analysis. You do not need to create an action plan for your strengths unless you believe you must take specific actions to ensure that you remain strong in an identified area.

The next step in the Planning phase is to bring together the results of the SWOT with the corresponding action plans into a single plan that will guide the Execute phase of the process improvement framework. Again, the best way to accomplish this is in a group setting in the form of a workshop. When establishing a plan for process improvement, you should take into account four different perspectives. The first is the perspective of *Process Management*, in which goals and tasks are directly related to continual process improvement activities and governance. The next perspective is *Project Management*, in which the goals and activities are related to the facilitation and oversight of the process improvement project. *Technology* is the third perspective, whose goals and activities relate specifically to software design, development, construction, testing, and deployment. The final perspective is *Support*, which deals with all goals and activities that support the other three perspectives. Support may include ordering hardware or software or even finding space for the process improvement team to work. Note how the sample planning grid shown in Table 6-5 breaks the plan into perspectives, iterations, and then further into goals and tasks.

Table 6-5   Simplified Process Improvement Schedule

Perspective	Iteration 1 Goals	Iteration 1 Tasks	Iteration 2 Goals	Iteration 2 Tasks
Process	Adopt code quality processes. Adopt design quality standards.	Integrate Testing and Uniting into Planning for new projects. Plan reviews for Requirements and Architecture for new projects.	Establish quality gates. Establish daily project feedback.	Develop release checklists. Trial run daily team meetings.
Management	Approve Team System budget.	Work with team to determine Team System costs.	Establish feed-back mechanisms.	Facilitate daily team meetings. Facilitate gathering of lessons-learned information.
Technology	Adopt code quality processes.	Research code standards.		Implement Team System.

Table 6-5   Simplified Process Improvement Schedule (Continued)

Perspective	Iteration 1 Goals	Iteration 1 Tasks	Iteration 2 Goals	Iteration 2 Tasks
Support	Prepare for Team System.	Get trained on Team System. Order Team System hardware/software.	Establish Project Learning Center.	Use Microsoft Windows Share-Point Services to establish repository for all project lessons learned.

The goals of the plan are kept separate to ensure that all team members know when they are complete. The goals and tasks you will use to populate the grid will come from the results of the SWOT analysis. Simply take the action plans you created for the highest priority weaknesses, opportunities, and threats, and work them into the plan with your team into iterations. The length of each iteration will depend greatly on your organizational constraints such as impact on other corporate commitments and service outages. Table 6-6 summarizes the Plan phase of the LPI framework.

Table 6-6   Summary of LPI's Plan Phase

Topic	Description
When can you begin?	Project charter accepted by business stakeholder.
	Resources and team allocated.
	Kickoff meeting held.
How do you know when you are finished?	Assessment results document completed and distributed to the team.
	Process improvement plan created and approved.
	Resources secured for plan execution.
Typical activities	Collect information on existing processes and technologies.
	Conduct one or more assessment workshops.
	Conduct one or more planning workshops.
	Review/approve the plan.
Deliverables	Assessment results document.
	Process improvement execution plan.
	Risk assessment.

Recognizing and Acting on the Brutal Facts

Sometimes the assessment and planning workshops described in this chapter bring out only a negative view of an organization's ability to develop software. For this reason, it is important that the strengths of the organization be considered first. With this in mind, however, you want your entire team to talk openly about their feelings and opinions on your existing processes, and you should be prepared to hear things you may not want to

> hear. You must acknowledge every team member's opinion equally because you do not want to establish any barrier that may prevent your team from hearing all of the cold hard facts that will help drive good decision making.

Executing and Monitoring Process Improvement

Simply put, during the Execution and Monitoring phase of the LPI framework, your project team will work toward achieving the goals and performing the activities decided on by the previous planning phase. This phase will end when you have achieved all your goals or time has run out. Just as in other projects, it is a good idea to segment the Execute phase into fixed-duration iterations. In a process improvement project, activities usually do not get performed with the same velocity as they might on regular projects because a process improvement project is typically run at the same time as normal projects. Therefore, iterations usually last at least 20 working days. The lengths of each iteration do not need to be the same, and you and your team should use common sense when deciding length.

As with regular projects, your process improvement team should meet regularly to review the progress of the project. In these meetings, the team raises any blocking issues or conditions that may require the project plan to be modified and the team to refocus. Don't be afraid to change your plan if changes will increase your chances of success.

The team should maintain the following mindsets during this phase of the project:

- Expect to make changes to your process improvement plan.
- Maintain momentum on all activities even though it is sometimes difficult because of other day-to-day responsibilities of team members.
- Try to achieve results early and often.
- Celebrate every achievement.
- Don't set yourself up for failure; keep the scope of the project under tight control, making sure not to take on more than your team can handle. If one part of the project needs to increase in scope, you should consider reducing scope in other areas.

Table 6-7 summarizes LPI's Execute phase.

Table 6-7   Summary of LPI's Execute Phase

Topic	Description
When can you begin?	Process improvement execution plan created.
	Resources secured.
How do you know when you are finished?	Goals and activities achieved or the end of the phase reached because of budget and schedule constraints.

Table 6-7   Summary of LPI's Execute Phase (Continued)

Topic	Description
Typical activities	Activities will vary from project to project and will depend on the results of the process improvement execution plan.
Deliverables	Deliverables specified by the process improvement execution plan.

Reviewing and Continuation of Process Improvement

The Review phase marks the transition between an Execute phase and the Plan phase of the LPI, when you will essentially start all over again. During the Review phase, the team and sponsors meet to take a peripheral look at the activities performed and goals achieved during the Execute phase. The team comes together to assess progress, and they plan to repeat the process.

As with all previous phases of the LPI framework, conduct a facilitated review workshop with your team to objectively reflect on the success of your project and each planned goal and activity. During the workshop, you should take a close look at the team's progress and record any learned lessons that should be incorporated into future Plan and Execute phases. The review session must be facilitated by a member of your team to stay focused on the following aspects of your project:

- Changes made to process, team models, and underlying tools and infrastructure.
- Comparison of the planned process improvement tasks and goals to actual results.
- The impact of the results towards the needs of the business.
- Team productivity improvements.
- Team morale and working condition improvements.

The project manager, in conjunction with the process improvement team, also schedules a planning workshop that will lay the framework for the next iteration of process improvement. More details on this phase are provided in Table 6-8.

Table 6-8   Summary of LPI's Review Phase

Topic	Description
When can you begin?	After the completion of the Execute phase.
How do you know when you are finished?	Planning phase meetings are scheduled and organized.
Typical activities	Review workshop.
Deliverables	Lessons learned document.

Improving Process by Reducing Uncertainty

From a project manager's perspective, one of the key objectives is to improve a team's ability to estimate effort and schedule. From a process improvement perspective, one of the only ways you can effectively accomplish this might not be obvious. Many organizations think that by recording the differences between estimated effort and actual effort on projects, they can adjust their future estimates accordingly. Unfortunately, this doesn't work for many different reasons, such as different team dynamics and ever-changing technologies. The best way to improve your team's estimating ability is to decrease the amount of unknowns on your project to increase the certainty of the estimates and by ensuring that the estimates reflect all aspects of a project. For example, most of the time developers will provide an estimate that includes only the time required to write the code for a solution. These estimates do not take into account the time required for developer testing, integration of the features into the product, the establishment of unit tests, deployment considerations, and so on. Make an estimating checklist to ensure that your team addresses each of these areas when providing an estimate.

With regard to reducing the unknown, start by emphasizing activities that increase the quality, not the velocity, of your projects. For example, asking a project team "How many bugs will you have in your next project?" would probably generate some blank stares. The answer to this question is impossible to even guess. However, asking your project team "How long will it take to write unit tests for this feature?" would likely yield a good estimate. So, if writing unit tests during the development of software reduces the unknown with respect to the time required to fix bugs, you should probably spend more time unit testing. This activity might be perceived as slowing the team down because fewer features can be developed in the same period of time, but you should do it anyway. Including activities in your project that increase the quality of requirements, designs, code, deployment packages, or even documentation increases the certainty of your estimates.

Technology change is a very important aspect of a project that tends to decrease overall certainty of estimates. For example, a developer may be quite certain how to write a particular function in Microsoft Visual Studio 2003 on version 1.1 of the Microsoft .NET framework but be uncertain of how long this same task will take using Visual Studio 2005 and version 2.0 of the .NET framework. This problem is compounded by the dramatic change of all aspects of technology. You can increase certainty, however, by ensuring that your team has easy access to abundant technical resources and is well educated about future technology in addition to current technology. For example, you could form *centers of excellence* in your organization that facilitate the sharing of experience and knowledge to decrease the amount of technical uncertainty your team experiences on a project. However, if there is a single ultimate truth that you should embrace with regard to estimation, it's that you can never get good estimates from bad requirements.

The Story of Process Improvement for Humongous Insurance

Chase and his team finally did it. They released an entirely new product line for Humongous Insurance on time and on budget. The management at Humongous Insurance is very impressed and realizes that Chase's team possessed something very special to have achieved this momentous challenge in such short a period of time. The company approached Chase to see whether he would be interested in taking on yet another challenge; spreading his best practices across the organization so that other teams could benefit from his approach.

After some deliberation and thought, Chase decides to accept this new challenge and to take a more practical approach to organizational process improvement. Chase understands that for process improvement practices to be used, all teams within the organization must embrace them, and that means that he must get them involved throughout the process improvement process instead of trying to force new practices on them without their input.

Chase's first job is to meet with Humongous Insurance management. Chase tries to determine exactly what the organization expects from process improvement such as how much money and how many resources the company is willing to invest into the project. Chase makes it clear that he will be needing time from virtually all the product groups in the organization to gather feedback and to perform certain process improvement activities. Chase wants to make it clear that project workloads and schedules will probably be affected in the short term, but the results will more than pay for the initial productivity loss. After his meeting with management, Chase captures these requirements and constraints in a Vision/Scope document for the process improvement project and asks management for explicit approval to begin the project.

Chase's first job is to select his project's primary team members. This group must best represent all of the roles and projects within the organization. He selects a number of lead developers, three developers from three different product lines, the corporate chief software architect, the lead testers of two other large projects, and two of the sales and marketing staff. Chase also contracts a well-known consultant to help facilitate and guide their assessment and planning workshops and calls a kickoff meeting with the entire team. During this meeting, Chase walks the team through the project charter document and discusses the expectations of the team as they move forward through process improvement. At this time, Chase also schedules a process improvement assessment workshop with his entire team to be facilitated by the consultant. The consultant asks the team member to prepare for the workshop by consulting with their colleagues in all the organization's development teams to compile lists of the tools, templates, and practices currently used through the company.

During the assessment workshop, the consultant leads the team through exercises designed to capture aspects of their software development processes that worked very well in addition to aspects that need improvement. The consultant also gathers opinions from the group as to what the team members think could be done to improve the weaker areas of their project and what might prevent them from successfully implementing those changes. During the assessment workshop, the energy of the team was heightened as everyone was more than happy to provide feedback into the organization that will eventually result in higher quality software, fine-tuned processes, and a more positive work environment. In order to better focus the team, the consultant decides to look at different aspects of the organization's software development practices individually, starting with program and product management areas, followed by software architecture, development, testing, operations, and finally, user experience. The assessment results are next distributed to the team for their review as the assessment will be the foundation for the process improvement planning workshop scheduled for the following week.

At the kickoff of the planning workshop, Chase begins by first thanking the team for their open and honest feedback on the organization's current software development practices. He's very happy that the initial discussions stayed positive and that the team worked to stay productive and focused. Chase explains that the planning exercises will need to be just as focused for the team to come to conclusions regarding the process improvement activities they will perform first. During the planning workshop, the consultant works with the team to further rank the results of the assessment. With the help of the entire team, the consultant begins to create a process improvement plan broken into twelve one-month iterations in which assigned work will be carried out by the team. The process improvement work that is derived from the highest priority areas of the assessment (for example, the greatest opportunities and mitigations for the highest-ranked process weaknesses) are scheduled first, making sure that everyone agrees on the results they are trying to achieve every iteration. The resulting plan is then sent to management for review and approval. Once approved, the team meets briefly one more time to begin the execution phase of the project.

During the process improvement Execution phase, many activities are undertaken by the team in different areas. For example, the entire organization will attend training on Visual Studio Team System. In addition, the product managers work more closely with the sales and marketing departments to set a better requirement management process that will be used with their existing customers to track requirements for their product line. The developers and the software architect work on processes that will have all teams conduct specific review meetings throughout the development process such as design planning meetings, design reviews, code reviews, and operational reviews. Another group will be setting methods of harvesting and communicating these new processes. This group will be responsible for updating Visual Studio Team System process templates to ensure that all new processes are reflected and accurately documented. They are also responsible for ensuring that any new document template, such as a Microsoft Office Word document template used to store the results of a design review meetings, are appropriately integrated into the Visual Studio Team System process template definitions.

During the execution phase of the project, Chase decides to track the project by using Visual Studio Team System. All work specified in the process improvement planning document is represented as work items within Visual Studio Team System. Chase also instructs the team to store all related process improvement documentation and templates in the project portal running under Windows SharePoint Services. The default reports that ship with Visual Studio Team System also provide an easy way to communicate project status with Humongous Insurance management.

As the project continues month by month, the project team realizes they may have taken on more than they can handle, and as a result, during a project review meeting at the end of the third iteration, the project team decides to refocus their activities to accommodate the December holiday season. The team also agrees to remove some goals from their current pass of process improvement because they have realized that achieving these goals will probably not result in the value they anticipated at the beginning of the project. The modification of the plan by the project team ensures that they will continue to meet every goal they have set out to meet at the end of every iteration and, thus, continue to breed results that resonate throughout the organization. Some of the other process improvements include establishing continuous build policies, manual testing practices, increased developer/tester interaction practices, and the creation of deployment and operational checklists and more refined software update and deployment processes.

At the end of the first execution phase of process improvement at Humongous Insurance, the results of process improvement have begun to become apparent through all aspects of the organization. For the first time, Humongous Insurance now has the ability to understand their software development processes starting from requirements received from customers and spanning the entire development life cycle reaching into operations and support. One of the key focuses of the initial phase of process improvement was the adoption of a quality-first mindset from every aspect of the business. As a result, the company now has the ability to measure efficiencies and quality in many areas of their business that traditionally seemed immeasurable. They have seen decreases in defect rates, higher-quality budgeting and estimating, and most importantly, greater customer satisfaction. What is even more apparent is the overall attitude of the organization's staff. Before the process improvement project began, the staff seemed very disconnected, if not apathetic to many aspects of quality and delivery throughout the organization. The staff members, starting with those directly involved with the process improvement project, now seem energized and enthusiastic and ultimately proud of their accomplishments after being empowered to embrace the responsibility of improving their roles within the organization. Chase was determined to maintain a steady rate of success throughout the process, and even those who doubted the impact of the project are now convinced of the value of practical and focused process improvement activities. It is this mindset shift that will form an even more important foundation for the next cycle of process improvement.

At project completion, twelve months after they began, Chase calls a project review meeting with the entire project team in addition to Humongous Insurance management. During this meeting, the team reflects on the previous twelve months and attempts to determine how they could improve the overall process for the future. Chase also asks the management team to discuss the impact of process improvement across the organization and compare the results with what they expected. Chase and management work together to set the focus of the next cycle of process improvement and once again provide confirmation of the constraints that will need to be adhered to during the next cycle. At the end of the review meeting, Chase schedules the next series of assessment and planning workshops that will guide the next cycle of process improvement.

Summary

In this chapter, we took a look at how you might want to improve your software development practices over time using a lightweight process improvement framework. This framework employs a practical team collective-based approach to improving organizational practices around software development using an iterative yet continual model of assessment, planning, execution, and review.

Tailoring Visual Studio Team System

- Review the list of available customizations in Microsoft Visual Studio Team System.

- Customize existing Team Projects.

- Use the Process Template Editor.

Overview of Visual Studio Team System Customization

Visual Studio Team System provides you with abundant features, and one of its most important capabilities is adapting to the changing needs of an organization or project. But wait a second—we've spent the entire book discussing how Visual Studio Team System can be used to enhance your team's ability to deliver software. Why would you need to customize Visual Studio Team System when it is capable of doing so much right out of the box?

In the world of technology and the software that drives it, the only constant is change, and every process we use and every tool that helps us do our job must embrace this fact. Change is inevitable and must be addressed to incorporate varying types of projects, ever-changing team dynamics, the integration of lessons learned, and unique market conditions that force us to continually innovate technologically on an ever-decreasing budget. The tools that we use to manage our teams must be as adaptable as the software industry they support if we expect them to provide us with any ongoing value. Throughout this book, we have established how Visual Studio Team System can be used to provide support for the software development life cycle; in this chapter, we will take a look at how you can extend this value by customizing various aspects of Visual Studio Team System to reflect your specific needs.

I'm sure you're wondering why customization of Visual Studio Team System is covered in a book about managing projects. Simply stated, it is extremely important that project managers understand how to extract the most value out of the Visual Studio Team System for their teams.

What Can You Customize?

Virtually every aspect of Visual Studio Team System can be customized to some degree, and we've already explored many ways you can do this, such as creating new work item queries and customizing areas and iterations. This chapter expands upon the most common customization scenarios, which were briefly introduced in the previous chapters. The following sections provide you with an overview of what you can customize in Visual Studio Team System . The details of how you can perform these customizations can be found later in this chapter. Figure 7-1 depicts the most common customizations of Visual Studio Team System from a project manager's perspective.

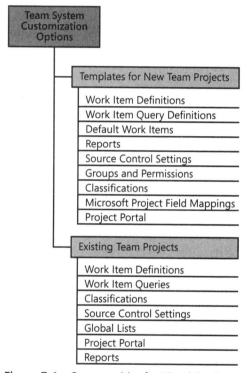

Figure 7-1   Opportunities for Visual Studio Team System customization

Work Item Customization

Work item customization is perhaps the most common type of customization you can make to Visual Studio Team System. As defined in earlier chapters, work items are specified by an XML file called a work item type definition. This open and declarative way of specifying work items provides you with the opportunity to customize virtually every aspect of a work item and provides the ability to create your own work item types and add them to Visual Studio Team System. In fact, one of the most common work item customization tasks many project managers make is to add new fields to a work item type definition to capture additional information that may be relevant to your project or organization. For example, suppose you are using Visual Studio Team System to manage bugs for your company's line of products, and you would like to track which customer discovered each recorded defect. In this case, you could add a *Customer* field to the Bug work item that would allow your team to capture this information. You could even display a list of all of your customers in a drop-down list to make it easier for your team to enter the appropriate value.

Another common work item customization is the modification of existing work item fields. There are many reasons why you might want to change various aspects of a work item field, such as its description, default values, drop-down list values, prohibited values, or even help information that describes the field and how to use it. You might also want to provide some additional rules that govern how each field is used, such as making a field required or read-only for certain groups of users. You will learn more about the details of work item field customization later in this chapter.

Another common work item customization is the modification to the workflow definition that each work item type describes. Each default work item type released with Visual Studio Team System as part of the default set of process templates specifies a certain set of workflow states and a set of paths that specify valid transitions between those states. For example, the Bug work item from the MSF CMMI process template has four states: New, Active, Resolved, and Closed. In your organization, you might want to have a fifth state called Validate, which could be used by the testing department to track which bugs must be manually verified prior to marking the bug as resolved, which is equivalent to transitioning the bug to the Resolved state. The work item type definition file will allow you to create new states and transitions that will help to accommodate this need.

The XML that specifies a work item also provides information regarding the layout of the fields when the work item is displayed from within Visual Studio. For example, the work item definition will specify the order of each of the fields displayed, the location of each field, the available field tabs, and field labels. Modifying the layout information contained within the work item definition XML files will allow you to control exactly how each field is placed on the screen, modify the structure and content of existing tab pages, and even create your own tabs to better organize your custom fields.

You can even create your own work item types and add them to existing Team Projects or to project templates to be used for future projects. Work items are simply structures that allow you to track the assignment and state of work. Microsoft conveniently includes a few definitions as part of the process templates installed by default in Visual Studio Team System; however, you can use the same very powerful feature to create different types of work items. For example, you might want to create a Persona work item type that will allow you to capture information about the users of your system. A Glossary work item type is another that is very commonly added to projects. Generally, if you need to track a list of items, you can typically represent each item as a work item in Visual Studio Team System. Figure 7-2 shows a work item that was created using a custom work item type called Glossary.

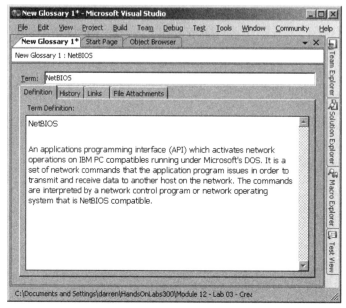

Figure 7-2   Custom work item type

Work Item Query Customization

Every method of accessing work item details requires a work item query, and so it is important that the entire team understands how to customize existing work item queries in addition
to creating and sharing new ones. In fact, during the course of most projects, you will want to
add new work item queries for your team that will make it easier to find and work with the
growing database of work items. Work item queries provide the criteria for the work item
search operation and establish the conditions that must be met for a work item to be returned
as a query result. For example, the Mitigation Action Status query returns a list of work items
that represent all mitigation actions in the Team Project. The criteria specified in the Mitigation Action Status query are listed in Table 7-1.

Using the Mitigating Action Status work item query as an example, you might want to create
a new work item query called Mitigating Action Assigned to Me, which would be modified to
add an additional query criterion, as shown in Table 7-2.

Table 7-1   Mitigation Action Status Query Definition

And/Or	Field	Operator	Value
	Team Project	=	@project
And	*Work Item Type*	=	Task
And	*Task Type*	=	Mitigating Action

Table 7-2   Mitigation Action Status Query Definition

And/Or	Field	Operator	Value
	Team Project	=	@project
And	Work Item Type	=	Task
And	Task Type	=	Mitigating Action
And	Assigned To	=	@Me

> **Note**   Notice the use of @Project and @Me in the work item query definition. These are examples of special parameters that are derived at the time the query is run. This will be discussed in more detail later in this chapter.

Work item query definition is typically an evolutionary process starting with the default work item queries provided to you out of the box by Visual Studio Team System and evolving based on the needs of your project team. Every time you need to view a different subset of work items, you need to either modify an existing work item query or create a new work item query with specific constraints that specify the details of the work items you would like to see. When you create new work items queries, you will have the ability to save the work items queries for the entire team to access or in a private area called My Queries, which is accessible only to you. If you have the appropriate permissions, you can also make copies of existing work item queries and change the names of existing queries.

Default Work Items

You might have noticed that whenever you create a new Team Project, you get a number of work items automatically created for you. These default work items are included within the process template you used to create your new project, and because of this, you will be able to modify the default work items list by changing the underlying process template definition. Changing default work items is essential when you want to integrate your own processes and methodologies into Visual Studio Team System. Default work items represent work that should always be performed when you are working on a project of a particular type. You might want to completely replace the MSF process templates' default work items with your own, perhaps to handle certain required organizational documentation, which might be unique to a particular project.

Classification Customization

Classifications are very important to work items and ultimately work item reporting because they provide ways in which you can categorize work item instances by specifying either a functional area or iteration that reflects blocks of time on your project. Classifications are easily modified from Team Explorer; however, you can also modify the default set of areas and iterations your projects will have after you create them. Once again, process templates specify the default set of areas and iterations that will be created for your project. Suppose that you wanted every project to be standardized on a pre-established set of areas such as User Experience, Business Facade, Software Interface, and Application Services (as depicted in Figure 7-3). All you would need to do is modify the default classification settings within a process template, and every new project that is based on the modified process template will have these same initial classifications.

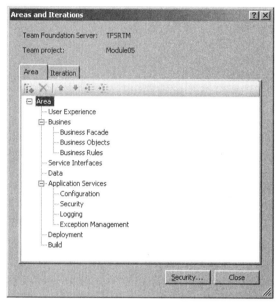

Figure 7-3   Example of area classification customization

Report Customization

The reports that Visual Studio Team System provides are really cool, and just like virtually every other aspect of Visual Studio Team System, they are completely customizable. Some, however, are sufficiently complex that they might require a senior developer to make certain changes to them. Nonetheless, it is actually quite simple to make certain changes, such as adding company logos or additional header and footer information, to these reports. Report definitions are referenced from within process templates but are actually constructed with Visual Studio's Report Designer for Microsoft SQL Server 2005. There are really two ways that you can modify reports: within a process template or after the report is deployed as part of your project. If you modify report definitions after you create your Team Project, note that the modifications will not be reflected in any new projects you create. For report customizations that you want to be reflected in all new projects, perform the customizations on the report definitions stored within the process template definition. Because Visual Studio Team System uses SQL Server 2005 Reporting Services to manage reports, you can also use the same tools Microsoft uses to create your own reports from the rich data stored within the Visual Studio Team System data warehouse.

> **Important**   To build even simple reports based on the data contained within the Visual Studio Team System data warehouse, you will need a deep understanding of the data and structure of the data warehouse. This book does not cover use of Visual Studio to author complex reports or details on the complex underlying structures of the Team Foundation Server data warehouse.

Source Code Control Customization

There are many customizations you can make to the Source Control features of Visual Studio Team System. Such modifications include making check-in notes to help capture additional metadata information regarding a check-in operation and source control policy settings, with which you can choose to have Visual Studio Team System check that certain conditions are met prior to the check-in operation, such as requiring the association of a check-in operation to a work item. Suppose, however, that you wanted to make sure that all code that enters the source repository has a copyright statement at the top of every file containing source code in your project. You can achieve this by creating new source control policies that implement rules specific to your environment and your needs. The creation of new source code policies is a job for a senior developer who is familiar with the Visual Studio Team System application programming interface (API) and is not covered in much detail in this book.

Default Security Customization

By default, all Visual Studio Team System projects specify a certain set of security groups and settings. These settings might not be appropriate for your project or your organization. You can choose to change the default project security settings after you create your Team Project, or you can modify the process template that specifies them in the first place. Modifying the default security configurations for new projects might be required if you want to have different roles (such as project managers, developers, testers, and project administrators) having different sets of permissions for every new project. In that case, you can create new roles (also known as *groups*) with specific security rights within a process template, and every new project will have these enforced automatically. Modifying security settings, however, is likely not related to the role of a project manager and is not covered extensively in this chapter.

Project Portal Customization

Visual Studio Team System uses Microsoft Windows SharePoint Services (WSS) as the project portal, and thus, you will be free to customize each portal according to the functionality of WSS. Visual Studio Team System adds functionality to the portal that you normally would not see in a typical WSS site such as links to Visual Studio Team System reports, a reporting Web part that displays the Remaining Work report on the main page of the WSS site, and links to process guidance, which can provide your team reference information regarding the methodology you chose to use for your project. WSS sites can do so much more than what you see, so much in fact that entire books have been written on the subject. For this reason, we won't go into a great amount of detail on how to extend WSS sites. Instead, let's summarize the realm of possible customizations you could make to project portal sites and leave the how for a book that specializes in WSS customizations.

Create custom lists   Windows SharePoint Services provides the ability to create SharePoint lists, which act much as work items in Visual Studio Team System. You may want to create lists of information in categories that do not make good sense to store in Visual Studio Team System, such as budget items or contact information.

Rearrange Web parts   SharePoint appears through Web parts. You don't need any programming skills to be able to extensively customize the content and location of these Web parts.

Alter themes   Users can change the theme and skin of a site to better represent the culture of the team or project.

Collaborate using Announcement, Links, and Events   Users can use Visual Studio Team System to collaborate with team members outside of Visual Studio Team System.

Tools for Customization

A great deal of the customization just mentioned can be performed right within Team Explorer. Other customizations are a bit more complex and will require some technical skills to accomplish. The following is a list of the additional tools you will need to perform the customizations discussed in this chapter:

XML Editor of Choice   The process templates used during the creation of new Team Projects provide a number of customization opportunities. Process templates are specified in XML, and you will need to have an XML editor, such as XML Marker or Notepad 2, to make these customizations. XML-editing features and is a good choice if XML requires direct modification.

Visual Studio 2005   For more extensive customizations, code will need to be written to take advantage of the extensive programmatic interfaces in Visual Studio Team System. (This book does not cover any details of this process.)

Process Template Editor   The Process Template Editor was originally created by Imaginet Resources Corporation and was intended to make the job of editing process templates less tedious. The Process Template Editor provides an intuitive graphical interface that makes it possible to edit virtually every aspect of a process template. The tool also provides a great deal of template validation to help ensure that you don't make any mistakes or configure a template in a way that would be inconsistent or in error. In addition, you can use the Process Template Editor to edit live information on your computer running Team Foundation Server, such as graphically editing a work item type in an existing project or adding values to a special server-side list called a *Global List*. The Process Template Editor is covered in more detail later in this chapter.

The remainder of this chapter provides a detailed discussion of customizations that can be performed by a non-developer. This means that many of the customizations mentioned in this chapter are not be covered. Please note that the following is a list of customizations that may require the aid of a software developer, and for that reason, are omitted from this chapter.

■ Custom source control policies

■ Complex editing of process templates

■ Non-trivial report customization

Important   Extensive programmatic customization and extension of Visual Studio Team System can be extremely complex and requires writing code. This book will not address deep extensibility of Visual Studio Team System, but it will highlight opportunities for such extensibility. To get more information about the programmatic interfaces provided by Visual Studio Team System, download the Visual Studio 2005 software development kit (SDK) from *https://affiliate.vsipmembers.com/*.

Before we continue, it is important to point out that there are two general ways to customize Visual Studio Team System. The first is on existing Team Projects. These customizations are important because they will allow your project team to gradually adapt the features of Visual Studio Team System to meet the changing needs of the project. The second grouping is on project templates. These customizations will not affect any existing project and will focus on new projects based on the modified templates.

Customizing Existing Projects

In this section, you will learn how you can customize an existing Team Project to reflect ongoing changes to your process and the needs of your team.

Work Item Queries

To recap, work item queries are the mechanism by which we can find and manipulate work items. The process templates that ship with Visual Studio Team System specify a set of work item queries; however, it is very common for organizations to create their own queries based on specific needs of their team or even rename the work item queries to be more congruous with organizational naming guidelines for work item queries. This section provides step-by-step guidance on how to perform the most common work item query customizations.

Note   Team Explorer allows for two general categories of work item queries: Team Queries and My Queries. Work item queries available from the Team Queries list in Team Explorer are available to anyone on your project who has the View Project-Level Information permission, which is granted to all project users by default. All project users can have their own work item queries in their own My Queries list. Regardless, renaming work item queries follows the same process in either case. When editing or renaming work item queries that reside in the Team Queries list, you must have the Edit Project-Level Information permission.

Creating a New Work Item Query

1. In Visual Studio Team Explorer, select your project and navigate to the Team Queries folder.

2. On the Team menu in Visual Studio, choose Add Query. Alternatively, you can right-click the Team Queries folder in Team Explorer and select Add Query. The New Query window will appear, allowing you to enter filter criteria for your query.

3. Add filter criteria for your query by populating the And/Or, Field, Operator, and Value columns. You can have many lines in your query with each representing a condition that work items must match for them to get returned in the query results. Use the Field column to specify the work item field you want to evaluate. For example, you might choose the Work Item Type field if you want to create a filter for certain work item types in your project. Use the Value column to specify the value of the field you are evaluating. Use the Operator column to specify the way in which you are evaluating the field value. The *And* and *Or* operators are used to specify how multiple filter expressions will be combined to create one complete work item query expression.

4. Run the query by pressing F5 or by selecting Run Query from the Team menu in Visual Studio to ensure that the results of the query match what you had anticipated.

5. Save the query by choosing Save New Query on the File menu or by pressing Ctrl+S. The save operation opens the Save Query As dialog box (shown in Figure 7-4), which you can use to name the query and save it in one of the following three forms/locations:

   ❑ As a Team Query so it appears in the Team Queries section of Team Explorer and is available to the all users with permissions to access your Team Project.

   ❑ As a My Query, which will save the query definition in the My Queries section of a product you can specify. This query will be available only to you.

   ❑ As a file with a name and directory that you specify.

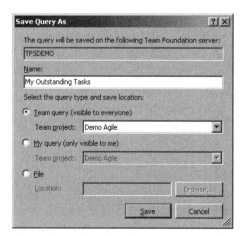

Figure 7-4   The Work Item Query Save Query As dialog box

> **Tip** Saving work item queries as files gives you some additional opportunities for collaboration. For example, as a project manager, you might want to send an e-mail message to instruct your team to review all of the tasks assigned to them and set the state of completed tasks as Closed. You could attach a work item query, called My Outstanding Tasks, that you had already saved to your computer, to provide a convenient way for developers to launch the query to find tasks assigned to them.

Use of Columns in the New Query Dialog Box

The query depicted in the Figure 7-5 searches for all work items in the current project assigned to you that are either a requirement or a change request work item type in a proposed work item state.

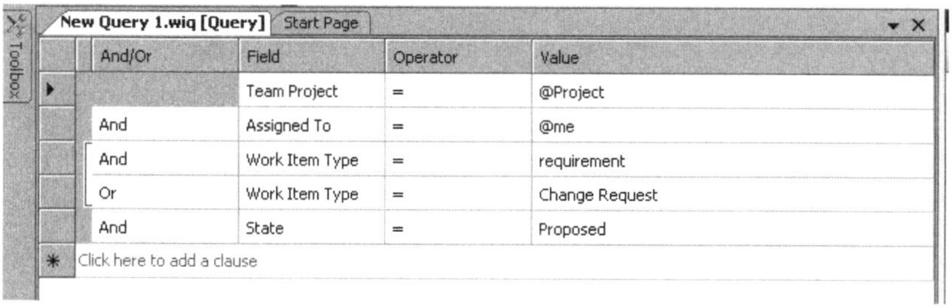

And/Or	Field	Operator	Value
	Team Project	=	@Project
And	Assigned To	=	@me
And	Work Item Type	=	requirement
Or	Work Item Type	=	Change Request
And	State	=	Proposed
	Click here to add a clause		

Figure 7-5   Grouping clauses in a work item query

Notice the bracket that connects the work item type clauses. This is a grouping clause and is used to group together more than one condition. In this case, the clause grouping is used to query for either requirements *or* change requests. Without this grouping, the query would return all proposed requirements or change requests assigned to me.

Figure 7-6 represents a slightly more complex query that you could construct to demonstrate the wide range of possibilities with respect to the work items you can create for yourself or your project team.

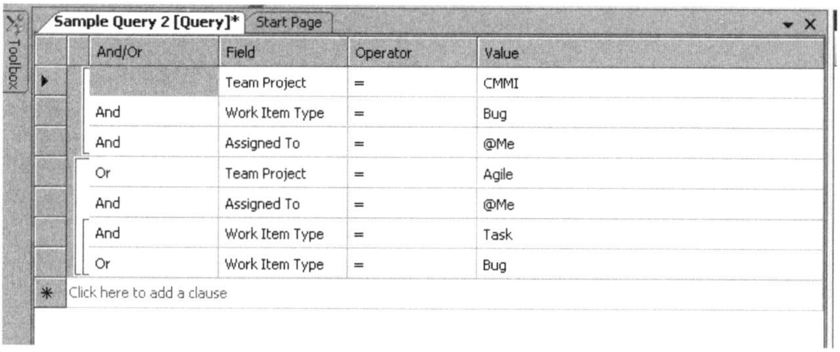

And/Or	Field	Operator	Value
	Team Project	=	CMMI
And	Work Item Type	=	Bug
And	Assigned To	=	@Me
Or	Team Project	=	Agile
And	Assigned To	=	@Me
And	Work Item Type	=	Task
Or	Work Item Type	=	Bug
	Click here to add a clause		

Figure 7-6   Example of a custom work item query

In the work item query shown in Figure 7-6, there are multiple sets of grouped clauses and an example of using a nested clause group.

When creating work item queries, you will need to be familiar with the usage of different operators. Refer to Table 7-3 for a description of the operators you can choose from when building your queries.

Table 7-3 Work Item Query Operator Summary

Operator	Description
=	Equals returns values in your work item query expression when there is an exact match to the values you specify.
<>	Does not equal returns values in your work item query when there is no match to the values you specify.
Under	This operator applies to the classification fields *Areas* and *Iterations*. You would use the Under operator to look for a value anywhere under a certain branch in the classification tree.
Not Under	The *Not Under* operator works exactly opposite of the *Under* operator; use it when you are looking for values that do not appear in any branch under a specified branch of the classification tree.
In	The *In* operator evaluates a value to determine whether it matches one of a set of values. For example, you can use *In* to determine if the Test Name value is Test 1, Test 2 or Test 3.
Contains	The *Contains* operator can be used to search for a substring anywhere in the field value. For example, you can create a query expression that states that the *Title* field must contain the text *test*, which will instruct Visual Studio Team System to return work items with titles such as "test1: Enter Description" or "Enter the test details into Visual Studio Team System."
Does Not Contain	This operator works in the exact opposite manner as the *Contains* operator, returning rows that explicitly do not contain specified text.
Was Ever	Used to determine if a field ever had a certain value at any time after its creation.

Similarly, you can use a few special comparison values when creating conditions to certain fields: @Project, @Me, and @Today. These comparison values are replaced with the actual values during the execution of the query. For example, @Project will be replaced with the name of the current project. Similarly, @Me will be replaced with the name of the person who is executing the query, and @Today will be replaced with the date that the query is run.

Of course, you can create many new simple queries that are not included in the process templates that ship with Visual Studio Team System. Here are some examples of queries you may want to construct:

- All Requirements
- All Functional Requirements
- Approved Functional Requirements

- My Outstanding Tasks from All Projects
- Tasks that have ever been assigned to me
- All Resolved Bugs in Iteration 1
- Bugs I have Resolved

Changing the Columns of Your Work Item Query

You will likely want to adjust the columns that appear as a result of a work item query. To add, remove, or reorder columns in work item queries, perform the following steps:

1. In Team Explorer, right-click a work item query you want to modify and choose View Query to open the Work Item Query Editor (if you already have the Work Item Query Editor open, you can skip this step).

2. Choose Column Options from the Team menu in Visual Studio to show the Column Options dialog box as shown in Figure 7-7.

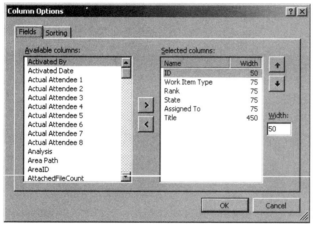

Figure 7-7   Changing the column options for a work item query definition

3. Select the displayed fields by clicking the appropriate arrow buttons in the middle of the Fields tab in the Column Options dialog box. To add a field to the selected columns list, choose the column from the Available columns list and click >. To remove a column from the Selected columns list, select the field from the Selected column list and click <. To change the order of the fields in the Selected field list, use the up and down buttons on the right side of the tab. You can also adjust the width of each displayed column by selecting the column and specifying the width, in pixels, in the width box on the right of the Selected columns list.

4. Adjust how the work item query will sort the list of work items it returns by clicking the Sorting tab in the Column Options dialog box. To specify a sort order of a column, add and remove columns to the selected columns list in a same way as adding field columns

in the previous step. To specify the sort order of a column, select the column from the selected column list and choose the direction of the sort (ascending or descending) by using the buttons to the right of the selected columns list.

5. Click OK to save the column options for your work item query.

Making a Copy of a Work Item Query

Sometimes it is better to make a copy of an existing work item query before making changes to its definition. A good example of this is taking a work item query that is a Team Query and copying it to your personal My Queries, where you are able to make changes to the work item type definition without affecting anyone else on your team. When you are finished, you can also copy the work item query you just modified back to Team Queries, either overwriting an existing work item query or adding it to the existing list.

To copy a work item query, perform the following steps:

1. Find the work item query you want to copy from either of the query lists Team Queries or My Queries.

2. Right-click the work item query and select Copy from the shortcut menu.

3. Select the destination of the work item query, either Team Queries or My Queries.

4. Right-click the destination list and choose Paste from the shortcut menu.

> **Tip** Moving work items queries between the Team Queries and My Queries lists is very similar to copying. Simply perform the preceding steps but choose Cut instead of Copy from the shortcut menu.

Renaming a Work Item Query

Renaming work item queries is very common and straightforward. It is common for organizations to completely change the names of all work item queries on a project to make it easier to navigate through large numbers of work item queries in Team Explorer. For example, instead of having work item queries called All Bugs and Active Bugs, project managers will rename the work item queries Bugs–All and Bugs–Active. This makes a lot of sense if there are a number of variations of Bug queries, because the queries are sorted alphabetically in Team Explorer to make it easier to find the set of work item queries that deal with bugs.

To rename a work item query, perform the following:

1. In Team Explorer, right-click the work item query you want to rename from either the Team Queries list or the My Queries list and select Rename.

2. Type the new name and press Enter.

Source Code Control

From a project manager's perspective, there are really only a few customizations you will need to make to the source control features of Visual Studio Team System: adding check-in notes, adding check-in policies, and changing permissions to source control folders. Again, in larger organizations, these tasks should likely be left up to the technology lead for the project, especially setting up permissions. However, on smaller and more agile teams, the project management role could be shared with the technology lead or software architect. This section will explore how to perform the most common customizations to source control to your existing Team Projects.

Modifying Check-In Notes

Check-in notes allow the developers to capture additional information about a check-in operation. Process templates provide three default check-in notes: Code Reviewer, Security Reviewer, and Performance Reviewer. Check-in notes can be made mandatory, preventing the check-in operation if ignored by the developer. You can easily modify the default list of check-in notes either by adding new check-in notes or by modifying existing ones. Again, you will need Edit Project-Level Information permission to perform this action.

To modify check-in notes, perform the following steps:

1. In Team Explorer, click the project whose check-in policies you want to modify. On the Team menu, point to Team Project Settings, and then click Source Control. The Source Control Settings dialog box appears.

2. Click the Check-in Notes tab to show the options for managing check-in notes.

3. To make an existing check-in note required, select the check box to the right of the corresponding check-in note.

4. To create a new check-in note, click Add to show the Add Check-in Note dialog box. Type a name for the new check-in note and indicate whether the new note is required or not. Click Add to add the new check-in note to the list of check-in notes for the project.

> **Warning**   Many organizations embrace check-in notes, going so far as making a number of them mandatory. This might initially seem like a good idea because it could help lead to greater conformity, but it won't make your developers very happy. As a general rule, you should try not to put many obstacles in front of your developers when they check in source code because this may discourage them from doing this when they need to. Mandatory check-in notes cannot be ignored, and if the developer is overloaded with notes that must be filled in, there is a greater chance that the value of the content of the notes will diminish or contain irrelevant information such as random key strokes.

Modifying Check-In Policies

A *check-in policy* is a rule that must be met before source code can be checked into Team Foundation Server. By far, the most common check-in policy is the Work Item check-in policy, which promotes the association of the check-in operation with one or more work items in a project. By default, Visual Studio Team System provides that plus two additional check-in policies: Testing Policy and Code Analysis. Testing Policy ensures that tests from specific test lists are successfully executed before checking in. Code Analysis requires that code analysis be performed on the project prior to check-in. You can easily change which default source control policies are enforced for your team by following these steps:

1. In Team Explorer, select the Team Project whose check-in policies you want to change.

2. On the Team menu, select Team Project Settings | Source Control to show the Source Control Settings dialog box.

3. Click the Check-in Policies tab, on which you can add, edit, remove, enable, and disable installed check-in policies.

4. To add a check-in policy, click Add and select from the list of available check-in policies. Some policies, such as the Code Analysis policy, require configuration—you will be prompted to specify the specific code analysis rules that will be executed.

> **Note**   It is possible to create a new check-in policy; but the procedure is quite technical and, therefore, beyond the scope of this book. It will suffice to tell you that user-created check-in policies appear in the list of check-in policies just as the three that are provided with the product.

Customizing Process Templates

Process templates specify virtually every aspect of a Visual Studio Team System project, from the type of work items and work item queries that your team will use to the templates of the documents your team will consume from the Team Portal. Process templates are used during the creation of new Team projects and are stored on the server for anyone with the appropriate permissions to use. The most important aspect of process templates is the fact that you can customize them to fit the unique needs of your organization or your projects.

Process templates are actually a collection of files in various formats such as XML, Microsoft Office document templates, Microsoft SQL Server report definitions, and work item query definition files. By default, Visual Studio Team System installs two process definitions for you on the server: MSF for Agile Software Development and MSF for CMMI Process Improvement. If you wanted to make changes to either of these process templates or to create your own from the base definitions of these templates, you will first need to download them to your computer.

> **Tip**   Due to the high complexity of a process template definition, you should not attempt to create a process template from scratch, but rather you should customize an existing process template and rename it to fit your needs.

The first step in editing process templates is to download a process template to a local working directory where you can make changes. To download a process template to your computer, follow these steps:

1. In Visual Studio 2005, on the Team menu, point to Team Foundation Server Settings and then click Process Template Manager to show the Process Template Manager window.

2. Select the process template you want to download from the list of available process templates stored on the computer running Team Foundation Server and click Download.

3. In the resulting dialog box, choose the location on your computer where you want to save the process template, such as your desktop, and then click Save.

The process template will be saved to your computer, and Visual Studio will notify you when the process has completed. The directory structure where the template is saved that should resemble Figure 7-8.

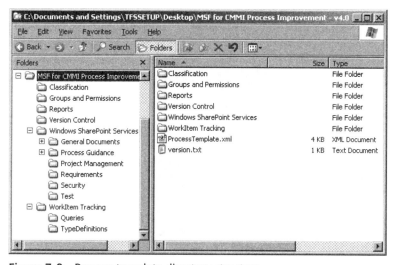

Figure 7-8   Process template directory structure

Important   You require the appropriate permissions on your Team Foundation Server to download and upload process templates. If you cannot obtain these permissions, your Visual Studio Team System administrator will need to perform these operations for you.

Every process template begins with one file, ProcessTemplate.xml. This file is essentially the index to all other aspects of a process template. Microsoft created process templates allowing for future components to be added to Team Foundation Server. It's the job of the Process-Template.xml file to point to other XML files that specify different configurations for different components of a Team Project. For example, ProcessTemplate.xml references a file called WorkItems.xml in the WorkItem Tracking directory. WorkItems.xml makes further reference to the work item definition files, stored in the Work Item Tracking\TypeDefinitions directory and work item query definitions stored in the Work Item Tracking\Queries directory. WorkItems.xml also provides a list of default work items that will be created when a new Team Project is created. Figure 7-9 depicts how the ProcessTemplate.xml references other XML files in the different directories within the process template directory structure, and Figure 7-10 depicts all the areas within the process template structure that you can modify.

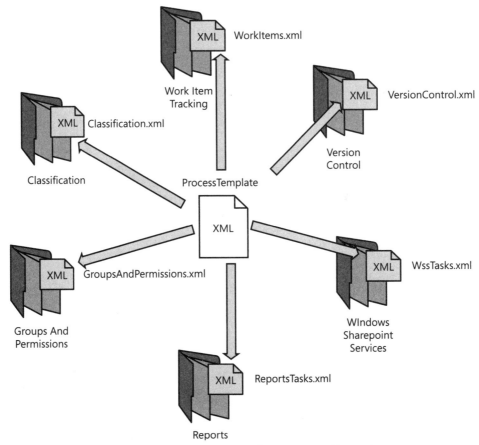

Figure 7-9 ProcessTemplate.xml points to XML files in plugin directories.

 Best Practices Process Templates should be treated as source code, and it is, therefore, a good idea to place process template definitions within the Visual Studio Team System source control system.

Since this book is not meant for developers, I won't go into greater details of the structure of the XML that makes up process templates. You might be left wondering how you will be responsible for editing the XML in a process template if you are not given more details. There is a simple answer to this problem: a tool called the Process Template Editor that you can use to edit your process templates.

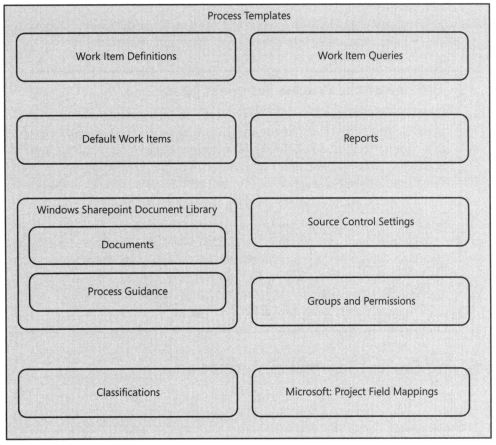

Figure 7-10   ProcessTemplate.xml points to other XML files for each Visual Studio Team System plugin.

The Process Template Editor

As you could probably imagine, the XML documents that constitute the process templates can get messy and complicated. The Process Template Editor eases the burden of process template modification by providing you with a graphical interface. The tool performs multiple forms of validation on the process template to help prevent making errors or inconsistencies within the process template.

Warning   Even though the Process Template Editor was created to make editing process templates much easier, you should still have some understanding of XML.

You can obtain the Process Template Editor as part of the Team Foundation Power Toys download available from the Microsoft Download Center (*http://www.microsoft.com/downloads*).

The Process Template Editor provides features that will make process template editing much quicker and easier. The following sections detail how to use the tool to customize process templates and work items for the benefit of your teams and organization.

Life before the Process Template Editor

Life before the Process Template Editor was not good for project managers. The only way to edit a process template was through the use of a text editor, because changes needed to be made directly to the XML files. Intimate knowledge of the structure and rules of the underlying XML was required, and mistakes were frequent. Also, there was no way to validate any of your changes until you imported the process template back into Team Foundation Server, making testing difficult and time consuming.

In addition, you needed a couple of important command-line tools if you wanted to manage work item type definitions and Global lists. WITImport and WITExport (WIT stands for Work Item Type) are tools that were used to import and export, respectively, work item types from a Team Project into and from XML files that needed to be edited by hand. Similarly, GLImport and GLExport are similar command-line tools that were used to import and export Global list definitions.

Modifying Process Template Information

You can launch the Process Template Editor from Visual Studio 2005. On the Team menu, point to Process Template, and then click Open Process Template. This will allow you to specify a process template that you wish to edit. To select this template, navigate to the location of the process template you downloaded from the Team Foundation Server until you find the ProcessTemplate.xml file. The next step you should take is to ensure that the Process Template Editor is connected to a Team Foundation Server. By default, the Process Template Editor does not connect to the default Team Foundation Server you configured in your Team Explorer. To specify a Team Foundation Server you wish the Process Template Editor to connect to, choose Connect from the drop-down list box in the top right corner of the Process Template Editor window to show a dialog box that will allow you to specify the Team Foundation Server. This may seem strange at first because the tool is used primarily to edit the XML-based process template files stored on your local computer or corporate file share. The reason for the required connection has to do with validation—the Process Template Editor uses Team Foundation Server itself to help validate the contents of the process templates as you go. If you choose not to connect to Team Foundation Server, by clicking the Work Disconnected button (Figure 7-11), you will still have the ability to edit process templates; however, some validation will not occur until you attempt to import the process template to Team Foundation Server. To have the Process Template Editor help validate your process template as you make changes, specify the name of your server in the Connect to Team Foundation Server dialog box (simply replace the name of your server between *http:// and :8080*). For example, if the name of your computer running Team Foundation Server is TeamFoundation01, the connection specified in the dialog box should be *http://Team Foundation01:8080*.

Figure 7-11   Specifying a computer running Team Foundation Server by using the Process Template Editor

After you open the ProcessTemplate.xml file, you will be presented with the Process Template Editor window, as shown in Figure 7-12. The left side of the Process Template Editor is a tree that represents the configuration areas of a process template. As you navigate through the tree, the right side of the process template will change to show you all of the available configuration options for the selected configuration area.

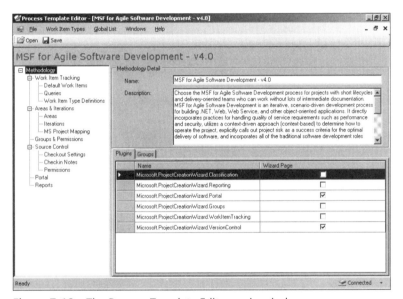

Figure 7-12   The Process Template Editor main window

The first set of options you will see when you open a process template is general methodology information, such as the methodology name, description, and a list of plugins that the opened process template makes reference to, of which only name and description can be edited. If you made a copy of an existing process template as the basis for a new process template, provide a unique name for your new template; otherwise, when you upload it, you will overwrite the existing version.

Editing Default Work Items

Let's start by looking at how you can maintain work item type definitions within a process template. If you have already opened up a process template within the Process Template Editor, you will see that the first configuration node in the process template configuration navigation area is called Work Item Tracking. Let's start by maintaining the default set of work items within a process template. Just to recap, a process template contains a set of work items that are automatically created for you when you create a new Team Project based on that template. For example, MSF for Agile Software Development ships with 15 default work items such as Set up: Set Permissions and Create Vision Scope Statement. The Process Template Editor provides you with a convenient way to modify this list, allowing you to add new default work items, edit existing work items, or delete default work items from the process template.

To add a new default work item to a process template, perform the following steps:

1. Click the Default Work Items node in the Process Template configuration navigation tree. This will display the Default Work Items tab and a list of all of the default work items in the process template.

2. On the Default Work Items tab toolbar, click New to specify the type of default work item you would like to add to your process template. Note that only work item types that are part of your process template are listed.

3. When you have specified the work item type, Risk for example, the Process Template Editor will display the form (as shown in Figure 7-13) associated with the work item type. Here, you will be able to provide details for your work item such as Title, Description, and any other details you want to add. When you are finished, click OK to add the work item to the list of default work items.

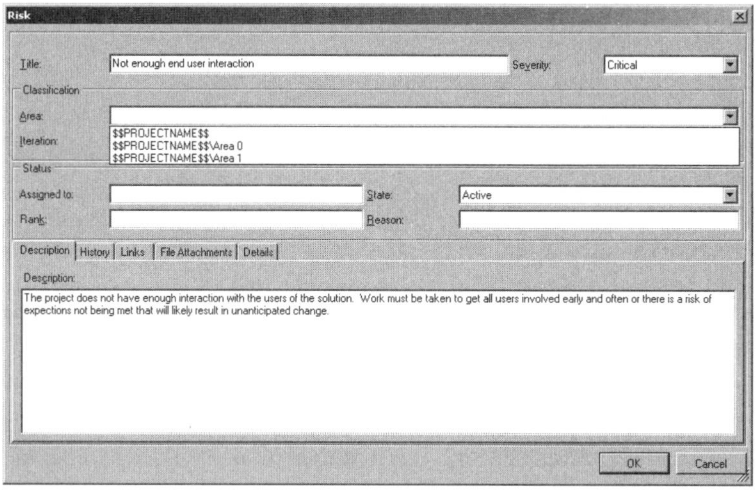

Figure 7-13   Adding a new Risk work item to a process template

There are some important aspects of the default work item form to point out. First, this form does not provide any of the validation you would normally see when filling out work item forms from within Team Explorer. Second, when you are typing classifications, you will see $$PROJECTNAME$$ in the drop-down lists for the *Area* and *Iteration* fields. This is a place-holder for the name of the project this work item will eventually be created under and will be replaced when the work item is created in projects that are created from the process template you are editing.

> **Tip**   One of the most common types of default work items added to process templates are Risk work items to help ensure that the most common issues your team deals with from project to project are specifically addressed during every project.

If you make a mistake when you are filling out the details of a default work item, don't worry—you can always go back and edit the default work item by selecting the work item from the list of default work items and clicking Open on the Default Work Item tab toolbar. Deleting default work items is simple: click the default work item you want to remove from the process template and then click Delete on the Default Work Item tab toolbar. Delete default work items with care because there is no undo feature in the tool.

Editing Work Item Queries

Work Item Queries are the very essence of how your team will find and work with work items. The Process Template Editor provides the ability to manage the default list of a Team Project's work item queries. It also provides you with the ability to create new simple work item queries through the Work Item Query Editor. To see the list of default work item queries in your process template (Figure 7-14), click the Queries node of the Process Template Editor's configuration navigation tree.

> **Note**   If there is one aspect of a Team Project that changes often throughout the life of a project, it is work item queries. Invariably, teams will create new work item queries for their projects no matter how much work they perform up front trying to identify queries they think they might need. In addition, Team Explorer makes editing work item queries almost trivial, and for this reason, many project managers choose not to spend a lot of time using the Process Template Editor to create many new work item queries.

When creating a new work item query by clicking New on the toolbar of the Queries tab, you will be prompted to specify a name for the query. From the same dialog box that prompts for the name of the query, you can click Edit Query Definition to show the Process Template Editor's work item query editor (shown in Figure 7-15).

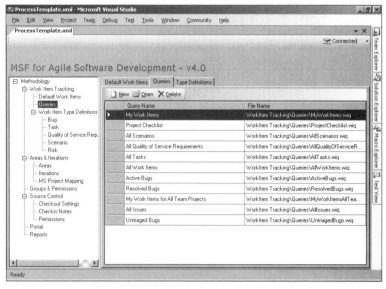

Figure 7-14 Managing work item queries by using the Process Template Editor

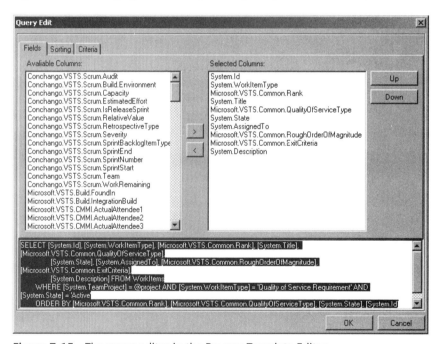

Figure 7-15 The query editor in the Process Template Editor

The query editor will allow you to add and remove fields from the query results (using the Fields tab), change the query result sort order, and specify the criteria for the query. The query editor also displays the details of the underlying query definition in SQL, which can also be edited in place to produce complex queries the editor isn't able to produce, such as nested query conditions. If you are already familiar with the Team Explorer work item query building interface, you will have no problems using the Process Template Editor's version of the tool.

> **Tip**   The Process Template Editor does not provide the same graphical abilities as Team Explorer for creating complex work item queries. It will be easier to create placeholders for the work item queries within the Process Template Editor and update their definition once you have created a new project.

Editing Work Item Types

For many project managers, work item customization is quite important because it allows them to control exactly what to track and how to track it. For this reason, the Process Template Editor helps to provide an environment that makes it much easier to edit work item type definitions. In fact, there are three ways you can modify work item type definitions by using the Process Template Editor: editing work item type definitions in a Process Template; editing in individual work item type definition files; and editing work item type definitions against a live Team Project, an operation that allows you to easily make changes to work items without having to create a new Team Project or use cryptic command-line utilities.

Let's start by looking at how you can manage work item type definitions as part of a process template definition. You will start by bringing up the list of work items in your process template by clicking the Work Item Type Definitions node of the configuration navigation tree. You can use the Process Template Editor to create new work item type definitions, edit existing definitions, remove definitions from the process template, and import work item type definitions from outside of the process template. Although you have the ability to create a work item type definition from scratch, this is rarely a good idea. You should always create a new work item type based on the definition of another, and for this reason, when you click New on the Type Definition tab's toolbar, you will get a dialog box that allows you to make a copy of an existing work item first, as shown in Figure 7-16.

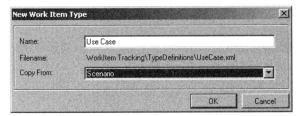

Figure 7-16   Creating a new work item from the definition of another

> **Caution**   If you create a work item type definition without first copying a definition from another work item, you will be responsible for adding all fields, workflow, and field layouts to the work item from scratch, which can be tedious and time consuming.

After you create a new work item, you can then edit its definition by clicking Open on the Type Definitions tab's toolbar to show the Work Item Type Edit window. This window contains three tabs. The Fields tab lists all work item fields associated with the work item type you are editing. The Fields tab will also allow you to create new fields or edit or delete existing fields. The Workflow tab will allow you to manage the workflow definition for the work item, and the Layout tab provides tools that will help you design the form users will use to fill out work item details.

Note   You might notice the View XML button on many of the tabs of the Work Item Type Edit window. Clicking this button displays the underlying XML of the section of the work item type you are working on. This feature is really only for more technical users of the tool to help understand how the Process Template Editor is managing the underlying XML of the work item type.

Editing Work Item Fields

Managing the fields of a work item is likely one of the first things you will do after creating a new work item type. You can add new fields to capture additional information within the work item (most typical), edit the definition of existing fields (such as to change field rules), or even delete fields. When you are either editing a field or creating a new field type, you will be working with the Field Definition dialog box (Figure 7-17), where you will be able to specify the name of the field, the field type, the internal reference name of the field, associated help information, and data warehouse integration parameters.

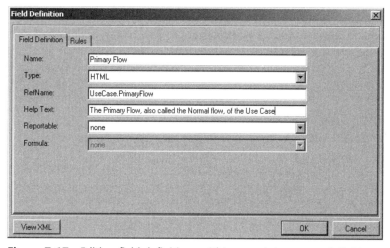

Figure 7-17   Editing field definitions within a work item type definition

After providing a name for your field, you will also need to specify a field type, details of which are provided in Table 7-4. The RefName value is used internally in Visual Studio Team System and must uniquely reference your new field within all Team Projects on the Team Foundation Server instance. The RefName value also needs to contain one period, and you may not use the words *System* or *Microsoft*. Some examples of RefNames include MyCompany.UseCase-Name and UseCase.NormalFlow. The Help Text field will help users understand how the field is to be used when they are filling out work item information. The Reportable field tells Team Foundation Server how to treat the value of the field with respect to the underlying data ware-house. The Reportable field value can either be *none*, *dimension* (which will allow the field value to act much as a pivot field in an Microsoft Office Excel pivot table), *detail*, or *measure*, which indicates that it is to be used as a calculated field. If you specify that the field value should be a *measure*, you must then specify the formula, selecting from sum, count, distinct count, average, minimum, or maximum data warehouse calculations.

Warning   Working with reportable fields should not be taken lightly. A detailed explanation of the Team Foundation Server data warehouse is beyond the scope of this book, and you must have a certain depth of understanding of this data warehouse before you work with reportable fields. So unless you are working with software developers who understand the structure and relevance of the underlying data warehouse, do not mark your fields as reportable.

Table 7-4   Work Item Field Types

Field Type	Usage
String	Used for simple field types that contain a small amount of text or numbers. The *Title* field in a work item is an example of a String field.
Integer	Used for numeric fields such as *Priority* (1–9) or *Probability* (1–100). The *Rough Order of Magnitude* field of a scenario is an example of an Integer field.
Double	Used to store more precise pieces of numeric information containing decimal points, for example, 100.25. The *Remaining Work* Field in a task is an example of a Double field.
DateTime	Used for fields that store either a date or a time value. Many built-in fields, such as *Created Date* or *Closed Date*, use this field type.
PlainText	Used to store larger amounts of non-formatted text or numerical data. Such fields types are good for allowing more space for a description than provided in a simple string field. The *Description* field of a work item is an example of a PlainText field.
HTML	HTML fields have the ability to contain rich content such as tables and textual formatting.
TreePath	Reserved for *Area* and *Iteration*. Do not use.
History	Reserved for the *History* field in a work item. Do not use.

Each field can have one or more rules associated with it. For example, you might want to create a mandatory field called *Customer Name* and provide a list of valid customers that will appear in a drop-down list. In this case, there are actually two rules: a mandatory rule and an allowed values list. To add a rule to a field, open the field definition and click the Rules tab (shown in Figure 7-18).

There are many available rules that you can apply to a field, which are described in Table 7-5. However, by far the most common rules you will use will be the Allowed Values, Default, Read Only, and Suggested Value Rules.

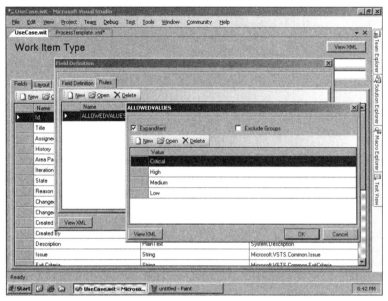

Figure 7-18 Work item field rules

Table 7-5   Available Work Item Field Rules

Field Rule	Description
ALLOWEDVALUES	Provides a list of values allowed for the field. The user must select from one of these values when filling out the form. You can also specify group names and global lists as an allowed value and specify that groups be expanded and listed individually in the field drop-down list. For example, you can specify [Project]\Contributors as an allowed value. If you select the Expand Item check box, the work item will display a list of all users who are a member of the current Contributors group in the Team Project in addition to the name of the Contributors group itself. If you select the Exclude Groups check box, only the members of the Contributors group are listed, and the group name will be omitted from the list.
ALLOWEXISTINGVALUE	Allows a field to retain an existing value, even if that value is no longer allowed.
CANNOTLOSEVALUE	Indicates that the value of the field cannot be lost.
COPY	Indicates that the value of the field should be copied from the system clock or the name of the current user.

Table 7-5   Available Work Item Field Rules (Continued)

Field Rule	Description
DEFAULT	Specifies a default value for the field. Default values can be obtained from the system clock (used, for example, for capturing a particular time a work item has changed), the name of the current user initiating the change (for example, the *Changed By* field would capture the name of the current user editing the work item), a particular value expression, or the value of another field in the work item.
EMPTY	The field value will be cleared on a work item save, and the user will not be allowed to enter any value. This rule can be made conditional by providing names of groups for which this rule will be invoked or specifically ignored. For example, you can represent a rule that requires a given field to remain empty for Project Contributors and not be required to remain empty for Team Foundation Administrators.
FROZEN	Specifies that after the field value has been set, it cannot change. This rule can be made conditional by providing names of groups for which this rule will be invoked or specifically ignored. For example, you can represent a rule that requires a given field to be frozen for Project Contributors and not required to be frozen for Team Foundation Administrators.
MATCH	Specifies that the string field must match a particular pattern or patterns. Valid values are *A*, *N*, and *X*. All other values are taken as literals. *A* represents an alphabetical character. *N* represents a numeric character. *X* represents any alphanumeric character. For example, the pattern XXX-XXX-XXX will allow values 123-abc-r4g and not allow values such as 123.455-23.
NOTSAMEAS	Specifies that a field value cannot be the same as the value of another field in the current work item.
PROHIBITEDVALUES	Provides a list of values that the field explicitly cannot contain.
READONLY	Indicates that this field is read only. This rule can be made conditional by providing names of groups for which this rule will be invoked or specifically ignored. For example, you can represent a rule that sets a given field as read only for Project Contributors and as not required for Team Foundation Administrators.
REQUIRED	Indicates that this field must be specified in the form. This rule can be made conditional by providing names of groups for which this rule will be invoked or specifically ignored. For example, you can represent a rule that causes a given field to be required for Project Contributors and not required for Team Foundation Administrators.
SERVERDEFAULT	This rule is similar to the COPY rule; however, this rule fills in a value when the work item is saved instead of when it is first opened, and the user cannot override the value. When this rule is turned on, fields will appear read-only on the form. This rule is used for fields such as *Last Changed By* and *Last Changed On* to support secure audit trails.
SUGGESTEDVALUES	This rule is very similar to the ALLOWEDVALUES rule except that using this rule, the users are free to type in any other value they want in the field, whereas the ALLOWEDVALUES rule forces them to select from a pre-established list.

Table 7-5   Available Work Item Field Rules (Continued)

Field Rule	Description
VALIDUSER	Displays a list of users of Team Foundation Server.
WHEN	Used for conditional rules. This rule specifies that further rules are enabled when a particular field has a particular value.
WHENNOT	Used for conditional rules. This rule specifies that further rules are enabled when a particular field does not have a particular value.
WHENCHANGED	Used for conditional rules. This rule specifies that further rules are enabled when a particular field has changed in a work item.
WHENNOTCHANGED	Used for conditional rules. This rule specifies that further rules are enabled when a particular field has not changed in a work item.

As you can see, you can be quite verbose with field rules, and it will likely take a bit of practice to get things right. I have learned from the experiences of many customers worldwide that field rules should be kept as simple as possible. Work items that contain many complex rules will dissuade your users from using work items. Use rules to make work items easier for your team members to use, not to make then more difficult.

Referring to Groups in Field Rules

You may have noticed that you can make reference to groups from certain field rules such as ALLOWEDVALUES and SUGGESTEDVALUES. Groups can be Visual Studio Team System Global groups, Active Directory groups, or Team Foundation groups. For example, you will notice that when adding a list item to a list rule such as ALLOWED-VALUES, there is a field drop-down list that also displays any Global groups on the server to which you are currently connected. By default, Team Foundation Server stores build numbers in Global lists on the server. If you specify a Global group as a list item and set it to expand by selecting the Expand Item check box, the values within the group will be listed in the field. You can also specify Team Foundation Security groups such as [Project]\Contributors or [Server]\Team Foundation Server Administrators or groups from Active Directory such as MyDomain\Domain Users.

Editing Work Item Workflow

After creating fields and their rules, you can also change the workflow specification for a work item. Each work item type specifies its own workflow specification, which consists of a set of states and a set of valid transitions between two states. To modify a work item type's workflow definition by using the Process Template Editor, click the Workflow tab of the Work Item Type Editor, shown in Figure 7-19.

The Process Template Editor will allow you to specify all of the valid states of a work item. Each state can also specify a set of rules that apply when the work item is in that state. For example, in the Task work item type that is shipped with the MSF Agile process template, the Active state specifies a few new rules, specifically that when the state of the work item is Active, the *Closed Date* and *Closed By* fields of the work item must be empty.

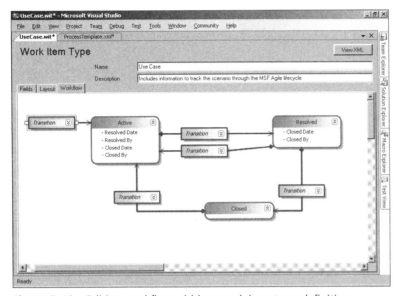

Figure 7-19   Editing workflow within a work item type definition

To create a new workflow state, perform the following steps:

1. Open the work item type definition for editing and click the Workflow tab to show the work item workflow designer. Ensure that the Visual Studio 2005 Toolbox window is visible by clicking Toolbox on the View menu. Drag a new state from the workflow designer toolbox onto the design surface.

2. Select the new state object on the workflow design surface and type the name of the state. The name of the state must be unique to the work item type.

3. Add rules that will be activated when a work item enters the new state. Right-click on the new state object on the workflow design surface and click Open Details from the context menu. To add a new rule to a field, click New. You will then need to specify a field you would like to add a new rule to and specify the rule you want to apply (shown in Figure 7-20). Use the same process as when creating rules for work item fields.

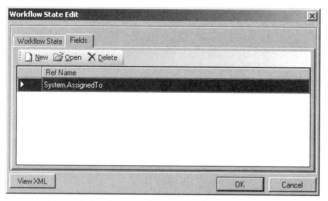

Figure 7-20 Selecting a field when adding a rule

Workflow transitions specify the rules that allow a work item to move from state to state. By default, when you create a new work item, it doesn't have any state at all. For this reason, you will need to have a transition specified from the "nothing" state to one of the states you just created. When creating state transitions, there are many options you can specify. To create transitions from the Process Template Editor, click the Transition object from the workflow designer's toolbox onto the design surface. Next, click the state you wish to create a transition from followed by the state you wish to make a transition to. To specify the details of the transition, right-click on the transition object that was just created for you on the workflow design surface, and click Open Details from the context menu. The result is shown in Figure 7-21.

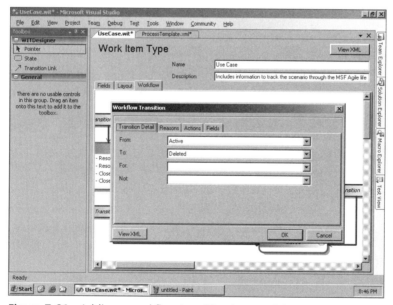

Figure 7-21 Adding a workflow transition to a work item

On the Workflow Transition form on the Transition Detail tab, you can specify the state you are transitioning from in addition to the state you are allowing transition to. In addition, you can use the For and Not drop-down lists to specify groups of people for whom this transaction is allowed or not allowed. For example, you may want to give only project managers the ability to reopen a work item, in this case moving a work item from the closed to active state. In this case, you can click [Project]\Project Managers in the For drop-down list if you have this group set in your process template.

Every state transition typically has a reason, which corresponds to the *Reason* field on a work item form. Reasons allow you to specify why a transition is being made. For example, you may have a transition from the Active to the Closed state because the work item has been completed, deferred, cut from scope, or has been deemed obsolete. Each of these reasons would be listed in the list of reasons for the transition definition. You can also specify the default reason that will automatically be chosen for you when you initiate state change. In the case of the workflow definition of a Task work item in the MSF Agile template, the default reason for the transition from Active to Closed transition is Completed. To make this even more complicated, every reason selected by a user during a transition can invoke even more field rules in the same way that workflow states can create new rules. Just when you thought it couldn't get more complicated, you should also know that transitions can also invoke additional rules. For example, for the transition from Active to Closed states for a Task in MSF Agile, the *Close Date* of the work item will have a SERVERDEFAULT rule, the value of the *Closed By* field will be from the current user (according to the COPY rule), must be a VALIDUSER, and is a required field as determined by the REQUIRED rule.

Workflow transactions can also be triggered by something called an *action*. For example, Microsoft provides a CheckIn action that gets triggered when a developer associates a work item during a check-in operation. When the check-in is performed by the developer, Visual Studio Team System will automatically trigger the appropriate transition associated with the action. Note that the check-in action is the only action you can associate with a transaction until Microsoft provides additional actions or tools that extend Team Foundation Server provide additional actions.

To create new field rules on transactions, perform the following steps:

1. While editing the details of a transition of a workflow in the workflow designer, click the Fields tab in the Workflow Transition dialog box to show a list of fields to which you want to apply rules.

2. Click New to add a field to the list or click an existing field to open its properties. From this point on, specifying a rule for the transition is very similar to adding rules to work item fields.

To modify the list of reasons for a transition, follow these steps:

1. While editing the details of a transition of a workflow in the workflow designer, click the Reasons tab in the Workflow transition details dialog box to show a list of reasons for the selected transition.

2. Click New above the list of reasons to create a new transition reason or Open to view an existing reason. You can also mark one of the reasons in the list as default by selecting the check box in the Is Default column.

3. On the Reasons tab, you will need to specify a name of the reason, which needs to be unique for the transition. The Fields tab in this dialog box is where you would add rules that will be activated when the reason is selected during a transition. Perform the same steps as you would when adding field rules in other areas of a work item type definition.

Customizing Work Item Layouts

Up until this point, you have learned how to add fields and control the workflow and rules that determine how work items behave. None of these new fields, however, will be visible until you ensure that they are properly displayed on the work item form. Each work item type has its own layout that determines how work items are displayed to users from within Visual Studio. The Process Template Editor provides the Work Item Layout Editor to help with the structure of the work item forms, allowing you to quickly change the entire look and feel of a work item for your team. While editing a work item type definition, you can click the Layout tab of the Work Item Type Edit window to view the layout details of the work item, as shown in Figure 7-22.

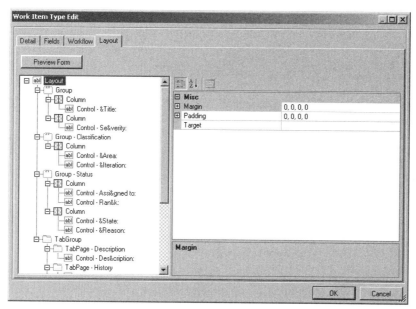

Figure 7-22 Editing a work item's layout

The layout of a work item consists of a number of different elements. Field controls are used to capture data for work item fields. Field controls can either be simple text boxes (called FieldControls in the Process Template Editor), Date and Time controls (referred to as DateTimeControls) that help capture date/time-based fields by adding a calendar to the drop-down list of the field, or HTML controls (referred to as HTMLFieldControls) that allow the capture of fully formatted text information for HTML-based fields. Work item forms can also contain Group controls, which act to group a number of related fields together on the screen. For example, if you view a Risk work item, you will see that the fields *Assigned to*, *State*, *Rank*, and *Reason* are grouped together on a Group control called Status. A Column is another element you must consider when modifying the layout of work item forms. For example, the Status group on the Risk work item just mentioned displays the four fields it contains across two columns. You will also notice that work item forms contain tabs that help to organize other controls such as group controls and other field controls. A cluster of tabs on a work item form is called a Tab Group.

When designing the layout of forms, you should be aware of some restrictions on where you can place certain controls. For example, Tab Group controls must be contained within a Tab Group. Group Controls must have at least one Column. Field controls can be placed just about anywhere on the form except for directly within Groups or Tab Groups; in both of these cases, field controls must be assigned to a Column contained within a Group. And finally, Columns must be contained with a Group or Tab Page. What you are left with is a hierarchy of work item form elements. In addition, each element that you can create (tab groups, tabs, groups, columns, and field controls) all have a set of properties, which are displayed as property pages in the Process Template Editor, which you can configure to control how the elements are displayed. Table 7-6 displays the available properties for each element type of a work item form.

Table 7-6   Work Item Layout Element Properties

Element Name	Property	Element Properties
Field Control	Dock	If specified, the dock property allows a field to stretch to fill the remainder of the container. Valid field docking values are Top, Bottom, Left, and Right.
	FieldName	Specifies the name of the underlying work item field the control will map values to.
	Label	Specifies text to help identify associated field contents.
	LabelPosition	Indicates where the label should be placed relative to the field data. Possible values are Top, Bottom, Left, and Right.
	Margin	Specifies the amount of room you want around the outside of the control (between it and its neighbors) in pixels. The amount of space can vary on each side.
	Padding	Specifies the amount of room you want around the border of the control (between it and its contents) in pixels.
	ReadOnly	Allows you to show a field in a control but not perform any editing.

Table 7-6 Work Item Layout Element Properties (Continued)

Element Name	Property	Element Properties
	Type	Specifies the type of the control.
Group/Tab	Label	Specifies the label of the group section.
	Margin	Specifies the amount of room you want around the outside of the control (between it and its neighbors) in pixels. The amount of space can vary on each side.
	Padding	Specifies the amount of room you want around the border of the control (between it and its contents) in pixels.
Column	FixedWidth	Specifies the column width as a number of pixels.
	Percentage-Width	Specifies the width the column should occupy as a percentage of the width within the containing element. *PercentWidth and FixedWidth are mutually exclusive.*
Tab Group	Margin	Specifies the amount of room you want around the outside of the control (between it and its neighbors) in pixels. The amount of space can vary on each side.
	Padding	Specifies the amount of room you want around the border of the control (between it and its contents) in pixels.

To add new controls or change the position of existing controls on the form, perform the following steps:

1. In the Work Item Type Edit window, click the Layout tab to show the control tree and the properties pane.

2. To add a control to the work item layout, right-click the area you want to add the control in and select from the valid list of controls that appear in the shortcut menu. Note that the Process Template Editor will show you only controls that you can add based on the area of the layout hierarchy you selected. For example, if you chose a Tab Group in the tree, the Process Template Editor will allow you to add only a Tab Page. Set the appropriate properties for the control in the properties pane on the right side of the Work Item Type Edit window.

3. To move a control to a different position in the layout tree, right-click the control you want to move, and on the shortcut menu, choose either Move Up or Move Down depending on the direction you want to move the control in the tree. Continue this operation until the control has moved into the desired location.

4. Click the Preview Form button in the Work Item Type Edit window to have the Process Template Editor give you a representation of what the work item will look like when you're finished.

Of course, as with anything else, save your work often. The work item type definition will not be saved until you choose to save the entire process template by clicking Save on the File menu (or pressing Ctrl+S) in Visual Studio 2005.

Other Work Item Features in the Process Template Editor

We have just covered how to edit work item type definitions that are part of a larger process template. The Process Template Editor provides a few extra handy features that provide you with more options on how you work with work item type definitions. Specifically, the Process Template Editor provides you with the ability to export work item type definitions from a Team Project to an XML file on your computer. To do this, select Process Editor >Work Item Types >Export WIT from the Team menu in Visual Studio 2005 The Process Template Editor will prompt you to identify a Team Project on the server you just made a connection to, and from there, you can select the work item type definition you want to export along with the name you want to give the file and location you want to export the definition into, as shown in Figure 7-23. The Process Template Editor allows you to edit the work item type definition independent of a process template definition.

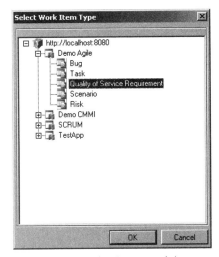

Figure 7-23   Selecting a work item to export

When you have successfully exported the work item, in Visual Studio 2005, on the Team menu, point to Process Editor, then point to Work Item Types, and then click Open WIT from File to open the work item type definition where you can use the Process Template Editor to perform all of the aforementioned work item modifications. When you're finished, you can save the work item type definition and then re-import to either the same Team Project or another Team Project on your server in Visual Studio 2005. On the Team menu, point to Process Editor, then point to Work Item Types, and then click Import WIT. During the import process, you will be given a chance to select a target Team Project you want to import the work item into. If you choose a Team Project that already has a work item with the same name, you will be asked whether you want to overwrite the version of the work item type stored on the server with the new version you are importing.

Another very handy feature is the ability to open a work item type definition directly in a Team Project without having to export, modify, and then re-import the work item type definition. To modify live work item types, on the Team mean, point to Process Editor, and then click Open WIT from Server and specify the Team Project and work item type you want to edit. When you are finished, simply save the work item type definition, and updates will be made to the server for you. The next time your team uses a work item of that type, they will be able to see the appropriate changes.

Warning   Be careful when editing work item type definitions on the server. If you make a mistake, it will affect your entire team. A good practice when editing work items involves having a test project available where changes can be made in isolation from other team members. After you have verified that all appropriate changes are acceptable, you can then use the Export and Import features of the Process Template Editor to move the work item type definition from your test project to the live Team Project for your team to start using.

Editing Global Lists by Using the Process Template Editor

Global lists are structures stored within Team Foundation Server that list items. An example of a Global list is a list of automated build numbers. These lists can be used to provide values for drop-down lists associated with work item fields, as described in previous sections of this chapter. Many organizations have taken the use of Global lists to the next level, using these lists to provide a convenient way of storing a single representation of available list options. For example, you can create a Global list called Allowed Ranks that contains the values {1,2,3,4,5}. You could then change the definition of the *Rank* field in all of your project's work item type definitions to use the Allowed Ranks Global list to specify the ALLOWEDVALUES field rule. When using the work item, the *Rank* field will allow you to select {1,2,3,4,5} from the drop-down list. Suppose at some point in the future it is decided that the possible *Rank* values should be changed to {1,2,3,4,5,6,7,8,9,10}; because you used a Global list to store these values, you could simply edit the Allowed Ranks Global list, and every field definition that uses this Global list will reflect this change instantly.

Similar to work item type definitions, the Process Template Editor provides you with the ability to edit Global lists directly on a server, export global lists to an XML file where it can be edited offline, and import Global list XML files back to Team Foundation Server. In Visual Studio, on the Team menu, point to Process Editor and then click Global List to perform these operations. Figure 7-24 depicts the Global List editor within Visual Studio Team System. Right-click any node in the editor to obtain a list of options. These options include New Global List, New Item (which will create a new value under an existing global list), and Delete (which will delete either an item in a list or the entire Global list itself).

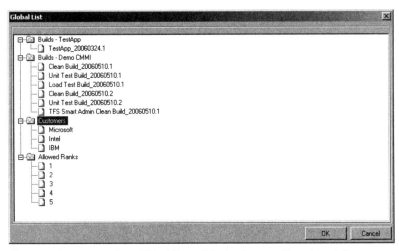

Figure 7-24   Managing Global lists with the Process Template Editor

Editing Classifications

Process templates also specify the default list of areas and iterations for new projects. This is why new Team Projects created from templates such as MSF for Agile Software Development come preloaded with three iterations. The Process Template Editor provides you with the ability to create default classification hierarchies in the same manner as you would from the Team Explorer interface, as shown in Figure 7-25. To navigate to the area of the Process Template Editor where you can manage these default classifications, open a process template definition and click the Areas & Iterations node in the configuration navigation tree.

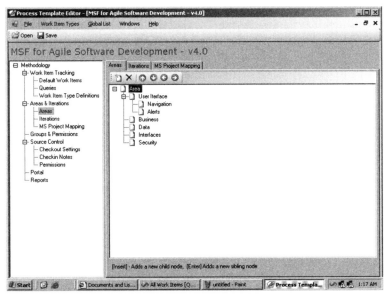

Figure 7-25   Managing default classifications by using the Process Template Editor

> **Tip** When editing classifications, you can press the Insert key to add new child nodes and the Enter key to quickly add new sibling nodes to the classification hierarchy.

Editing Microsoft Office Project Field Mappings

As a project manager, you no doubt have some experience with Microsoft Office Project to plan and manage projects. Visual Studio Team System provides the ability to integrate work items with Office Project, with each task in an Office Project file mapping to a work item in Visual Studio Team System. Unlike Office Excel, however, Office Project has built-in columns such as Predecessor, Resource, Work, and Duration. These fields do not have a one-to-one relationship with fields specified in a work item, especially if you have made considerable changes to a work item by adding and removing fields. The process template specifies how work item fields map to fields in Office Project, and the Process Template Editor provides a way of managing this mapping. By clicking the Office Project Mapping node in the Process Template Editor's configuration container, you can view and change these default mappings. The Office Project Mapping section displays a list of mapped fields represented by four columns. The Work Item Tracking Field Reference Name represents the work item field you want to map into Office Project. The Project Field column represents the name of the field in Office Project you are targeting. Note that the field name is prefixed with *pjTask*. The Project Name column specifies a change in the name of the target column in Office Project. For example, the *System.State* field gets mapped to the Text13 column in Office Project. The value in the Project Name column is State, which indicates that Office Project should display State instead of Text13 when displaying the column. The Project Units column identifies the unit of measurement that will be assumed when values are mapped from work items to a numeric field in Office Project. For example, the work item field *Completed Work* contains a numeric value, and the field mapping *pjHour* specifies that Office Project should treat that value as an hour instead of a day, week, or month.

You can either add new field mappings by clicking New on the Office Project Mappings toolbar or Open on an existing mapping to show the Project Mapping dialog box. The Project Mapping dialog box contains one extra option not displayed on the field mapping list called Publish Only. The Publish Only option indicates that the Microsoft Office Project Visual Studio Team System add-in will receive information for this field from Visual Studio Team System and will never be used to update work item information during a Publishing action.

Editing Default Security Settings

Process templates also specify the default security groups and their permissions for new Team Projects. The Groups & Permissions node in the configuration container of the Process Template Editor allows you to create groups and set their default permissions. By default, the MSF Agile template specifies three groups: Readers, Contributors, and Build Services. You might want to change this list to something such as Developers, Testers, Customers, Project Managers, and Architects with each group having its own set of permissions. Click New and Open on the Groups & Permissions toolbar to create or edit groups.

Setting permissions by using the Process Template Editor is a bit more complex. After you create a group, you can click the group in the list to show the permissions assigned to that group in the permission grid. The permission grid has two perspectives, the right to perform an activity, and the Visual Studio Team System component on which you can perform that activity. The Process Template Editor lists all of the available permissions in the first column of the grid under the group listings. Along the top of the grid is a list of the objects that can apply permissions. The cell that is at the intersection of the permission and the target object specifies the appropriate permission. For example, if you select the Readers group in the list of security groups, the grid will display an Allow value in the cell at the intersection of GENERIC_READ and PROJECT. This indicates that the Readers Group can read project-level information. Cells that are gray indicate that the combination of the permission and the target object, which intersect at that cell, cannot exist. For example, the PUBLISH_TEST_RESULTS permission makes sense for a project, but it doesn't make much sense for EVENT_SUBSCRIPTION. Table 7-7 explains the listed permissions, and Table 7-8 provides an explanation of the target objects listed in the grid.

Table 7-7 Process Template Permissions

Permission Name	Description
GENERIC_READ	Ability to read information from the target
GENERIC_WRITE	Ability to update information about the target
WORK_ITEM_READ	Ability to read work items
PUBLISH_TEST_RESULTS	Ability to publish test results to Team Foundation Server
WORK_ITEM_WRITE	Ability to write work item information
START_BUILD	Ability to launch a build process
UPDATE_BUILD	Ability to update a build
EDIT_BUILD_STATUS	Ability to edit the build status after a build has completed
MANAGE_EVERYONE_GROUP	Permission to manage the Everyone group
CREATE_PROJECTS	Ability to create new Team Projects
ADMINISTER_WAREHOUSE	Ability to configure settings on the Visual Studio Team System data warehouse
CHECK_IN	Ability to check in code
DELETE	Ability to perform a delete operation
DELETE_TEST_RESULTS	Ability to delete recorded test results from the server
ADMINISTER_BUILD	Ability to administer a build
CREATE_CHILDREN	Ability to create child notes of a classification tree
UNSUBSCRIBE	Ability to unsubscribe from alerts

Table 7-8   Process Template Permission Targets

Target Name	Description
PROJECT	A Team Project
CSS_NODE	Classification Notes (Areas and Iterations)
NAMESPACE	Team Foundation Server
EVENT_SUBSCRIPTION	Team Foundation Server events

Editing Default Source Control Settings

The Process Template Editor also allows you to configure Team Project default source control settings such as enabling/disabling multiple checkouts, default check-in notes, and default permissions. To edit these settings from the Process Template Editor, click the Source Control node in the configuration container, as shown in Figure 7-26. The Process Template Editor mimics how Team Explorer configures checkout settings and check-in notes as described earlier in this chapter.

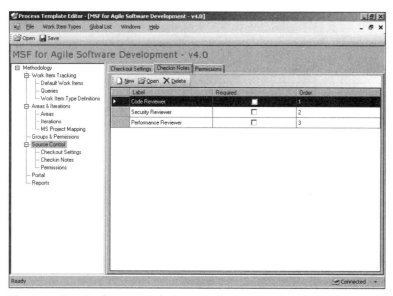

Figure 7-26   Configuring default source control settings in the Process Template Editor

Editing Default SharePoint Structure and Contents

Microsoft Windows SharePoint Server sites act as the project portal for each Visual Studio Team System project. The process templates used to create new projects specify the default document libraries and their contents for each new site. You can use process templates to deposit all of the appropriate templates and documents your project will need so that your team will never have to search for the appropriate documents again. The Process Template Editor allows you to create document libraries and their contents so that you can embed your own organization's content and policies for all new projects.

To create a new document library for your Team Projects:

1. Click to the Portal node of the Process Template Editor to show the Portal document library and contents configuration pane (shown in Figure 7-27).

2. Right-click the root of the Portal tree and choose New Document Library from the shortcut menu, on which you will be prompted to specify a name and a description.

3. To add documents, for example, templates or empty delivery artifacts ready to be filled out by the team, right-click your new document library and click Import from the shortcut menu. Note that you can also choose New Folder from the shortcut menu, allowing you to create a hierarchy of folders underneath the document library you just created.

4. After choosing Import, you will be prompted to specify a directory of files you want to import. Click Browse to navigate to this folder. You can also specify that the Process Template Editor retrieve the entire contents of the specified directory, including all subdirectories. Click Import to add the selected folder and its contents to the document library definition. The Process Template Editor takes a copy of the files you specify and moves them into the appropriate location within the process template document structure.

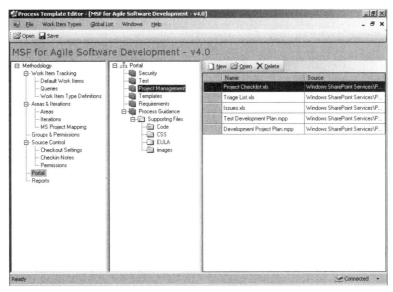

Figure 7-27   Editing default document libraries and documents

Editing Report Listings and Parameters

As already mentioned, the modification of report definitions used by Visual Studio Team System to provide the rich reporting capabilities will not be covered in this chapter. Modifying the list of reports that get installed during the creation of a new Team Project, however, is something that is managed by the Process Template Editor, because all report definitions are actually part of the process template definition files.

Reports are stored in files with the extension .rdl. To see the list of reports for your project, click the Reports configuration node in the Process Template Editor. From a nontechnical project manager's perspective, there really isn't much to do with this list other than to remove reports from this list. Each listed report has a configured set of technical parameters such as cache expiration, report parameters, and data source declarations. These should be modified only by software developers familiar with Microsoft SQL Server Reporting Services and Visual Studio Team System reports.

Uploading the Modified Process Template

When you have completed all of your changes to the process template, as long as you have the appropriate permissions, you can now upload them back into Team Foundation Server. To upload the process template, launch Visual Studio and Team Explorer. On the Team menu, point to Team Foundation Server Settings, and then click Process Template Manager to open the Process Template Manager dialog box. Click Upload and navigate to the location of the process template you want to import into Visual Studio Team System. Note that if the process template you selected has the same name as a process template that already exists within Team Foundation Server, you will be prompted to confirm an overwrite. If you choose to overwrite, there is no undo option, so be very careful. If you are uploading a template whose name is different than that of any others on the server, it will be added as a new process template and be available to be the basis of the next Team Project.

> **Note**   Process templates are used only during the creation of new Team Projects. If you make a modification to a process template that was the basis of existing Team Projects, those projects will not be affected by any update you make.

Tailoring Process Guidance

The process template also contains all of the files that represent process guidance. Remember what process guidance is; it's the Web pages that describe how the process works, what the work items do, and generally who does what by when (Figure 7-28). As you make changes to the underlying process templates, such as creating new work items or changing the definitions of existing work items, it would be nice to have these changes reflected in the process guidance. Unfortunately, this is not very easy or very practical because there is no tool that will make this job easier for you. In fact, this is such a complicated task that project managers will likely always call upon a developer to perform these modifications. Details of process guidance editing will not be provided in this book because you would need a deep understanding of XML to do it. If you are still interested in how you can modify process guidance for your teams or organization, the best action to take is to read the six-part article on this task that you can download from *http://msdn.microsoft.com/library/default.asp?url=/library/ en-us/dnvs05/html/MSF_buildprocess.asp.*

> **Note**   Process guidance data is actually stored in a document library definition and can be viewed by using the Process Template Editor when performing maintenance on the portal configuration area.

Figure 7-28   A Team Project's process guidance

Summary

In this chapter, we reviewed the most common and powerful customizations you can perform in Visual Studio Team System from the viewpoint of a project manager. These customizations will allow you to change how the product works to best fit your team and process methodology.

Capability Maturity Model Integration (CMMI)[1]

- Understand what CMMI is today and where it evolved from.

- Understand the structure and key components of CMMI.

- Understand the relationship between CMMI and MSF 4.0 for CMMI Process Improvement.

If you ponder how quickly the business and technological landscape changes from year to year, you might wonder how any organization can survive. An organization's ability to simply exist depends directly on its ability to adapt. However, change is a tricky subject. Most organizations understand that change is good, but they struggle with the question of what should be driving the business changes. Change may be essential to survival; however, change without direction, purpose, or control could be detrimental.

What if we take the problem of change to the paradigm of software development? Let's face it: in general, most organizations aren't very good at software development. When it comes to the construction of software, organizations tend to struggle to understand what they are about to build, how to design it, how to plan for it, and how to deliver on time and on budget without sacrificing quality. If you are part of a savvy organization, you'll likely learn from your mistakes, and you might evolve your software development practices and methodologies to better suit your company's specific needs. You might wonder, however, whether there could be a common way for organizations to advance their software development processes. Can a model of gradual and continual improvement be created that allows organizations to increase their productivity while increasing the quality of the software they create? This is where the Capability Maturity Model comes in.

---

1 Special permission to use "Capability Maturity Model Integration® (Version 1.1): CMMI® for Systems Engineering, Software Engineering, Integrated Product and Process Development, and Supplier Sourcing" (CMMI-SE/SW/IPPD/SS, V1.1), Copyright 2002 by Carnegie Mellon University, in Managing Projects with Microsoft Visual Studio Team System is granted by the Software Engineering Institute.

   THIS CARNEGIE MELLON UNIVERSITY AND SOFTWARE ENGINEERING INSTITUTE MATERIAL IS FURNISHED ON AN "AS-IS" BASIS. CARNEGIE MELLON UNIVERSITY MAKES NO WARRANTIES OF ANY KIND, EITHER EXPRESSED OR IMPLIED, AS TO ANY MATTER INCLUDING, BUT NOT LIMITED TO, WARRANTY OF FITNESS FOR PURPOSE OR MERCHANTABILITY, EXCLUSIVITY, OR RESULTS OBTAINED FROM USE OF THE MATERIAL CARNEGIE MELLON UNIVERSITY DOES NOT MAKE ANY WARRANTY OF ANY KIND WITH RESPECT TO FREEDOM FROM PATENT, TRADEMARK, OR COPYRIGHT INFRINGEMENT.

   The SEI and CMU do not directly or indirectly endorse this publication.

   ®Capability Maturity Modeling, CMM and CMMI are registered in the U.S. Patent and Trademark Office by Carnegie Mellon University.

The Capability Maturity Model Integration (CMMI) was developed at the Software Engineering Institute (SEI) to provide organizations with a framework of process improvement. CMMI was formed to provide guidance around improving an organization's processes and their ability to manage the development, acquisition, and maintenance of products and services. CMMI is probably best known for its appraisal techniques that work to quantify and qualify existing organizational processes. You might have heard of CMMI Level 3 or Level 5 as a way to indicate the relative maturity of an organization according to this model. You might have also heard the rumor, likely started by developers, of CMMI being the prohibitor of creativity, replacing an organization's dexterity with ceremony, processes, and endless documentation. Although it is true that the level of record keeping and tracking required to achieve higher levels of CMMI certification is increased, the pain associated with this effort is much more a function of the tools used to track and record related information than it is the need for the information itself. The goal of CMMI was never to smother creativity with documentation and process but to increase the ability to repeat success through predictable quality and productivity.

> **Note** The SEI was founded in 1984 to advance the state of the practice of software engineering and to serve as a national resource in software engineering and technology. The SEI is a federally funded research and development center sponsored by the United States Department of Defense and operated by Carnegie Mellon University in Pittsburgh. Although the SEI's primary customers are defense contractors, any organization is welcome to take advantage of the many available resources on their Web site (*http://www.sei.cmu.edu/cmmi*).

The information contained within the walls of CMMI helps to paint a picture of what your processes should accomplish and provides guidance for your ongoing process improvement initiatives. These initiatives span an entire spectrum of activities and focus areas required to develop, acquire, and maintain products and services. CMMI not only provides targets for your processes and practices, it also lays down a framework that supports ongoing process improvement, recognizing that change needs to be managed and cultured for it to be successful. CMMI does all of this by focusing on improving your organization's process infrastructure through training and standardization in addition to providing guidance on how to plan for and support process improvement, adoption, and standardization activities.

A Brief History of CMMI

The CMMI project was sponsored by the U.S. Department of Defense (DoD) under the Office of the Undersecretary of Defense, Acquisition, Technology, and Logistics (OUSD/AT&L), which is, we agree, quite a mouthful even on a good day. A government organization may have been the primary sponsor of CMMI, but it took a committee of members from industry, government, and the SEI at Carnegie Mellon University to develop the CMMI framework, which is actually a combination of integrated CMMI models, an appraisal method, and all the supporting products and documentation you could want.

In all truth, CMMI is not really the first of its kind. As a matter of fact, the word *Integrated* in the title should have tipped you off that CMMI is a result of an integration of existing models, specifically:

- SW-CMM for Software
- EIA/IS 731 for System Engineering
- IPD-CMM for Integrated Product and Process Development

SW-CMM

In the 1970s and 1980s, the United States Department of Defense saw many of its large software development projects result in spectacular failures. It needed a tool for evaluating the software development capabilities of defense contractors to avoid costly setbacks in the future. In 1986, Watts Humphrey, the Software Engineering Institute (SEI), and the Mitre Corporation responded to a request by the U.S. government and created a software maturity framework and associated questionnaires and appraisal methods. By 1991, the SEI published the Software Capability Maturity Model (SW-CMM) version 1.0, a comprehensive model that described the principles and practices that drive software process maturity, providing an evolutionary path to disciplined software development. By 1993, version 1.1 was released after two years of evaluation and further refinement.

Electronic Industries Alliance/Interim Standard (EIA/IS) 731

The evolution to and from EIA/IS 731, as intuitive as it may sound, wasn't as clear cut as CMM for Software. EIA/IS 731 deals with the concept of systems engineering, which is a term used to group almost all system-related disciplines together under one umbrella term. Even before there was an official EIA/IS 731 standard, two different organizations attempted to model the process of systems engineering practices. The Enterprise Process Improvement Collaboration (EPIC) group, consisting of industry, academia, and government, released the Systems Engineering Capability Maturity Model (SE-CMM). Virtually at the same time, another group, called International Council on Systems Engineering (INCOSE), created a method for evaluating the capabilities of systems engineering organizations based on existing engineering standards. This method slowly evolved into its own maturity model called the Systems Engineering Capability Assessment Model (SECAM). At that time, both organizations decided to work closely with one another under the Electronic Industries Alliance (EIA) and ended up merging the models into a single standard now called the EIA/IS 731, also known as the Systems Engineering Capability Model (SECM).

IPD-CMM for Integrated Product and Process Development

Integrated Product and Process Development (IPPD) is a much more grand vision of change management because it deals with the way an organization works, its organizational structure, and overall behavior of its leaders. IPPD emphasizes the involvement of business stakeholders from all perspectives and throughout the entire life cycle. The IPD-CMM development team, which was established by EPIC and supported by many from the CE-CMM, took more than two years to make their submission to the CMMI effort, and they struggled to put together many incongruent and new IPPD concepts.

There are literally dozens of other standards that have influenced CMMI and its evolution. In fact, you can clearly see influences from ISO 15504, People CMM, Software Acquisition CMM, and System Security models. Each of these maintains its own structures, formats, and terms, which makes them somewhat difficult for anyone to integrate. Not only did CMMI work to build an initial set of integrated models and eventually improve upon the best practices from its underlying source models, it also worked to establish a framework to help integrate future models and create an associated set of appraisal and training residuals, as shown in Figure A-1.

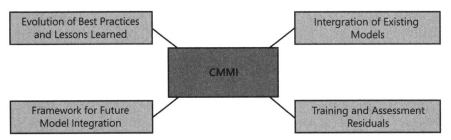

Figure A-1   CMMI is truly an evolutionary offspring of many other models and provides a platform for future extensibility.

Objectives of CMMI

Contrary to what most developers believe, CMMI's sole purpose isn't to make their life difficult. In fact, it's just the opposite. In their book, *CMMI Distilled: A Practical Introduction to Integrated Process Improvement* (Addison-Wesley, 2003), Ahern, Clouse, and Turner paint a picture of the business objectives of CMMI that include having the ability to consistently produce higher-quality products and services, create additional value for sponsors and corporate stakeholders by implementing cost saving techniques and best practices, increasing market share by increasing both quality and velocity, and, believe it or not, increase employee satisfaction. As we've already stated, CMMI represents an integration of many models and provides a more unified approach for model integration and consolidation. This achievement means that CMMI helps to eliminate inconsistencies between various similar underlying models, increases clarity and consistency, and provides a common glossary and set of terminology. This integrated model also works to provide a more repeatable and consistent style of constructing maturity models while at the same time respecting legacy efforts.

Truly, CMMI is not about authoring documents but rather gaining efficiencies in the construction of software or delivery of service. We have observed, however, that this persona has arisen due to reasons much less about structure of CMMI than about the methods by which CMMI goals and practices have been implemented, which usually employ a more traditional document artifact–based model. In many cases, the recommendation that is provided by CMMI is to track information. The CMMI model does not dictate the method by which information is tracked. Traditional methods have chosen document-based artifacts for this purpose, a method the authors of this book do not necessarily endorse. For example, take the CMMI Engineering Requirements Development and Requirements Management process areas. Nowhere in the definition of this process area does it state that team members have to create lengthy documents by using Microsoft Office Word; in fact, what this process area suggests is that your teams should simply develop product requirements. If you can do that with a user sitting right next to you, fantastic! Let's think about the Project Management process areas as another example. One of the practices within this process area is to manage risk and to monitor the project against a plan. Even agile development has some level of a plan (it might not be overly specific, but it's a plan)—yet it doesn't need to be in a thick document or follow a CMMI-prescribed document template to be compliant with CMMI. Many organizations choose to adopt a document-driven approach to help govern and control the process ("When this document is submitted and approved, go to step 2"). In fact, CMMI SCAMPI Distilled suggests that more than 400 document types and 1000 artifacts are required to facilitate a CMMI appraisal—that's a lot of documents, none of which were likely fun to create (*CMMI SCAMPI Distilled: Appraisals for Process Improvement*, SEI Series in Software Engineering, by *Ahern, Armstrong, Clouse, Ferguson, Hayes*, and Nidiffer, Addison-Wesley Professional, 2005). We should not confuse the act of collecting and tracking information (and the information that can be further inferred from it) with the creation of documents. Ultimately, you will need to track information; however, the manner in which you choose to store that information should best suit the needs of your organization—and in our opinion, documents are rarely adequate.

One reason that CMMI is associated with obsessive documentation is the need to provide objective evidence for a CMMI appraisal. Objective evidence consists of qualitative or quantitative information, records, or statements of fact pertaining to the characteristics of an item or a service or to the existence and implementation of a process element (*Software Engineering Institute: Standard CMMI Appraisal Method for Process Improvement [SCAMPI]*, Version 1.1: Method Definition Document, December 2001, page 1–11 and Glossary).

> **Note**   Microsoft Visual Studio Team System uses several different approaches to help an organization produce objective evidence for a CMMI appraisal. First, evidence gathering is a by-product of the normal development cycle. In other words, Visual Studio Team System captures process-related evidence automatically in the normal course of using the tool. Second, Visual Studio Team System generates reports, not documents, as the artifact-generation tool.

The most important aspect of CMMI is its underlying theme of continual process improvement and the management of organizational change. This aspect of CMMI will force you to look at your processes and say, "Yeah, that didn't work, let's try something new," instead of simply continuing to make bad choices or relying upon heroics for varied results. On the other hand, you may find things that worked really well and say, "Hey, let's make sure we do that again." If you find that your organization is producing too much documentation without making any positive impact on the quality of your process, software, or services, CMMI promotes a model that encourages you to change to help ensure that the highest degree of value is flowing through and out of your team and your organization. CMMI stresses gradual change because it is very difficult to simply jump to a high level of CMMI maturity or capability. This gradual and yet continual model of positive change is really the end goal of CMMI, achieved at Level 5, which focuses on continual process improvement that encourages organizational improvement and innovation around process and technology.

The Pieces of CMMI

This book is likely not the best reference for any great detail regarding the inner workings of CMMI. We have decided, however, to include a bit of a discussion of its basic premise and highlight the structures that you should be familiar with to help you navigate the Microsoft Solution Framework's (MSF) implementation of CMMI Level 3, called MSF 4.0 for CMMI Process Improvement.

The Big Picture

Before jumping headlong into any CMMI implementation, you should be aware that CMMI has two representations: Continuous and Staged. What's the difference? Well, consider two perspectives you can take regarding process improvement. The first perspective is a representation of how well your organization can perform a certain type of task, such as managing requirements or managing projects. This perspective would be equivalent to the Continuous representation of CMMI. In this case, capability is assessed by establishing baselines and then measuring improvements in each of the individual processes specified by CMMI. The other perspective may be based on how well the entire organization is able to deliver software solutions. This perspective is equivalent to CMMI's Staged representation. A Staged CMMI representation takes a look at clusters of processes that are used to establish distinct stages of maturity across an organization, providing much more of an organizational roadmap to process improvement. Figure A-2 depicts CMMI's representations and highlights some of the other aspects of each model.

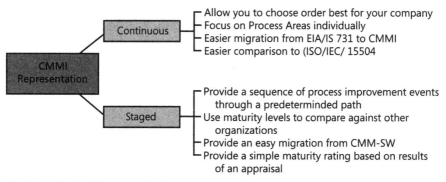

Figure A-2   CMMI representations

Another key concept within any representation of CMMI is that of a process area. *Process areas* are groupings of the most significant topics of process improvement. Each process area has a very specific process improvement target. In addition, each process area has a set of goals that describe the results of a successful process. Each goal, in turn, has a set of practices that can aid in the achievement of the goal. Any goal that is specific to a process area is called a *specific goal* (SG). Every process area must have a goal, and in this light, specific goals are referred to as *required material* with regards to the definition of a process area. Goals that can be applied to all process areas are called *generic goals* (GGs). When you achieve a generic goal in a process area, you are demonstrating control over the planning and implementation of that process area, which provides an indication that the processes are more likely to be effective and repeatable. According to the definition of a process area, *practices* are activities performed to achieve a goal. When a practice is unique to a process area, it is called a *specific practice* (SP) and is considered to be an *expected material* in the definition of a process area. Why expected and not mandatory? The purpose of all process areas is to achieve certain goals. How you choose to achieve those goals isn't mandatory, and the practices provided are also not mandatory. When a practice is associated with a generic goal that applies to multiple practices areas, it is called a *generic practice* (GP). Process areas can also describe other pieces of information called *informative materials*, such as references, formal names, notes, typical work products, subpractices, and something called *discipline amplifications*, which is differentiation information of the process area for a given discipline. Figure A-3 represents the relationship between goals and practices with regards to a process area definition.

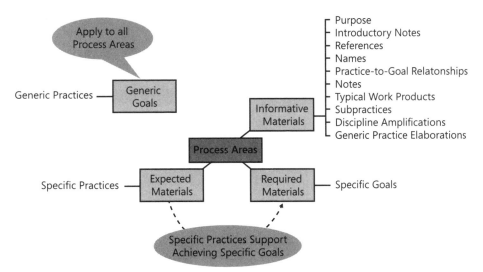

Figure A-3   Structure of a process area definition

CMMI specifies 25 different process areas across four process area categories: Process Management, Project Management, Engineering, and Support. Table A-2 at the end of this appendix contains a summary of these process areas grouped by process area categories along with a summary of their purpose.

CMMI encompasses many different disciplines, including systems engineering (SE), software engineering (SW), integrated product and process development (IPPD), and supplier sourcing (SS), as shown in Figure A-4. These disciplines are unique enough to demand special attention within the CMMI model, and for this reason, we have discipline amplifications within the process area definitions.

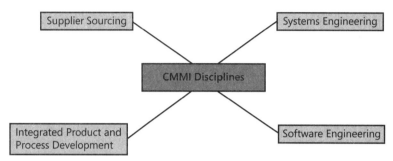

Figure A-4 Structure of a process area definition

CMMI provides you with the ability to obtain specific versions of the model that are more tuned to different disciplines. Table A-1 summarizes the available combinations.

Table A-1 Available Downloads for CMMI

Downloadable Document	Description
CMMI-SW	Covers only the Software Engineering discipline
CMMI-SE/SW	Covers the Software Engineering and Systems Engineering disciplines
CMMI-SE/SW/IPPD	Covers the Software Engineering, Systems Engineering, and Integrated Product and Process Development disciplines
CMMI-SE/SW/IPPD/SS	Covers all four disciplines

For more information about the details of each process area, refer to the Software Engineering Institute's Web site. In addition, this site provides you with the ability to download the specifications, in either PDF or Office Word format, for the CMMI model according to discipline.

Staged Representation

CMMI provides a staged representation that works to supply a detailed roadmap consisting of five stages of a process improvement initiative from an organizational perspective. Each of the five stages is called a *maturity level*, and each has a set of associated process areas that guide the organization's focus at that level. The staged representation relies upon a maturity dimension, as opposed to a capability dimension, as its measuring stick, with each maturity level having a characteristic or theme associated with it in much the same way that capabilities are described in a Continuous CMMI representation. The maturity levels specified in the Staged representation, along with their associated process areas, are depicted in Figure A-5.

Organizations can have a formal assessment conducted by qualified CMMI appraisers to determine the maturity level for which they comply. If you have ever heard of a company being appraised at Level 3, the maturity level within the Staged representation is likely what was being referred to. The appraisal process works to evaluate the entire organization by taking a look at how many goals have been achieved for each process area. For example, if an organization has been appraised at Level 3, this means that all of the specific goals for each process area identified with Level 3 have been achieved along with the specific goals in all lower levels, in this case, Level 2 (there are no process areas associated with the maturity level of 1).

> **Note**   CMM-SW was one of the first representations to introduce a similar five-level model of maturity.

Level	Process Areas	Result
Level 5: Optimizing Continuous Improvement	Organizational Innovation and Deployment Causal Analysis and Resolution	Productivity Quality
Level 4: Managed Quantitative Management	Organizational Process Performance Quantitative Project Management	
Level 3: Defined Quantitative Management	Requirements Development Technical Solution Product Integration Verification Validation Organizational Process Focus Organizational Process Definition Organizational Training Integrated Project Management for IPPD Risk Management Integrated Teaming Integrated Supplier Management Decision Analysis and Resolution Organizational Environment for Integration	
Level 2: Repeatable Individual Initiative	Requirements Management Project Planning Project Monitoring and Control Supplier Agreement Management Measurement and Analysis Process and Product Quality Assurance Configuration Management	
Level 1: Initial Heroic Efforts	Design Code Compile Test	Risk Waste

Figure A-5   Staged maturity model

Continuous Representation

The Continuous representation of CMMI does not provide any specific guidance regarding the order in which you choose to conduct your process-improvement activities. The practices and processes in a continual model are organized in a way that supports achievements in individual process areas in a manner that best suits the needs of your organization. With this model, each process area is appraised at its own capability level, resulting in an organization that will likely have different process areas rated at different capability levels, as depicted in Figure A-6.

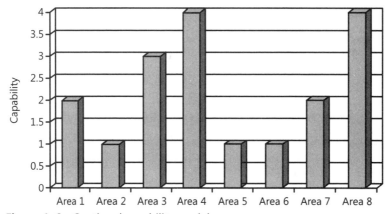

Figure A-6   Continual capability model

There are five levels of capability represented in the Continual model based on the capability dimension, as opposed to the maturity dimension used in the staged representation. Like the maturity dimension, each level is given a name that works to depict the theme associated with that particular level. The names of the capability levels are:

- Level 1: Performed
- Level 2: Managed
- Level 3: Defined
- Level 4: Quantitatively Managed
- Level 5: Optimizing

Although the names of the maturity levels seem to correspond to the names of capability levels, they are still quite different because capability levels are applied to individual process areas, whereas maturity levels apply to a set of process areas and their associated specific goals.

Note   Continuous representation includes a method called *equivalent staging*, which enables the results of appraisals using Continuous representation to be translated into maturity levels (Software Engineering Institute: *Capability Maturity Model Integration (CMMI)*, Version 1.1, Continuous Representation, March 2002, Appendix F).

Choosing Between Representations

Staged, Continual—where do you start? Which one is right for you? A lot of organizations begin with the Staged model, primarily because it's been used very successfully with very good results for a number of years. A Staged representation provides a clean path from working to improve project management to providing organization-wide process definitions, to using quantitative analysis techniques for improving and optimizing behavior. Continual models of process improvement precede Staged models, yet they are likely used less often in practice. Most CMMI practitioners who value the Continual model do so because of its flexibility and freedom. With the Continual model, organizations can better align the order and priority of process-improvement activities based on the needs of the business and team. Many also like the amount of detail Continual models provide with respect to reporting—the ability to see an individual process area's capability specifically. Figure A-7 demonstrates these concepts and possible benefits that you might realize as a result of choosing one model over another.

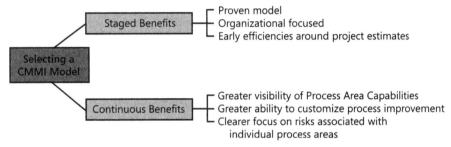

Figure A-7   Benefit comparison between Staged versus Continuous representation

CMMI Process Area Reference

Table A-2 summarizes process areas, categorizing them and explaining the purpose of each.

Table A-2   Lists and Definitions of Process Areas

Process Area	Purpose
Process Management Areas	
Organizational Process Focus	To plan and implement organizational process improvement based on a thorough understanding of the current strengths and weaknesses of the organization's processes and process assets.
Organizational Process Definition	To establish and maintain a usable set of organizational process assets.
Organizational Training	To develop the skills and knowledge of people so they can perform their roles effectively and efficiently.
Organizational Process Performance	To establish and maintain a quantitative understanding of the performance of the organization's set of standard processes in support of its quality and process-performance objectives and to provide the process's performance data, baselines, and models to quantitatively manage the organization's projects.

Table A-2   Lists and Definitions of Process Areas (Continued)

Process Area	Purpose
Organizational Innovation and Deployment	To select and deploy incremental and innovative improvements that measurably improve the organization's processes and technologies. The improvements support the organization's quality and process performance objectives as derived from the organization's business objectives.
Project Management Areas	To establish and maintain plans that specify project activities.
Project Planning	To provide an understanding of the project's progress so that appropriate corrective actions can be taken when the project's performance deviates significantly from the plan.
Project Monitoring and Control	To manage the acquisition of products from suppliers for which there exists a formal agreement.
Supplier Agreement Management	To establish and manage the project and the involvement of the relevant stakeholders according to an integrated and specified process that is tailored from the organization's set of standard processes. For Integrated Product and Process Development, Integrated Project Management also covers the establishment of a shared vision for the project and a team structure for integrated teams that will carry out the objectives of the project.
Integrated Project Management for IPPD	To identify potential problems before they occur so that risk-handling activities may be planned and invoked as needed across the life of the product or project to avoid adverse situations and deal with them effectively if they do occur.
Risk Management	To form and sustain an integrated team for the development of work products.
Integrated Teaming	To proactively identify sources of products that may be used to satisfy the project's requirements and to manage selected suppliers while maintaining a cooperative project-supplier relationship.
Integrated Supplier Management	To quantitatively manage the project's specified process to achieve the project's established quality and process-performance objectives.
Quantitative Project Management	To establish and maintain plans that specify project activities.
Engineering Process Areas	To provide an understanding of the project's progress so that appropriate corrective actions can be taken when the project's performance deviates significantly from the plan.
Requirements Management	To manage the requirements of the project's products and product components and to identify inconsistencies between those requirements and the project's plans and work products.
Requirements Development	To produce and analyze customer, product, and product-component requirements.

Table A-2   Lists and Definitions of Process Areas (Continued)

Process Area	Purpose
Technical Solution	To design, develop, and implement solutions to requirements. Solutions, designs, and implementations encompass products, product components, and product-related life cycle processes either singly or in combinations as appropriate.
Product Integration	To assemble the product from the product components, ensure that the product, as integrated, functions properly, and deliver the product.
Verification	To ensure that selected work products meet their specified requirements.
Validation	To demonstrate that a product or product component fulfills its intended use when placed in its intended environment.
Support Process Areas	
Configuration Management	To establish and maintain the integrity of work products by using configuration identification, configuration control, configuration status accounting, and configuration audits.
Process and Product Quality Assurance	To provide staff and management with objective insight into processes and associated work products.
Measurement and Analysis	To develop and sustain a measurement capability that is used to support management information needs.
Decision Analysis and Resolution	To analyze possible decisions using a formal evaluation process that evaluates identified alternatives against established criteria.
Organizational Environment For Integration	To provide an Integrated Product and Process Development (IPPD) infrastructure and manage people for integration.
Causal Analysis and Resolution	To identify causes of defects and other problems and take action to prevent them from occurring in the future.

Summary

This appendix provided an overview of the CMMI model, and we looked at the Staged and Continuous representations. We observed some of the structures of the CMMI model, explored some of its history and origins, and discussed how to choose among the available representations.

Microsoft Solutions Framework

- Understand what MSF is today and where it evolved from.
- Understand the structure and key components of MSF.
- Understand Agile software development methods.

Overview of MSF

Microsoft Solution Framework (MSF) is an Agile software development process framework for building software solutions. It incorporates the latest software development methods used by teams both inside and outside Microsoft. MSF utilizes proven Agile development techniques, extends the Agile approach to all phases of the development life cycle and provides specific guidance for each role on the software development team.

The latest version of the Microsoft Solution Framework, MSF 4.0, is built from the ground up with Microsoft Visual Studio Team System in mind. Why tie the methodology so tightly to the development environment? One of the biggest problems to plague most development methodologies is the lack of good tools to support the methodology. Development teams are often left to struggle with poorly integrated tools that were never meant to support the process. As a result, the team comes to view the methodology itself as a cumbersome impediment. Visual Studio Team System offers a set of tightly integrated tools, and MSF 4.0 is designed to take full advantage of those process tools. In this way, MSF and Visual Studio Team System complement one another; MSF is the methodology that guides the process, whereas Visual Studio Team System is the tool set that enacts the process.

Visual Studio Team System includes two versions of MSF. *MSF for Agile Software Development* (MSF Agile) is geared toward an adaptive process for smaller teams. *MSF for CMMI Process Improvement* (MSF CMMI) is geared toward a refinement process for teams that require a more rigorous approach. It is designed to accelerate the achievement of CMMI Level 3 with an emphasis on automation rather than documentation.

Each MSF version is implemented as a *process template*, which is a set of configuration files that tells Visual Studio Team System how to set up a new Team Project. The process template effectively sets the methodology for the project by specifying which tools will be used and how those tools will be configured and by installing the process guidance documentation.

Visual Studio Team System provides a framework for process innovation that allows the process template to be readily customized for individual projects. Each project can run a separate version of a process, yet the metrics can be consolidated across all projects, regardless of process choice.

A Brief History of MSF

MSF was first introduced in 1994 as a loose collection of best practices from Microsoft's product development efforts and Microsoft Consulting Services engagements. MSF has evolved based on learning from the successful, real-world best practices of Microsoft development groups, Microsoft partners, and Microsoft customers.

MSF is managed and developed by a dedicated product team within Microsoft with guidance and review from an international advisory council of subject matter experts. MSF also continues to draw upon current Microsoft experience. The best practices from these internal project efforts are consolidated and distributed outside of Microsoft through MSF.

Note　The MSF product team encourages feedback from the growing community of practitioners though a public forum on the MSDN Web site. This is an excellent place to get your questions answered and see what others are saying about MSF. You can access the forum at *http://forums.microsoft.com/msdn/showforum.aspx?forumid=63.*

Microsoft conducted market research to determine what should be included in MSF for Visual Studio Team System. This research indicated that the market wanted a method for enacting Agile software development. Most of this demand was coming from North America. However, there was also a significant demand for the ability to enact and accelerate CMMI appraisal to Level 3. This demand was coming mostly from Asia, but it also included large defense contractors in North America.

Agile Software Development

MSF utilizes a lightweight, adaptive approach known as *Agile software development*. Agile software replaces the traditional phased approach to software development, known as the *waterfall life cycle model*, with a more nimble approach that utilizes iterative, incremental development based on short delivery cycles. Each iteration is of fixed duration, typically 2 to 8 weeks. The goal of each iteration is to produce working software–a product that may not be feature complete but that is shippable. This technique, also referred to as *timeboxing*, minimizes risk by breaking up a software development project into a series of mini projects, each with a fixed time frame. These mini projects are much easier to manage than one large monolithic project, and they offer the opportunity to change course, or adapt, from one iteration to the next.

Although Agile software development has its roots in various iterative and incremental delivery methods going back several decades, the mid-1990s saw the emergence of a variety of lightweight methods that later came to be known as *Agile*.

Manifesto for Agile Software Development

The term *Agile* was first applied to software development in 2001 by a group of prominent thinkers who represented various philosophies, including Extreme Programming, Scrum,

Dynamic Systems Development Method (DSDM), Adaptive Software Development, Crystal, Feature-Driven Development, and Pragmatic Programming. Later known as the *Agile Alliance*, this diverse and outspoken group of individuals introduced the world to the concept of Agile software development by way of a manifesto, complete with underlying principles. You can read the manifesto on the Agile Alliance Web site.

Innovations in MSF

Although MSF is built on Agile methods that are popular in the mainstream development community, it adds many new twists. Here are some of the ways that MSF extends Agile software development methods:

- MSF is the first Agile methodology that covers the entire software development life cycle and all of the team roles.

- MSF incorporates the notion of designing for operations, which is similar in concept to designing for manufacturing. This means that deployment and maintenance are taken into consideration early in the development process, not after the fact.

- MSF takes a unique approach to risk management. The Team Model in MSF offers seven constituencies of risk concern: Product Management, Program Management, User Experience, Architecture, Development, Test, and Release and Operations. Each of these constituencies must have at least one advocate to ensure appropriate coverage of concerns to mitigate risk. Roles within MSF are mapped against Team Model constituencies as advocates. Risks are identified based on prior data and experience from the advocates of each risk constituency. The probability of occurrence is weighed against the cost of mitigation and the impact of occurrence. Mitigation actions are then planned and managed to reduce the likelihood of occurrence, and consequently, they reduce variation in capacity. The advocates are then responsible for day-to-day risk monitoring.

- MSF utilizes lean project management with staggered planning. This approach is based on the assumption that creating software is a process of discovery. There are too many unknowns at the beginning of a project to create a detailed project plan. Furthermore, the requirements often change during the course of development. For this reason MSF takes an adaptive approach that involves an initial project plan that describes the overall approach and scope of the project and also establishes iteration length. The planning for each iteration occurs during the previous iteration so that the transition from one iteration to another can occur quickly and smoothly. In this way, planning is done progressively throughout the project, as needed, just in time, which makes the planning process highly adaptive.

- MSF specifies a system in terms of Scenarios and Quality of Service (QoS) requirements. A *Scenario* describes a specific user interaction with the system, a sequence of steps with a clearly defined result. A *QoS requirement* describes characteristics of the system such as security, performance, load, availability, stress, accessibility, serviceability, and maintainability.

- MSF uses *personas* to describes the various groups of users. Each persona is a composite description of the relevant characteristics of a particular user group.

- MSF introduces an Agile architecture design technique called *shadowing*. A leading shadow describes the architecture to be implemented in an iteration. As pieces of the leading shadow are implemented, they are moved to the trailing shadow. When the iteration is complete, the leading shadow is empty because all of the implemented parts have moved to the trailing shadow. In this way the trailing shadow is the accumulation of the architectures implemented so far. In other words, the trailing shadow always represents the architecture of the system as currently implemented.

- MSF utilizes test thresholds, which are metrics that specify the minimum quality required to release the product. Each test threshold acts as a quality gate. If the product doesn't measure up to the test threshold, it doesn't ship. Test thresholds are determined by the project team based on QoS requirements. The testing strategy is then based in part on these test thresholds. A typical test threshold is code coverage, that is, the percentage of the total code actually executed by unit tests. Simple projects that are not critical to the business may have a very low code coverage threshold, whereas complex applications involving life safety will have a very high code coverage threshold.

- MSF separates governance from capacity. *Governance* involves the allocation of resources to projects. It's the management process used to maximize the flow of value to the customer by selecting the best projects to work on. *Capacity* involves the people, processes, and tools used to implement projects. Capacity seeks to maximize the flow of value to the customer by continually improving productivity and quality. *Governance* and *Capacity* both work to optimize the effectiveness of the software development effort in different yet complementary ways.

- MSF utilizes the automated reporting capabilities of Visual Studio Team System to create trustworthy transparency. Visual Studio Team System automatically tracks work item progress and links it to version control. In this way, collection of process data is an automatic by-product of the development process, and the work products are directly tied to this process data. As a result, the data generated by Visual Studio Team System is both transparent and trustworthy. MSF takes advantage of trustworthy transparency by focusing on the use of reports to drive objective, rational management decisions and interventions. MSF metrics are self-generating, relevant, and leading (or predictive) indicators of project health. Trustworthy transparency leads to realistic schedules, reliable estimates, sustainable pace of work, and professional maturity rather than a reliance on heroic efforts.

Components of MSF

MSF is a framework made up of various conceptual components. These components, shown in Figure B-1, represent a set of practices that complement each other in such a way that the sum of the practices is greater than each one used in isolation.

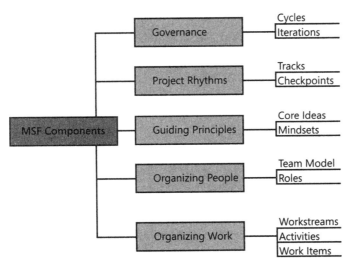

Figure B-1   MSF components

Cycles and Iterations

Software development projects based on MSF utilize an iterative development process. In other words, a project is split up into a series of mini-projects called *iterations* that last a few weeks each. As such, MSF-based projects are cyclical in that each iteration starts with planning, followed by execution, and wrapped up with a retrospective evaluation. Although the work performed changes from one iteration to the next, the cyclical nature of the iterations give the project a rhythm that helps the project team perform. The repetition produces a sense of familiarity, and with each iteration the team gets better at what they are doing—fine-tuning the process, increasing their velocity and improving their productivity.

Every iteration, except the first, begins with an iteration plan. An *iteration plan* specifies the Scenarios, QoS requirements, and bug allotments that are scheduled for the iteration. In the first iteration, the second iteration is planned. In the second iteration, the development and test team work on the tasks that they have chosen from this plan. Meanwhile, the third iteration is planned. In this way, there is only one checkpoint: the end of one iteration and the beginning of another. The retrospective and iteration planning meeting mark this checkpoint.

Advantages of iterative development include:

- Continuous learning and refinement.
- Mid-course corrections can be made.
- Reduced margin of error in your estimates.
- Fast feedback about the accuracy of your project plans.

Each iteration results in completion of a stable portion of the overall system. In many internal IT projects, each iteration also results in the a new release of the application. This allows the development team to deliver useful results to the customer early and often. In MSF, putting useful software into the hands of the customer is known as *flow of value*.

Governance

Governance involves the management of resources with the goal of maximizing the flow of value to the customer. MSF governance concerns itself primarily with aligning IT projects toward the benefit of the overall organization and its stakeholders. To that end, MSF governance ensures that each project obtains the required approvals and direction at clearly specified checkpoints throughout the project life cycle (Figure B-2).

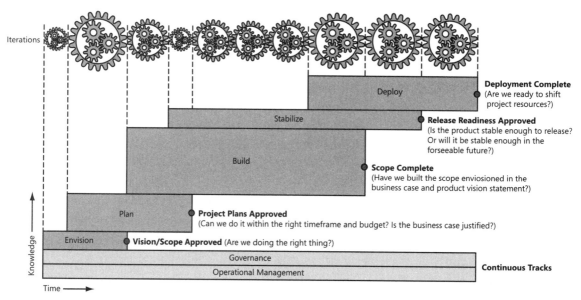

Figure B-2   MSF tracks

MSF specifies five tracks with each track representing a logical group of activities associated with a specific governance checkpoint. Each checkpoint is like a go-no-go gate through which the project must successfully pass in order to continue. This go-no-go gate consists of one or more governance questions. The answers to those questions result in a management decision, and the management decision brings the track to an end.

Principles and Mindsets

The behavior of a highly effective software development team can be described in terms of the principles that guide the team's actions. Principles empower the team by providing a framework that guides the team's day-to-day decisions. MSF offers a set of principles that the team can use as a starting point as it establishes its own principles.

Core Ideas

MSF divides principles into core ideas and mindsets that complement one another. The core ideas embody an overall philosophy, whereas the mindsets suggest a way of thinking that motivates the actions of individual team members. The core ideas are as follows:

Partner with Customers   Software development is a process of discovery. As mentioned before, many software development projects start with ambiguous, incomplete requirements. For this reason, it is important that the project team work closely with the customers to better understand their needs and to frequently solicit their feedback as work progresses. This partnership is vitally important for the project team to deliver the greatest value to the customer.

Foster Open Communications   People are competitive by nature. To that end, some folks are reluctant to share information with their teammates because they think it will give the others a competitive advantage. This sort of attitude is counter-productive because it hurts overall team performance. It is important that every team member understands that their indivual success is tied directly to the success of the team. When team members think of success in these terms, communications will flow freely thoroughout the team. People make better decisions when they have all the facts at their disposal. It's interesting to note that this free flow of information helps the team because it maximizes individual effectiveness. In this way, the person who shares information freely with the rest of the team is more likely to be personally successful than the team member who withholds information.

Work Toward a Shared Vision   Think about it—every great team achieves outstanding performance when all the members share a common vision of the team's ultimate objective. A software development team is no different. That shared vision focuses the team members on a common goal, which naturally leads to an alignment of interests. A shared vision promotes cooperation and collaboration within the team based on a sense of common purpose.

Quality Is Everyone's Business Every Day   Enlightened manufacturers have learned that quality is not something you can achieve by inspecting the product after it is produced. Quality must be built into the product at every step in the process. This is true for any type of product, from toasters to televisions to automobiles. Software is no different in this regard. All the team members should feel a sense of responsibility for software quality regardless of their roles. The quality of the final product—the software—depends on each step in the development process, from design to implementation to deployment. Defects can be introduced at any point in the process. Of course, testing is still important to ensure that the software performs as expected. However, Agile project teams don't wait until the software is complete to perform testing. Rather, they utilize testing throughout the development cycle to verify that each new feature added is performing correctly and that all previously implemented features continue to work properly. In general, the earlier a defect is caught, the less expensive it is to repair. However, the best defect is the defect that never happened. To that end, pride of workmanship and continuous improvement are very important to software quality.

Stay Agile, Adapt to Change   We live in a turbulent world of uncertainty and change. Your project team must function in this environment. Change is a fact of life: new opportunities pop up; problems occur; platform technologies evolve; new patterns and practices emerge; project team members come and go; and so on. The best way to cope with change is to embrace it, and the best way to embrace change is to take an incremental approach. Don't try to plan too far ahead. Do work in short iterative cycles. At the end of each iteration, evaluate the results, make adjustments, and then do it again. This approach forms the basis for Agile software development.

Make Deployment a Habit   One area where software development teams run into problems is deployment. Frequently, software works perfectly in the development environment, but when the team goes to deploy it, all sorts of problems crop up. The deployment environment might use a different version of the operating system, or maybe it's missing some required components. And then there is the common issue of misconfigured permissions that prevent things from working. By making deployment a habit and by practicing and testing deployment procedures, even with early–life cycle prototypes, the whole team learns how to make deployments run smoothly and predictably.

Flow of Value   The flow of value refers to the delivery of business value in the form of software from the project team to the customer. It's a subtle but important distinction for a team to realize that its objective is not to deliver software per se, but rather to deliver business value. When team members start thinking of their work in terms of the flow of value it produces, then value-added practices start replacing wasteful practices, which in turn leads to increased productivity, increased throughput, reduced costs, improved quality, and increased customer satisfaction.

Mindsets

Quality Is Specified by the Customer   Software exists to satisfy the needs of its intended audience—the customer. To that end, it's the customer who ultimately determines quality in terms of the software's ability to meet its intended purpose. A customer-oriented mindset means that the project team's number one priority is to understand and solve the customer's business problem.

Pride of Workmanship   The quality of a software solution tends to be directly related to the pride the project team takes in its design and construction. Team members who take pride in their work pay attention to the details that make the difference between merely satisfactory software and really great software. Pride of workmanship comes from within each team member, but as a project manager, you can reinforce this sense of pride through recognition for a job well done.

Team of Peers   Each member of a software development project team contributes to the development process. This team-of-peers mindset places an equal value on each of the team members and the roles they play. No one team member is more important than another. This sense of equality produces more open and transparent communications as well as a common sense of accountability for the outcome of the project.

Frequent Delivery   Historically software development teams delivered a software solution only after it was feature complete; i.e., it met all the requirements. Iterative development methods allow a project team to take a different approach by delivering the software solution incrementally. Frequent incremental delivery offers many benefits. The most important benefit is that it accelerates the flow of value to the customer. In most cases software does not need to be feature complete to be of value to the customer. By implementing the most valuable features first—as determined by the customer—and then delivering the software incrementally as features are completed, the project team allows the customer to realize that value as soon as possible. The team establishes credibility when it delivers useful results to the customer early and often. What's more, frequent delivery provides important customer feedback that allows the team to detect and resolve risks, bugs, and missing requirements in a timely manner. Frequent delivery also allows the team to validate and improve its processes and infrastructure.

Willingness to Learn   Software development teams perform best when their members have a thirst for knowledge. Software development is a rapidly changing field in which technical knowledge quickly becomes obsolete. Team members who keep up on the latest advances in tools and methods are in the best position to evaluate alternatives and maximize the flow of value to the customer. But a willingness to learn goes beyond keeping up with technology. Each project, indeed each iteration, offers an opportunity for the team to learn from its successes and mistakes and apply those lessons learned to their ongoing efforts. As a project manager, you can foster a learning environment by scheduling time for reviews, retrospectives, and training activities.

Get Specific Early   Analysis and design are important aspects to every software development project. However, it's possible to have too much of a good thing. In other words, the team can spend too much team designing an elegant solution instead of tackling solvable problems. This mindset encourages the team to define the big picture in broad strokes, then define specific goals through scenarios, and then describe specific implementation through the use of storyboards and prototypes. Getting specific early provides concrete examples that facilitate communications which, in turn, provides a rich source of feedback that further informs the design process. Getting specific early is key to clearly understanding both the problem and the solution, which is key to effectively building working code, passing tests, and creating deployable bits.

Qualities of Service   Software development teams have a natural tendency to focus on features initially and defer quality of service considerations such as performance, security, and scalability. It's important to keep in mind that quality of service requirements are often just as important as features in terms of value to the customer. A system with unacceptable response time is just as useless to a customer as a system with the wrong features. Failure to consider quality of service requirements early in the project can lead to expensive rework later. A quality-of-service mindset looks at the solution and develops plans based on every aspect of the customer experience.

MSF Team Model

The Team Model, depicted in Figure B-3, describes a team of peers who represent all of the constituencies involved in the production, use, and maintenance of the product. Each team member acts as an advocate on behalf of the constituency that he or she represents. There is no hierarchy involved—no team member is more important than another. This approach reduces risk by producing a system of checks and balances that guides the team toward the right solution.

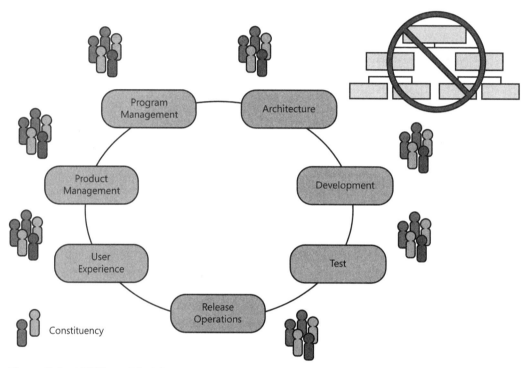

Figure B-3 MSF Team Model

The fundamental principles of the MSF Team Model are:

- A *team of peers* with clear accountability, shared responsibility, and open communications. Each role is accountable for a specific share of the quality of the overall solution.

- *Advocacy* for all key constituencies who must be represented on a successful software project. Every perspective is represented to provide the checks and balances that prevent errors of omission and lopsided decisions.

- *Stretch to fit* to the scale necessary for the specific project. Constituencies may be combined in small teams or further refined as teams scale for larger projects.

Roles

Each member of the project team plays at least one of the roles and is accountable for advocating on behalf of the constituency that that role represents within the Team Model.

Table B-1 shows how MSF Roles relate to the MSF Team Model advocacy groups.

Table B-1   Mapping MSF Roles to the MSF Team Model

	Roles	
Team Model Advocacy Groups	**MSF Agile**	**MSF CMMI**
Program Management	Project Manager	IPM Officer
		Project Manager
Architecture	Architect	Infrastructure Architect
		Solution Architect
Development	Developer	Build Engineer
		Developer
		Development Manager
		Lead Developer
Test	Tester	Test Manager
		Tester
Release/Operations	Releaser Manager	Release Manager
User Experience	Business Analyst	User Education Specialist
		User Experience Architect
Product Management	Business Analyst	Auditor
		Business Analyst
		Product Manager
		Sponsor
		Subject Matter Expert

Workstreams, Activities, and Work Items

MSF organizes work into workstreams and activities and then tracks work by using work items. A *workstream* is a group of activities that flow logically together and are often associated with a particular role. An *activity* is work performed to accomplish a specific objective. For instance, Define Personas is an activity that produces a specific work product—namely a Personas document.

Roles are assigned to each workstream and activity by using a common project management technique called RACI, which is an acronym that represents the four assignment categories:

- **Responsible** One or more roles responsible for performing the work.
- **Accountable** The one role with overall responsibility for the workstream or activity.

- **Consulted** The roles that provide input.

- **Informed** The roles the members of whom should be kept informed, that is, they have a vested interest.

A work item is a database record on the Visual Studio 2005 Team Foundation Server that is used to track the assignment and state of work, as shown in Table B-2. Each version of MSF has its own unique set of work items, which you can customize to meet the needs of your organization or project. You can add or remove work items and even add or remove fields for each work item.

Table B-2   MSF Work Items Track the Assignment and State of Work

MSF Agile	MSF CMMI
Bug	Bug
QoS requirement	Change Request
Risk	Issue
Scenario	Requirement
Task	Review
	Risk
	Task

MSF at a Glance

The MSF Process Guidance, the Web-based documentation built into the MSF process templates, does a great job of providing context-based guidance at each step of a project. As a project manager, you will most likely click the Roles tab, select Project Manager, select the appropriate track, and then view the relevant workstreams, activities, work items, examples, and templates.

Sometimes, though, it's helpful to see the big picture. Understanding the overall structure of MSF gives context to the individual activities and work items. There are many different dimensions to MSF: tracks, workstreams, activities, roles, responsibilities, and so on. As a result, it's difficult to show all these dimensions at once, especially when you need to represent it in two dimensions on the page of a book.

As it turns out, the Responsibility Matrix, a familiar project-management tool, does a pretty good job of showing the overall structure of MSF at a glance. Figure B-4 shows a portion of the Responsibility Matrix for MSF Agile. You can find the complete Responsibility Matrix for MSF Agile as a PDF document at *http://blog.arrowrock.com/sourceart/2006/02/07/MSFAnalysis-Tool.aspx*. This article also includes a PDF document containing the Responsibility Matrix for MSF CMMI.

Track/Workstream/Activity	Architect	Business Analyst	Developer	Project Manager	Release Manager	Tester
Envision						
Capture Project Vision						
Define Personas		R				
Write Vision Statement		R				
Plan an Iteration						
Determine Iteration length			C	R		
Plan						
Guide Project						
Assess Progress				R		
Review Objectives		C		R		
Build						
Create Solution Architecture						
Create Architectural Prototype	R					
Create Infrastructure Architecture	R					
Determine Interfaces	R		C			
Determine Performance Model	R		C			
Develop Threat Model	R					
Partition the System	R		C			
Implement a Development Task						
Cost a Development Task			R			
Perform Code Analysis			R			
Write Code for a Development Task			R			
Plan an Iteration						
Divide Quality of Service Requirements into Tasks	C		C	R		C
Divide Scenarios into Tasks	C		C	R		C

Figure B-4   Responsibility Matrix: MSF for Agile Software Development
(Entire chart available at *http://blog.arrowrock.com/sourceart/2006/02/07/MSFAnalysisTool.aspx*)

Index

X–Z

Joel Semeniuk

Joel Semeniuk is a Microsoft Regional Director and a Microsoft MVP in Team System with more than a decade of software project management experience. He has worked with Visual Studio Team System since its early development and has travelled the world lecturing, teaching, and helping customers adopt Team System. Joel is the author of two other books on programming software, and he blogs regularly about Visual Studio Team System and software development best practices.

Martin Danner

20 years and is a Project Management Professional (PMP) as well as a Microsoft Architect Most Valuable Professional. Martin contributed to a Microsoft Press book and Microsoft courseware on Visual Studio Team System during its development. Martin is a Senior Software Engineer at Healthwise, and he also provides training and consulting services through Accentient.

Additional Resources for C# Developers
Published and Forthcoming Titles from Microsoft Press

Microsoft® Visual C#® 2005 Express Edition: Build a Program Now!
Patrice Pelland • ISBN 0-7356-2229-9

In this lively, eye-opening, and hands-on book, all you need is a computer and the desire to learn how to program with Visual C# 2005 Express Edition. Featuring a full working edition of the software, this fun and highly visual guide walks you through a complete programming project—a desktop weather-reporting application—from start to finish. You'll get an unintimidating introduction to the Microsoft Visual Studio® development environment and learn how to put the lightweight, easy-to-use tools in Visual C# Express to work right away—creating, compiling, testing, and delivering your first, ready-to-use program. You'll get expert tips, coaching, and visual examples at each step of the way, along with pointers to additional learning resources.

Microsoft Visual C# 2005 *Step by Step*
John Sharp • ISBN 0-7356-2129-2

Visual C#, a feature of Visual Studio 2005, is a modern programming language designed to deliver a productive environment for creating business frameworks and reusable object-oriented components. Now you can teach yourself essential techniques with Visual C#—and start building components and Microsoft Windows®–based applications—one step at a time. With *Step by Step*, you work at your own pace through hands-on, learn-by-doing exercises. Whether you're a beginning programmer or new to this particular language, you'll learn how, when, and why to use specific features of Visual C# 2005. Each chapter puts you to work, building your knowledge of core capabilities and guiding you as you create your first C#-based applications for Windows, data management, and the Web.

Programming Microsoft Visual C# 2005 Framework Reference
Francesco Balena • ISBN 0-7356-2182-9

Complementing *Programming Microsoft Visual C# 2005 Core Reference*, this book covers a wide range of additional topics and information critical to Visual C# developers, including Windows Forms, working with Microsoft ADO.NET 2.0 and Microsoft ASP.NET 2.0, Web services, security, remoting, and much more. Packed with sample code and real-world examples, this book will help developers move from understanding to mastery.

Programming Microsoft Visual C# 2005 *Core Reference*
Donis Marshall • ISBN 0-7356-2181-0

Get the in-depth reference and pragmatic, real-world insights you need to exploit the enhanced language features and core capabilities in Visual C# 2005. Programming expert Donis Marshall deftly builds your proficiency with classes, structs, and other fundamentals, and advances your expertise with more advanced topics such as debugging, threading, and memory management. Combining incisive reference with hands-on coding examples and best practices, this *Core Reference* focuses on mastering the C# skills you need to build innovative solutions for smart clients and the Web.

CLR via C#, Second Edition
Jeffrey Richter • ISBN 0-7356-2163-2

In this new edition of Jeffrey Richter's popular book, you get focused, pragmatic guidance on how to exploit the common language runtime (CLR) functionality in Microsoft .NET Framework 2.0 for applications of all types—from Web Forms, Windows Forms, and Web services to solutions for Microsoft SQL Server™, Microsoft code names "Avalon" and "Indigo," consoles, Microsoft Windows NT® Service, and more. Targeted to advanced developers and software designers, this book takes you under the covers of .NET for an in-depth understanding of its structure, functions, and operational components, demonstrating the most practical ways to apply this knowledge to your own development efforts. You'll master fundamental design tenets for .NET and get hands-on insights for creating high-performance applications more easily and efficiently. The book features extensive code examples in Visual C# 2005.

Programming Microsoft Windows Forms
Charles Petzold • ISBN 0-7356-2153-5

CLR via C++
Jeffrey Richter with Stanley B. Lippman
ISBN 0-7356-2248-5

Programming Microsoft Web Forms
Douglas J. Reilly • ISBN 0-7356-2179-9

Debugging, Tuning, and Testing Microsoft .NET 2.0 Applications
John Robbins • ISBN 0-7356-2202-7

For more information about Microsoft Press® books and other learning products,
visit: **www.microsoft.com/books** *and* **www.microsoft.com/learning**

Additional Resources for Visual Basic Developers

Published and Forthcoming Titles from Microsoft Press

Microsoft® Visual Basic® 2005 Express Edition: Build a Program Now!
Patrice Pelland • ISBN 0-7356-2213-2

Featuring a full working edition of the software, this fun and highly visual guide walks you through a complete programming project—a desktop weather-reporting application—from start to finish. You'll get an introduction to the Microsoft Visual Studio® development environment and learn how to put the lightweight, easy-to-use tools in Visual Basic Express to work right away—creating, compiling, testing, and delivering your first ready-to-use program. You'll get expert tips, coaching, and visual examples each step of the way, along with pointers to additional learning resources.

Microsoft Visual Basic 2005 *Step by Step*
Michael Halvorson • ISBN 0-7356-2131-4

With enhancements across its visual designers, code editor, language, and debugger that help accelerate the development and deployment of robust, elegant applications across the Web, a business group, or an enterprise, Visual Basic 2005 focuses on enabling developers to rapidly build applications. Now you can teach yourself the essentials of working with Visual Studio 2005 and the new features of the Visual Basic language—one step at a time. Each chapter puts you to work, showing you how, when, and why to use specific features of Visual Basic and guiding as you create actual components and working applications for Microsoft Windows®. You'll also explore data management and Web-based development topics.

Programming Microsoft Visual Basic 2005 *Core Reference*
Francesco Balena • ISBN 0-7356-2183-7

Get the expert insights, indispensable reference, and practical instruction needed to exploit the core language features and capabilities in Visual Basic 2005. Well-known Visual Basic programming author Francesco Balena expertly guides you through the fundamentals, including modules, keywords, and inheritance, and builds your mastery of more advanced topics such as delegates, assemblies, and My Namespace. Combining in-depth reference with extensive, hands-on code examples and best-practices advice, this *Core Reference* delivers the key resources that you need to develop professional-level programming skills for smart clients and the Web.

Programming Microsoft Visual Basic 2005 Framework Reference
Francesco Balena • ISBN 0-7356-2175-6

Complementing *Programming Microsoft Visual Basic 2005 Core Reference*, this book covers a wide range of additional topics and information critical to Visual Basic developers, including Windows Forms, working with Microsoft ADO.NET 2.0 and ASP.NET 2.0, Web services, security, remoting, and much more. Packed with sample code and real-world examples, this book will help developers move from understanding to mastery.

Programming Microsoft Windows Forms
Charles Petzold • ISBN 0-7356-2153-5

Programming Microsoft Web Forms
Douglas J. Reilly • ISBN 0-7356-2179-9

Debugging, Tuning, and Testing Microsoft .NET 2.0 Applications
John Robbins • ISBN 0-7356-2202-7

Microsoft ASP.NET 2.0 *Step by Step*
George Shepherd • ISBN 0-7356-2201-9

Microsoft ADO.NET 2.0 *Step by Step*
Rebecca Riordan • ISBN 0-7356-2164-0

Programming Microsoft ASP.NET 2.0 *Core Reference*
Dino Esposito • ISBN 0-7356-2176-4

For more information about Microsoft Press® books and other learning products, visit: **www.microsoft.com/books** *and* **www.microsoft.com/learning**

Additional Resources for Developers: Advanced Topics and Best Practices

Published and Forthcoming Titles from Microsoft Press

Code Complete, Second Edition
Steve McConnell • ISBN 0-7356-1967-0

For more than a decade, Steve McConnell, one of the premier authors and voices in the software community, has helped change the way developers write code—and produce better software. Now his classic book, *Code Complete*, has been fully updated and revised with best practices in the art and science of constructing software. Topics include design, applying good techniques to construction, eliminating errors, planning, managing construction activities, and relating personal character to superior software. This new edition features fully updated information on programming techniques, including the emergence of Web-style programming, and integrated coverage of object-oriented design. You'll also find new code examples—both good and bad—in C++, Microsoft® Visual Basic®, C#, and Java, although the focus is squarely on techniques and practices.

More About Software Requirements: Thorny Issues and Practical Advice
Karl E. Wiegers • ISBN 0-7356-2267-1

Have you ever delivered software that satisfied all of the project specifications, but failed to meet any of the customers expectations? Without formal, verifiable requirements—and a system for managing them—the result is often a gap between what developers think they're supposed to build and what customers think they're going to get. Too often, lessons about software requirements engineering processes are formal or academic, and not of value to real-world, professional development teams. In this follow-up guide to *Software Requirements*, Second Edition, you will discover even more practical techniques for gathering and managing software requirements that help you deliver software that meets project and customer specifications. Succinct and immediately useful, this book is a must-have for developers and architects.

Software Estimation: Demystifying the Black Art
Steve McConnell • ISBN 0-7356-0535-1

Often referred to as the "black art" because of its complexity and uncertainty, software estimation is not as hard or mysterious as people think. However, the art of how to create effective cost and schedule estimates has not been very well publicized. *Software Estimation* provides a proven set of procedures and heuristics that software developers, technical leads, and project managers can apply to their projects. Instead of arcane treatises and rigid modeling techniques, award-winning author Steve McConnell gives practical guidance to help organizations achieve basic estimation proficiency and lay the groundwork to continue improving project cost estimates. This book does not avoid the more complex mathematical estimation approaches, but the non-mathematical reader will find plenty of useful guidelines without getting bogged down in complex formulas.

Debugging, Tuning, and Testing Microsoft .NET 2.0 Applications
John Robbins • ISBN 0-7356-2202-7

Making an application the best it can be has long been a time-consuming task best accomplished with specialized and costly tools. With Microsoft Visual Studio® 2005, developers have available a new range of built-in functionality that enables them to debug their code quickly and efficiently, tune it to optimum performance, and test applications to ensure compatibility and trouble-free operation. In this accessible and hands-on book, debugging expert John Robbins shows developers how to use the tools and functions in Visual Studio to their full advantage to ensure high-quality applications.

The Security Development Lifecycle
Michael Howard and Steve Lipner • ISBN 0-7356-2214-0

Adapted from Microsoft's standard development process, the Security Development Lifecycle (SDL) is a methodology that helps reduce the number of security defects in code at every stage of the development process, from design to release. This book details each stage of the SDL methodology and discusses its implementation across a range of Microsoft software, including Microsoft Windows Server™ 2003, Microsoft SQL Server™ 2000 Service Pack 3, and Microsoft Exchange Server 2003 Service Pack 1, to help measurably improve security features. You get direct access to insights from Microsoft's security team and lessons that are applicable to software development processes worldwide, whether on a small-scale or a large-scale. This book includes a CD featuring videos of developer training classes.

Software Requirements, Second Edition
Karl E. Wiegers • ISBN 0-7356-1879-8

Writing Secure Code, Second Edition
Michael Howard and David LeBlanc • ISBN 0-7356-1722-8

CLR via C#, Second Edition
Jeffrey Richter • ISBN 0-7356-2163-2

Additional SQL Server Resources for Developers

Published and Forthcoming Titles from Microsoft Press

Microsoft® SQL Server™ 2005 Express Edition
Step by Step
Jackie Goldstein • ISBN 0-7356-2184-5

Teach yourself how to get database projects up and running
quickly with SQL Server Express
Edition—a free, easy-to-use
database product that is based
on SQL Server 2005 technology.
It's designed for building simple,
dynamic applications, with all
the rich functionality of the SQL
Server database engine and
using the same data access APIs,
such as Microsoft ADO.NET, SQL
Native Client, and T-SQL.

Whether you're new to database
programming or new to SQL Server, you'll learn how, when, and
why to use specific features of this simple but powerful database development environment. Each chapter puts you to work,
building your knowledge of core capabilities and guiding you
as you create actual components and working applications.

Microsoft SQL Server 2005 Programming
Step by Step
Fernando Guerrero • ISBN 0-7356-2207-8

SQL Server 2005 is Microsoft's
next-generation data management and analysis solution that
delivers enhanced scalability,
availability, and security features
to enterprise data and analytical
applications while making them
easier to create, deploy, and
manage. Now you can teach
yourself how to design, build, test,
deploy, and maintain SQL Server
databases—one step at a time.
Instead of merely focusing on

describing new features, this book shows new database
programmers and administrators how to use specific features
within typical business scenarios. Each chapter provides a highly
practical learning experience that demonstrates how to build
database solutions to solve common business problems.

Microsoft SQL Server 2005 Analysis Services
Step by Step
Hitachi Consulting Services • ISBN 0-7356-2199-3

One of the key features of SQL Server 2005 is SQL Server Analysis
Services—Microsoft's customizable analysis solution for business
data modeling and interpretation. Just compare SQL Server
Analysis Services to its competition to understand the great
value of its enhanced features. One of the keys to harnessing
the full functionality of SQL Server will be leveraging Analysis
Services for the powerful tool that it is—including creating a cube,
and deploying, customizing, and extending the basic calculations. This step-by-step tutorial discusses how to get started, how
to build scalable analytical applications, and how to use and ad-
minister advanced features. Interactivity (enhanced in SQL Server
2005), data translation, and security are also covered in detail.

Microsoft SQL Server 2005 Reporting Services
Step by Step
Hitachi Consulting Services • ISBN 0-7356-2250-7

SQL Server Reporting Services (SRS) is Microsoft's customizable
reporting solution for business data analysis. It is one of the key
value features of SQL Server 2005: functionality more advanced
and much less expensive than its competition. SRS is powerful,
so an understanding of how to architect a report, as well as how
to install and program SRS, is key to harnessing the full functionality of SQL Server. This procedural tutorial shows how to use the
Report Project Wizard, how to think about and access data, and
how to build queries. It also walks through the creation of charts
and visual layouts for maximum visual understanding of data
analysis. Interactivity (enhanced in SQL Server 2005) and security
are also covered in detail.

Programming Microsoft SQL Server 2005
Andrew J. Brust, Stephen Forte, and William H. Zack
ISBN 0-7356-1923-9

This thorough, hands-on reference for developers and database
administrators teaches the basics of programming custom applications with SQL Server 2005. You will learn the fundamentals
of creating database applications—including coverage of
T-SQL, Microsoft .NET Framework, and Microsoft ADO.NET. In
addition to practical guidance on database architecture and
design, application development, and reporting and data
analysis, this essential reference guide covers performance,
tuning, and availability of SQL Server 2005.

Inside Microsoft SQL Server 2005:
The Storage Engine
Kalen Delaney • ISBN 0-7356-2105-5

Inside Microsoft SQL Server 2005:
T-SQL Programming
Itzik Ben-Gan • ISBN 0-7356-2197-7

Inside Microsoft SQL Server 2005:
Query Processing and Optimization
Kalen Delaney • ISBN 0-7356-2196-9

Programming Microsoft ADO.NET 2.0 Core Reference
David Sceppa • ISBN 0-7356-2206-X

---

*For more information about Microsoft Press® books and other learning products,
visit:* **www.microsoft.com/mspress** *and* **www.microsoft.com/learning**

Microsoft
Press

Additional Resources for Web Developers

Published and Forthcoming Titles from Microsoft Press

Microsoft® Visual Web Developer™ 2005 Express Edition: Build a Web Site Now!
Jim Buyens • ISBN 0-7356-2212-4

With this lively, eye-opening, and hands-on book, all you need is a computer and the desire to learn how to create Web pages now using Visual Web Developer Express Edition! Featuring a full working edition of the software, this fun and highly visual guide walks you through a complete Web page project from set-up to launch. You'll get an introduction to the Microsoft Visual Studio® environment and learn how to put the light-weight, easy-to-use tools in Visual Web Developer Express to work right away—building your first, dynamic Web pages with Microsoft ASP.NET 2.0. You'll get expert tips, coaching, and visual examples at each step of the way, along with pointers to additional learning resources.

Microsoft ASP.NET 2.0 Programming
Step by Step
George Shepherd • ISBN 0-7356-2201-9

With dramatic improvements in performance, productivity, and security features, Visual Studio 2005 and ASP.NET 2.0 deliver a simplified, high-performance, and powerful Web development experience. ASP.NET 2.0 features a new set of controls and infrastructure that simplify Web-based data access and include functionality that facilitates code reuse, visual consistency, and aesthetic appeal. Now you can teach yourself the essentials of working with ASP.NET 2.0 in the Visual Studio environment—one step at a time. With *Step by Step*, you work at your own pace through hands-on, learn-by-doing exercises. Whether you're a beginning programmer or new to this version of the technology, you'll understand the core capabilities and fundamental techniques for ASP.NET 2.0. Each chapter puts you to work, showing you how, when, and why to use specific features of the ASP.NET 2.0 rapid application development environment and guiding you as you create actual components and working applications for the Web, including advanced features such as personalization.

Programming Microsoft ASP.NET 2.0
Core Reference
Dino Esposito • ISBN 0-7356-2176-4

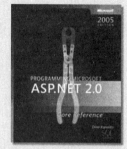

Delve into the core topics for ASP.NET 2.0 programming, mastering the essential skills and capabilities needed to build high-performance Web applications successfully. Well-known ASP.NET author Dino Esposito deftly builds your expertise with Web forms, Visual Studio, core controls, master pages, data access, data binding, state management, security services, and other must-know topics—combining definitive reference with practical, hands-on programming instruction. Packed with expert guidance and pragmatic examples, this *Core Reference* delivers the key resources that you need to develop professional-level Web programming skills.

Programming Microsoft ASP.NET 2.0
Applications: *Advanced Topics*
Dino Esposito • ISBN 0-7356-2177-2

Master advanced topics in ASP.NET 2.0 programming—gaining the essential insights and in-depth understanding that you need to build sophisticated, highly functional Web applications successfully. Topics include Web forms, Visual Studio 2005, core controls, master pages, data access, data binding, state management, and security considerations. Developers often discover that the more they use ASP.NET, the more they need to know. With expert guidance from ASP.NET authority Dino Esposito, you get the in-depth, comprehensive information that leads to full mastery of the technology.

Programming Microsoft Windows® Forms
Charles Petzold • ISBN 0-7356-2153-5

Programming Microsoft Web Forms
Douglas J. Reilly • ISBN 0-7356-2179-9

CLR via C++
Jeffrey Richter with Stanley B. Lippman
ISBN 0-7356-2248-5

Debugging, Tuning, and Testing Microsoft .NET 2.0 Applications
John Robbins • ISBN 0-7356-2202-7

CLR via C#, Second Edition
Jeffrey Richter • ISBN 0-7356-2163-2

For more information about Microsoft Press® books and other learning products,
visit: **www.microsoft.com/books** *and* **www.microsoft.com/learning**

What do you think of this book?

We want to hear from you!

Do you have a few minutes to participate in a brief online survey?

Microsoft is interested in hearing your feedback so we can continually improve our books and learning resources for you.

To participate in our survey, please visit:

www.microsoft.com/learning/booksurvey/

...and enter this book's ISBN-10 number (appears above barcode on back cover*). As a thank-you to survey participants in the United States and Canada, each month we'll randomly select five respondents to win one of five $100 gift certificates from a leading online merchant. At the conclusion of the survey, you can enter the drawing by providing your e-mail address, which will be used for prize notification only.

Thanks in advance for your input. Your opinion counts!

* Where to find the ISBN-10 on back cover

ISBN-13: 000-0-0000-0000-0
ISBN-10: 0-0000-0000-0

Example only. Each book has unique ISBN.

Microsoft®
Press

www.microsoft.com/learning/booksurvey/